Women In Changing Society

Women In Changing Society

Edited by

I. Sarkar
Department of History
North Bengal University, Darjeeling

SERIALS PUBLICATIONS
NEW DELHI (INDIA)

First Published-2008

ISBN: 978-81-8387-178-5

Published by

SERIALS PUBLICATIONS
4830/24, Prahlad Street, Ansari Road
Darya Ganj, New Delhi-110002 (India)
Phone : 23245225 Fax : 91-11-23272135
E-mail: serials@satyam.net.in

CONTENTS

FOREWORD

The collection of essays *Women in Changing Society,* edited by *Dr. I. Sarkar,* addresses a broad range of topics important to the study of women and gender in South Asia. The collection spans the centuries from ancient times to modern, with most of the writers addressing twentieth century issues. The topics included: The freedom movement, women's studies, work, education, literature, economic development, empowerment and violence provide an introduction to concerns of Women's Studies/Gender Studies scholars in South Asia. But what is especially significant about this collection is not the topics included, it is the regions studied. The authors of these essays have focused their attention on the neglected northeast and eastern areas of the subcontinent. Unlike most collections of essays on women in South Asia, this book has papers on Assam, Tripura, Nepal, Bangladesh and North Bengal. In her essay on "Paradigm Shifts in Women's Studies", Malini Bhattacharya writes: " ... it is its indigenous relevance that has given Women's Studies in India its relevance." This is also true about this collection- These essays have indigenous relevance. *Dr. I. Sarkar* is to be commended for bringing them together in a book.

Geraldine Forbes
Distinguished Teaching Professor
Department of History
State University New York Oswego
Oswego, New York.

CONTRIBUTORS

Malini Bhattacharya—Professor of English Literature and Director, School of Women's Studies, Jadavpur University.

J.C. Debnath—Professor, Department of Economics, North Bengal University, Darjeeling.

Vidyawati Agarwala—Lecturer, Department of Political Science, Raiganj University College (Uttar Dinajpur).

Sangh Mittra—Deputy Director Indian Council of Historical Research, New Delhi.

Chitrarekha Gupta—Professor, Department of Archaeology, Calcutta University.

Anita Bagchi—Lecturer in History, North Bengal University, Darjeeling.

S.L. Barua—Professor of History, Sri Sri Aniruddhadev Chair, Dibrugarh University, Assam.

Sutapa Bhattacharya—Professor, Department of Bengali, Visva-Bharati, Birbhum.

Tahmina Alam—Associate Professor, Department of History, Rajshahi University, Bangladesh.

I. Sarkar—Professor, Department of North Bengal University, Darjeeling. Editor of the Volume.

Satyadeo Poddar—Reader in History, Tripura University, Agartala.

Shirin Akhtar—Professor, Department of History, Jahangir Nagar University, Bangladesh.

Anuradha Dutta—Professor, Department of Political Science, Guwahati University.

Puspa Ghimre (Nirula)—Lecturer, Women's Studies Programme, Tribhuvan University, Kathmandu, Nepal.

Neera Shrestha—Lecturer, Women's Studies Programme, Tribhuvan University, Kathmandu, Nepal.

Aparna Mahanta—Professor, Department of English Literature and Director, Centre for Women Studies, Dibrugarh University, Assam.

Laxmikeshari Manandhar—Director, Women's Studies Programme, Tribhuvan University, Kathmandu, Nepal.

Marieta Banez Sumagaysay—Associate Professor, UPV Talcoban College, University of the Philippines.

Anil Bhuimali—Professor, Department of Economics, North Bengal University, Darjeeling.

R.K. Bhadra—Professor, Department of Sociology, North Bengal University, Darjeeling.

Soumyajit Samanta—Professor, Department of English, North Bengal University, Darjeeling.

ACKNOWLEDGEMENTS

The essays incorporated in this book were written by the contributors over the Past-Six years or so in various occasions of academic gatherings and personal initiatives. I am deeply grateful do the men and woman who shaped the stories of this book and have helped a lot to bring all the articles in this present book form. Some of the articles have been thoroughly revised and those who shared their experiences and allowed me entry into their world have changed my way of thinking and learning the women issues at present perspectives. I express my gratitude to Professor Geraldine Forbes for kindly writing a Foreword for the book.

The staff of the Serials Publications, New Delhi have always been a pleasure to work and they deserve my heartiest thanks for their unflinching courtesy and efficiency.

I. Sarkar
Department of History
University of North Bengal
Darjeeling
December-2006

INTRODUCTION

A vindication of the Right of Women by Mary Wollstonecraft first published in England in 1792 advocated the issue of women's emancipation and equality. It is through this book that the authoress perhaps for the first time launched the challenge to the structure of superiority and privileges enjoyed by the male folks over the centuries. Among many points she particularly accused was the hypocrisy of her time and condemned unequivocally the immorality and political subversion that makes a woman an object of fun and ridicule.

The time and society experienced by Mary Wollstonecraft is over but even today in 21st century the 'sad plight' of women does not have substantial change and all the more has evoked multifarious inquiries among those who are somehow concerned with the welfare of our human society. These responses have opened avenues to trace the changes, if any, in the life pattern and attitude of women and, if possible, to explore and examine the issues over the years. The objective being to boost up the changing profile of women in course of the changes which mould our life today from various standpoints. So it is a time to see both historically and psychologically how women could respond on the question of greater involvement in body politics, propagation in favour of rule and legislation for their needs and problems and on the other hand proved worthy of ensuring all round development of our society.

Post colonial period in economically backward countries like India, Nepal, Bangladesh has generated various contradictory currents. While the growth of economic development vis-a-vis socio-political movements have led loose the trend of liberal attitude towards women and issues like dowry system, sexual harassment, marginalization of women in service sectors communal and caste discrimination have not only victimized women but also devalued their social dignity in many respects. There should be strong voices against such injustice and initiatives be taken to explore the avenues glorifying women in terms of our social progress.

Under the above situation, to write or think about women today invariably to deal with the issues associated with emancipation of women-an old phrase that has drawn the attention of many scholars including India. The notion of equality and right has thus become a focal point of discussion which eventually takes a form of movement popularly called women liberation identifying the women's problems. The literature on such issues which has so far come down to us has a wide perspective but have many gaps which deserve to be filled up with meaningful researches.

Keeping in view such a background the present book entitled *Women in Changing Society* is comparatively a new academic venture. This is a collection of some articles written from various perspectives centering around women and covers up precisely sociological, historical and economic problems and issues of this particular class and so on. In most of the article attempt has been made to show, by and large, how the women are on the way to achieve a 'status' in our society by dint of their activities and engagements. It may be noted as a lesson of this study that whatever may be the role in the social functions, women are always to be located not as separate identity but their actions are valuable in removing obstacles or discrimination hampering the progress of human society and civilization.

It seems to be true that all the contributors have honestly tried to enlighten the distinctive features glorifying 'womanhood', an identification and expression which tends to root out exploitation and ensure dignity and status instead. In most of the writings incorporated in the present book, there are references and answers to many feminist readers who always question notions of progress and development. The history of such questioning is as old as our civilization but there are protests against many unnecessary stress that has been given by many of our social thinkers who have put much importance to women's sexuality. But it is highly irrational and can be proved its vagueness through our historical knowledge. The present book and its essays may open a new forum of investigation and thinking of such a trend of studies on women problems.

It sounds well that with the beginning of the 21 st century women have raised more voices for their desired goals. They have learnt to extend their demands in the form of human rights discourse which was so far taken to be the rights of the powerful. In this light the article by Malini Bhattacharya entitled *Paradigm Shifts in Women's Studies* is worthy of mention. Ih her studies she has made a thorough evaluation of some recent works and in her opinion women studies has become more productive when it has responded directly or indirectly to the needs of women's movement. In her studies she has warned about many age long conception of women problems and concludes that women studies has an "inbuilt proneness to this like studies of other oppressed or deprived groups". She even asserts that women can become, through her aware, a participant of the process of change which may ensure self confidence and with an ultimate prize of empowerment.

J.C. Debnath through his article *'Is Feminism a New Paradigm Shift in Sciences?* Wants to clarify the assertation of the feminists who want to establish that women have a different way of knowledge which is as valid as that of the males and "sciences can be fully correct if both in male and female stand points are combined together". Professor Debnath has also analyzed the debate on it and concludes that feminism is not a new paradigm shift in sciences though in specific instances it can correct male bias and make sciences more neutral and universal.

Women question in the light of feminism has been discussed by Vidyawati Agarwal in her article entitled *Feminist Thinking and Women in India*. In her attempt she shows how feminism is a proposal for social transformation as well as a movement that strives to end the oppression of women. Here Vidyawati has presented her evaluation of the treatment of women in India through the ages. In this respect she has fairly cited the arguments of some western scholars who have studied the issue in depth.

Sangh Mittra's article named *Lesser Known Women in the Ramayana* is another important and interesting incorporation of this volume having highlighted the lesser known women in the Ramayana. Her assertion is that the role of Urmila, Mandavi, Sulabha, Sunayana etc. is as significant as that of some leading women like Kaushalya, Kaikeya and Sumitra and even Sita. Sangh Mittra's appears to have consulted many original sources in support of her observations.

Working women of Ancient India presented by Chitrarekha Gupta is a thought provoking article having a new dimension of historical investigations on the women of Ancient India. She wants to establish the fact that women of Ancient India were not only *Patibrata* but were engaged in various works and occupations of economic life of that period.

Anita Bagchi has made a systematic study on the issue of *Involvement of Women in Scientific Activities of Ancient India*. Referring various documents, namely inscriptions, *Rigveda*, Atharaveda, *Kamasutra, Arthasastra,* etc she has tried to give a new idea of the development of agriculture, medicine, horticulture and so on in Ancient India. The contribution of women in the field of this scientific knowledge is something unique in the development of knowledge process of India.

State, patriarchy and Women. A Re-appraisal on Phuleswari Konwari is an article by S.L. Barma in which one may trace an interesting example how in the past-women, too, were often used as instrument in politics and indirectly exploited by powerful and selfish nobles to serve their desired ends. She illustrates her contention by taking up the case of Phuleswari Konwari, the consort of the Ahom King Shiva Singh (1714-1744) of Assam who was apparently vested with all political power with the title Baro-Raja (Great king) but in reality her power was "controlled and regulated by her hen-hearted husband" in order to keep the image of the king (her husband) clear and high.

The title of the article like *Liberation to Emancipation Through the Eyes of Women* by Sutapa Bhattacharya suggests how women were excluded from public life and deprived of true freedom. Mrs. Bhattacharya wants to establish how "men are as largely free as women are enslaved". She has referred many literary works and contemporary documents available in various centres of Bengal which record the voices of women on this question of bondage by the male-dominated society.

Tahmina Alam in her article entitled *Bengali Muslim Women in Post-Rokeya Period: Samsunnahar Mahmud* and *Fazilatunnesa* has given a lively description of the tenacity and boldness of two Muslim women as mentioned who in the post-Rokeya period took the lead of the Muslim women in Bengal and set examples of 'modern women' in various adverse circumstances.

The Role of Women in the Tebhaga Movement of North-Bengal by I. Sarkar, the editor of this volume is an attempt to pick up the issues that tempted the women, particularly the Rajbanshis and a few tribal communities of the region to participate in the Tebhaga Movement of 1946-1947 of North Bengal. Here a special attention is made to show that these women were a part and parcel of the socio-economic condition of North-Bengal and the age long exploitation and humiliation by the Zamindars induced them to stand beside the man-folks who raised their voices against the Zamindars and Jotedars of the region.

Satyadeo Poddar's article *Participation of Women in the Police Administration of Tripura* is a scholarly attempt to present the nature of police administration of Tripura during the time when it was a princely state. His whole paper is devoted to trace the problems and prospects of women participation after the merger of this state to the Indian union in 1948. The article is based on administrative reports and personal interviews of some people connected with the police administration of Tripura.

Shirin Akhtar has made a thorough study on the issue of gender justice in Bangladesh. In her study one may come across how post-colonial nationalist-ideas have provided impetus to the socio-economic upliftment among the middle class urban women of Bangladesh. The issues like emergence of secular family, representation in the legal bodies and also theorizing of women's status as an essential part of modernizing process of Bangladesh have been fairly presented by Shirin in her article entitled *Towards Gender Justice in Bangladesh*.

The nature of violence on women of North-East India is the key issue of the article presented by Anuradha Dutta. In her article Anuradaha wants to highlight how women of the above mentioned region are victims of suffering in various ways such as displacement, loss of home and property and close relatives, physical torture, sexual harassment etc. In this respect she has indicated the 'link' between militarism and violences.

Puspa Ghimire (Nirula) and Neera Shrestha have presented a lively picture of the condition of women in Nepal and specially they highlight contributions of the women folk in the field of economic, social, cultural and political development of the country. They have divided their study in four phases and have laid main emphasis on how in the changing phases of Nepal women have started coming out from household economy and are getting employment in industry and other sectors of the country.

Women in Discourses of Nation and Community and the politics of the personal: A Study of Northeast India by Aparna Mahanta is one of the unique contributions of this volume. In her study Mrs. Mahanta argues very firmly in favour of empowerment of women for self development and that women should not be trapped in the myth of nation or community. In her opinion, politics of the women's personal identity as an individual can only counter the threat of violence on women. She has cited some cases of North-east where there are examples like Bhawani Devi who were raped, tortured or killed on the excuses and blames being identified witches in the society. Mrs. Mahanta concludes at last, "developing the study of the politics of personal in women's studies could restore this lost dimensions".

In her article entitled *Women Development and Gender Equality Towards Twenty First Century-Issues, Challenges and Opportunities (Case studies of Nepal)*, Laxmi Keshari Manandhar has analyzed issues of development of present Nepal and the participation of women of Nepal in it. Marieta

Banez-Sumagaysay's article entitled *Correlates of Married Women's Labor Force Participation in Private Sales and Service Sectors* is self-explanatory. She has, in fact given a unique picture of the present society of the philippines. She shows how women of this country are being shifted from the household duties as wives and prefer working sector. In her analysis she has indicated that this trend has boosted up the economic growth of the country and in her words, it stands as a trend of "family welfare" of the nation as a whole.

Women in Education: An Emphasis on Dis-advantaged Women by Anil Bhuimali is a result of thorough study on dis-advantaged women. In this article Bhuimali lays emphasis on female literacy which may empower the women to achieve equality in the family, community and society. It is an analysis regarding rural-urban disparity among women. There is also a comparative study in this paper relating to female literacy in rural and urban settings.

In his paper entitled *'The Changing Status of women in India: The Areas of Role Conflict,* R.K. Bhadra attempts to clarify the 'role conflict in a situation of our modern society when women are playing two or more roles at one time. He opines that this situation happens particularly with those women who are engaged in services outside home along with a commitment to their traditional domestic affairs.

Many interesting issues have been focused by Saumyajit Samanta in his essay *Feminist Response to Cultural Imperialism: A Study of some selected Indo-Anglican Women Novelist* and having taken into consideration some outstanding novels by the Indian writers he wants to show how "the attempt of cultural domination by the colonizer over the colonized (i.e., India) becomes an apt metaphor for the annexation of feminist narratives by male-oriented discourse".

I. Sarkar
Department of History
North Bengal University, Darjeeling
December, 2006

Malini Bhattacharya

1

Paradigm Shifts in Women's Studies

Women's Studies is a fairly young branch of study. Even in the West, it developed in the 1960s. Susan Brownmiller associates its rise in the U.S. in the late'60s with campus activism and the critique by militant students of the existing education system. The core of Women's Studies as a critical and subversive activity developed on the margins of the academic world at a time when radical student movements saw knowledge as colluding with existing structures of powers and reinforcing them. In India too, the history of Women's studies goes back to the early 1970s. *Towards Equality,* the first Status Report on Indian women, published in 1974, can be taken as a watershed and an early model for Women's Studies in India. So, Women's Studies has really been with us for about a quarter of a century. If we are talking of 'paradigm shifts', we have to think first whether some important changes have taken place in the overall context in which Women's Studies developed.

In fact, a "paradigm shift", had been envisaged by Maithreyei Krishnaraj, one of the leading lights of Women's Studies in India, in her article "Women's Studies: Case for a new Pradigm", published in *Economic and political Weekly,* April 30,1988. This coincided with the moment when the University Grants Commission had admitted the need for introducing Women's Studies in University curricula and funds were being released for setting up of Women's Studies Centres. Krishnaraj's major argument was that the prevailing paradigm in Women's Studies was a compensatory model, i.e., women are seen as a disadvantaged group, for whom facilities, benefits etc. must be created. The development model remained the same, the power structure remained the same, only women were being allowed a little more space within the model. Her critique was that "much of the empowerment today is in the form of more elbow-room". Thus Krishnaraj anticipated the replacement of the 'welfare' or 'development' model by the "empowerment" model- true empowerment that should mean rejection of the top-down approach in development, decentralisation of power, participation of the subjects in decision-making.

One can only guess whether he foresaw that in the '90s, during the discussions and debates preceding the Beijing Conference of Women (1995), the "empowerment" model would gain such wide currency and would even be rapidly incorporated into Government Policy. India's Country Daper (1995) prepared for the Beijing Conference acknowledged this in the statement that:

"The approach of the eighth plan marks a progress from the goal of development to that of empowerment of women".

What Krishnaraj had called for–a new paradigm, has become so widely accepted today that even those who have the most retrograde views of women's status and condone "Suttee" and the dowry system as sacred Indian traditions, can identify 2001 as "Stree Shakti Varsh", and announce various schemes and programmes meant to 'empower' women. So when we are talking of a "paradigm shift" we are referring to what has already happened between 1998 and 2000, or are we proposing another set of new paradigms?

Let us look back a little more critically at the phases that Women's Studies has gone through. How is Women's Studies different from Studies in Social Sciences focussing on Women that went on before the 1970? What sort of break did *Towards Equality* signify? While earlier also, Studies of societies had or had not included chapters on women- e.g. women in Vedic Ages, women in the Freedom Struggle etc., from the 1970s the problem is patriarchy as imbricated into social structures, as affecting all aspects of social life. The question becomes a political one: to what extent does 'history' erase or marginalise 'her-story'? Then *Towards Equality* was published, one of the contributors said: we did not know that these problems existed, that women's lives were like this, before we took up the study. From this stage Women's Studies has highlighted its political objective-that deconstructing the ideological component in existing structures of knowledge, it has laid bare the extent to which knowledge itself is structured by ideology, it has intervened into different disciplines to expose areas of silence or distortion. Such intrusions have enabled these disciplines to break down boundaries and to recognise and negotiate problems for which no space had been allowed earlier. Women's studies has been a form of academic activism even when it has had no direct connections with Women's Movements. Of course, this means that one has to admit that a form of activism can be provided by pedagogy and research themselves at a certain level.

Let me also state clearly at this point I do not think that there has been any sharp dichotomy between academics and activists in Women's Studies in India, although some eminent figures in Women's Studies are of this view. Of course, it is for the academics, interested in the subject to push through Women's Studies in teaching and academic institutions; that is a necessary aspect of activism. But even from the 1970s, Women's Studies has been most productive when it has responded directly or indirectly to the needs of Women's Movements: movements arising from the Mathura Rape Case, the case of Roop Kanwar and the Muslim Women's Bill to mention only a few. This itself bears witness to the fact that it is its indigenous relevance that has given Women's Studies in India its liveliness. It is not a foreign import, as it has been alleged from time to time. In fact, it even seems to me that today this is still the distinguishing mark of Women's Studies in India and is to be contrasted with the situation in advanced countries, like the U.S. where the links between Women's Studies and Women's Movements today seem to be much more minimal.

The wider political context of the rise of Womes's Studies in India should not be missed. 1975 was International Women's Year; in the same year a women Prime Minister at home was curtailing democratic rights of the people by declaring Internal Emergency in order to stem the rising tide of dissatisfaction against the major ruling party. Bina Majumdar, one of the members of the Commission that brought out the "Towards Equality" report, tells us that although it had been set up by the Indira Gandhi government itself in 1971 expressed sharply critical tone of the Report produced by it upset the government and it was pushed under the carpet. It was difficult even to get copies of the Report. She says that throughout the Emergency period any small follow-up on the Report could be initiated only surreptitiously. Thus the basic element of heterodoxy seemed to brand Women's Studies as a source of danger for the status quo- at least that is how it was seen by the authorities. Yet it may also be observed that those in power were seeking to privilege women's issues, perhaps with the intention of drawing attention away from the concentrated attack they were making on the democratic rights of men and women in general. This was an indication of their inner contradiction.

It is also from that time that ruling ideologies have tried to corrupt and make use of the 'autonomy' of women's issues, by misrepresenting this as their 'apolitical' nature. This makes it all the more important for us to take cognizance of the interpenetration of the politics of gender with other kinds of politics: to explore whether there can be a 'pure' women's movement in isolation from all other political issues. The logic of the autonomous women's movements developing in the 1970s and 1980s was that while women have actively participated in different political movements from the time of the Freedom Struggle, these movements have generally by passed specifically women's issues or made them subservient to the 'larger cause'. Just as in the Gandhian movement women's agency had been tolerated only in a limited sense and as an extension of their role within the family, so in left movements too, patriarchy as a basic component in the structure of socio-economic repression has rarely been highlighted.

Therefore women's issues require a space of their own outside such discourses of power, and the function of women's studies is to create such space that the very parameters of these discourses may be radically changed. But this logic has led some of the autonomous women's groups to dissociate themselves as 'apolitical' in this sense because they feel that this is the only way in which the marginalisation of women's issue can be prevented.

The point I am trying to make is that such depoliticization of women's issues may in fact move towards undoing what the autonomous women's movements have achieved through long struggles; this would be the surest way of *ghettoising and institutionalising* the women's question instead of looking at it as a critical tool for destabilizing larger and more complex hierarchies of knowledge and power. Thus institutionalized, and put in its *niche*, Women's Studies would lose its sting for ruling ideologies because these latter would prefer that Women's Studies should keep within the ambit of women's issues, study them as problems that can be redressed by some localized schemes, some modifications in law here and there. The invisible warning sign here would be: You will get assistance and funding but do not meddle with the questions of overall power structures in society since these are of no concern to the women.

This tendency becomes apparent when women's issues are isolated from the question of what are the power structures that supplement and reinforce partriarchy. Then we find Women's Studies turning itself into something canonical, developing its own orthodoxies, losing the self-reflexivity that is the essence of cognitive endeavour. As a matter of fact, Women's Studies has an in-built proneness to this like studies of other oppressed or deprived groups. There is an ingrowing self-righteousness of the oppressed, this is perhaps a part of their self-righteousness of the oppressed, this is perhaps a part of their self-consciousness and helps them to survive, but which at the same time perpetuates the structure of oppression, becomes a way in which the oppressed internalizes the system. "I am the oppressed, the sufferer"-this itself may become my *raison,* d'être. Subjectivity comes to be interpreted in a rigid, ahistorical and superficial manner responding exclusively to some abstract generalized 'women's issues'. For instance, when the subject responds to colonialism/feudal oppression as a social being, such response comes to be regarded as an imposition of forces that are external to a women's self. Such study to exclude ways in which the gender dimension may change over time, to exclude the over-determination of the specific historical moment owing to which class or race dimensions may have priority over gender in the subject's consciousness. There is another side to this whole question also. If you think that subjectivity based on gender is wholly autonomous then you cannot logically prioritize this over the autonomy of subjectivity based on caste or community. The only way in which the synchronic notions of gender, caste, community, race etc. may be linked up with one another is through a diachronic historical category. As an unregenerated Marxist who thinks becoming a Marxist involves becoming a feminist too, I think that class in such a diachronic category. This is not to deny the distinct existence of categories like gender, caste, community, race, but to emphasize that they are useful as critical tools only when some way of understanding how they change in time and place has been devised. Otherwise we are likely to be pushed into a position where Hindu feminism, Islamic feminism, Dalit feminism etc. have to be posited as constraints within which women's movements and Women's Studies have to adjust themselves. This would be abdication of the privilege that all critical knowledge may claim of breaking given boundaries. On the other hand, this would also mean that a non-Hindu/non-Muslim man/woman would be prevented from intervening even academically into specific social structures to which he or she does not belong. Only a woman then would write on or study women or only a Hindu/ Muslim/Dalit would be able to do research on his or her own community.

Coming back to my original point about paradigm shift to empowerment, it is necessary for Women's Studies to scrutinize what makes the nation so readily acceptable to existing structures of power, so glibly replicable in government rhetoric. Is not it precisely this idea of 'women's empowerment' as marked off from•other invisible yet immutable and unquestionable structures of power? Krishnaraj's demand has to be looked at more closely. Words 'ship, slide, perish'. Krishnaraj's word is being used but is her meaning retained? That the development model had by-passed women is a generally accepted idea today; so the question of development is now rejected altogether so that 'empowerment' becomes a more cultural matter, a question of advocacy and awareness raising. Even while all those 'fruitless' general welfare measures like public distribution system and education and health subsidies are taken away, we think we may succeed in raising self-confidence in women, in instilling into them an 'awareness' of empowerment. We think she can become through her more aware, a participant in the process of change. In other words, we completely erase the political implications of 'empowerment', namely, decentralization of power, subversion of existing power structures. That would merely be a model of a paradigm shift to 'empowerment' without ideologically breaching the bastions of power. It seems to me that the model has gained a great deal of visibility today. My question is: will Women's Studies go with this or will it, as it has in the past, question the vary basis of the structures of knowledge generated in an inequitious and insupportable social system?

J. C. Debnath

2

Is Feminism a New Paradigm Shift in Sciences?

Feminist criticisms[1] of physical and social sciences have been quite vocal during the second half of the twentieth century and are, according to some observers, gradually taking the shape of some sort of a paradigm shift in scientific discourses. There are three broad feminist criticisms: (i) that women have been under-estimated in sciences. (ii) that women have been under-paid or not paid at all for their work in workplaces and at home and this has been justified by sciences, notably economics and (iii) that women have been under-represented in scientific professions.

UNDER-ESTIMATTION OF WOMEN IN SCIENCES

Scientists have often under-estimated the capabilities and contributions of women in various fields. Social scientists[2] have often justified women's inferior position in various walks of life by arguing that the gender division of labour—including exclusion of women from high positions in religion, politics, economic affairs or even sciences—is inaccordance with women's innate nature, and hence good for the society.

In the nineteenth century biological sciences[3] one could hear the echo of religious fundamentalism when the scientists proclaimed that females should not be educated as it would damage their reproductive organs. Scientists also tried to prove the intellectual inferiority of women by measuring their skulls and weighing their brains. Even in contemporary socio-biology, neuro-biology and endocrinology attempts are made to justify women's subordinate position and oppression. All these suggest that our sciences like all other pursuits of human beings are afflicted with *andro-centrism*.

Feminists have criticised neo-classical economics[4] from the point of view of its three basic features: rationality postulate (which is interpreted as the pursuit of self-interest), free choice and absence of any power relation. Feminist historians, philosophers and economists have persuasively argued that the concept of *rationality* has been fashioned to conform to the emotional and intellectual needs of the males—who are selfish, calculating, independent and separated from other persons and the surroundings. Love or altruism has no place in neoclassical economics and hence women's self-less service to the family and to their loving offsprings is utterly overlooked in neoclassical economics.

The options facing women are so limited and so different from those faced by men that to talk of *free choice* on the part of women is extremely misleading. Men have free choice, but not women. Gender identities are so constructed by the family and the society that women are compelled to take major responsibility for children and housework compared to men. There are also social sanctions ranging from *rebuke* to economic, social and legal penalties for violationg the gender norms. Under such circumstances "free choice" is a misnomer.

Marxists have for long been criticising neoclassical economics for its abstraction from *power relations* in the society. Many feminist economists argue that Marxist economics provides a more satisfactory analysis of women's problems than neo-classical economics. Whereas neo-classical economics tries to establish mutually beneficial optional solutions. Marxist analysis focusses on the exploitative power relations which is a reality and which explains and highlights women's real problems and their solutions.

UNDER-PAYMENT OR NON-PAYMENT FOR WOMEN'S WORK

Very often women get less pay and status than their male counterparts even though they may be doing the same work. Strangely, neo-classical economics explains and justifies this irregularity as a result of free and rational choice based on biological differences between the sexes assuming a hypothetical society where there is no exploitative power relation. According to this school of economics differentials in wages equal differentials in *marginal productivity* of labour. So, the lower wage rate for women and higher rate for men are justified on the basis of the assumption of female inferiority and male superiority.

Another pathetic irony is that even in countries where women have got their so-called emancipation and are working side by side with males in offices and work-places, they have failed to persuade their husbands to share their domestic responsibilities, thereby making themselves *doubly burdened*.

It seems what is really required is a genuine *change in the male perception* of women's position and problems, and a recognition of gender equality. This may be illustrated by an anecdote. Once there was a spurt of night-time assault on women in Israel. A male minister suggested that a curfew for "women only" be imposed at night so that women remained indoors after dusk. Ms. Golda Meir, the then Prime Minister, intervened and argued that since it was men who were attacking women the curfew should keep men indoors, not women. The iron-lady, however, could not implement her suggestion because it was an anathema to the male-dominated Israel.

Women's unpaid work in the household is not included in the measurement of *national income* on the plea that there are problems of measurement. Well, problems may be there, but there should have been attempts to solve them. Regretably, no such attempt has yet been made. The *Human Development Report*[5]*, 1995* published by the United Nations Development Programme estimated that world-wide women perform $11 trillion worth of non-monestised work that is not included in the national income accounts of the world, the global income being $23 trillion. So, about half of global income generated by women is not counted at all which means that much of women's contribution is unrecognised and unpaid.

UNDER-REPRESENTATION OF WOMEN IN SCIENTIFIC PROFESSIONS

The issue of under-representation of women in scientific professions can best be illustrated by examining *women's position in economics profession*[6]. Economics is the most male-dominated of social sciences and under-representation of women in this discipline is quite stark. The USA is economically the most powerful country in the world and have most of the leading economists of the world. It is also the leading democratic country and advocates equal opportunity for all. But its record of gender-equality is disappointing.

In the 1970's in the USA only eight percent of the total Ph.D. degrees was awarded to women candidates. Many universities in the USA and also elsewhere have no female member in the economics faculty. Alice Rivlin was the first woman president of the American Economic Association in 1987 in the hundred years of the association's existence. Labour economics is the field where gender discrimination is one of the most important issues. But when the University of Chicago started the *Journal of Labour Economics* there was no female member in its editorial board. Again, in a study of gender bias in the acceptance of papers by economic journals it was seen that women's papers had lower acceptance rate than men's when the referees know their names, but their papers had higher acceptance rate than men's when the referees didn't know their names. The picture in physical sciences was not different, whether in the USA or elsewhere.

Why is the picture so deppressing? It is because there are a number of *obstacles, familial and social,* that women very often find difficult to overcome. The socialisation by families, religious, educational institutions and the media persuade them that they lack the logical, mathematical and quantitative abilities that are required for careers in science or that such careers are unwomanly. Moreover, scientific careers are so structured that it is very difficult for a womn to reconcile to the demands of the family and the career. If she happens to be the wife of a scientist she has to support her husband in his profession as well as look after her family—and after that she hardly has any energy or time to pursue her own scientific studies or take a scientific profession.

FEMINISM AND SCIENTIFIC KNOWLEDGE

Feminism attempts to give a voice to women's problems and to correct the male-oriented perspective of sciences. It is inspired by research works such as *Women's Way of Knowing*[7] that argues that women learn and express themselves differently than men. Feminism is a perspective, not a method and it uses a wide range of research methods to carry out critiques of non-feminist sciences and establish women's own point of view. It is trans-disciplinary and attempts to bring about a more gender-egalitarian social change.

Western thought including scientific thought is pervaded by *dualisms*—mind and body, reason and emotion, culture and nature, objectivity and subjectivity and so on in which the first of each pair is associated with masculine and the second with feminine standpoint, and there has always been dominance of the former over the latter. Feminists want to end this androcentric dominance and bring a balance in the character of sciences. Harding identifies three basic instances[8] taken by feminist science critics which she calls (i) feminist empiricism, (ii) feminist standpoint epistemology, and (iii) feminist post-modernism.

Feminist empiricism accepts the prevailing empiricist methodology but wants to correct the andro-centric bias. Were more women engaged in sciences quite different and more adequate sciences might have emerged. As Seiz says: "If knowledge is indeed importantly shaped by the social identity of the inquires (i.e., males), a large-scale influx of women into the scientific professions might be expected to improve scientific knowledge. Women scientists might ask new questions, obtain new observations, suggest new explanations, and uncover and correct the flaws produced by andro-centric bias. Thus, having more women practising science may be seen as not merely a question of fairness (i.e., equal opportunity) but also one of truth."[9]

Feminist standpoint epistemology holds that not only old empiricism but also new methodologies will be required for making sciences more balanced by incorporating women's standpoint or ways of knowing the natural and social reality. If science have so far developed mainly by the males, they have incorporated only one standpoint, hence the prevailing sciences are partially correct. Sciences can be fully correct if both the male and female standpoints are combined together.

One can ask, why should there be a different standpoint of females? There are two explanations for this: The first traces its origin to women's childhood experiences that are dissimilar and often discriminatory. The other is sociological in nature and resembles the Marxist stance. It says that male and female standpoints have their roots in the discriminatory adulthood experiences including gender division of labour.

Feminist post-modernism goes a bit further and says that all explanation of reality are necessarily partial and hence it is better to accept that there are many truths rather than a single truth explaining a phenomenon. If we try to achieve a single truth as explanation it will really be a partial truth forcibly imposed on others by the dominant group—it will be a false universalisation of particular truth. Hence, feminist post-modernists are against any compromise, co-operation or complementary status with the andro-centric scientists—they want to tread a completely new track.

Apart from the substantial differences among the three stances, there would also be further differences if we take into account women of different races, religions, nationalities, classes and cultures. So, to accept a unitary women's standpoint is to engage in the same sort of false universalisation that the feminists have so far deplored in the andro-centric nature of sciences.

Mankind is divided into males and females for reproductive purpose, but basically they are the same and hence there is no fundamental difference between these two sections of the human race which implies that there should not be fundamental difference between the male and female views of sciences. While the age-old deprivation of women must be redeemed, a feminist over-reaction is uncalled for and injurious to the development of sciences.

NOTES AND REFERENCES

1. For feminist criticisms see Harding, S. (1986), *The Science Question in Feminism* (Ithaca: Cornel University Press) and Tuana, N. ed. (1989), *Feminism and Science* (Indianapolis: Indiana University Press).
2. For gender bias in social science see Harding, S. (1987), *Feminism and Methodology: Social Science Issues* (Bloomington: Indiana University Press) and Hess, B. and Ferree, M.M. eds. (1987), *Analysing Gender: A Handbook of Social Science Research* (Newbury Park: SAGE Publications).
3. For Gender bias in biological sciences see Bleier, R. (1984), *Science and Gender: A Critique of Biology and Its Theories on Women (New York,* Pergamon Press).
4. For feminist criticism of neo-classical economics see Folbre, N. and Hartman, H. (1988), "The rhetoric of Self-interest and the Ideology of Gender" in Arjo Klamer et. al. eds. *The Consequences of Economic Rhetoric* (New York: Cambridge University Press).
5. For Women's unpaid and unrecognised work see *Human Development Report* (yearly since 1990). United Nations Development Programme, U.N.
6. For Women's positions in economics profession see Seiz, J.A., "Fender and Economic Research" in Neil de Marchi, ed. (1992), *Post-Popperian Methodology of Economics* (Boston: Kluer Academic Publishers).
7. For women's perception of truth see Belenky, M.F. et.al. (1986), *Women's Ways of knowing* (New York: Basic Books.)
8. For three feminist stances see Harding, S. (1986). For three other types of feminism (liberal radical and socialist) see Jaggar, A (1983), *Feminist Politics and Human Nature* (Totowa, NJ: Rowman and Allenheld).
9. For the theory of paradigm shift see Kahn, T.S. (1970), *The Structure of Scientific Revolutions* (Chicago: University of Chicago Press).

Vidyawati Agarwal

3

Feminist Thinking and Women In India

"Women question", the term should be understood by using the work "Feminism" which seeks to highlight women's specific oppression in relation to men, preventing this from being submerged, amidst all other unequal relationship existing in society. Thus feminism is sometimes confined to women's struggle against oppressive gender relationships. In practice, however, women's action both now and in the past, often have been against inter connecting relation of inequality and have involved many aspects of resistance, around daily life and culture that are not simply about gender.

Feminism is a proposal for social transformation as well as a movement that strives to end the oppression of women. As peafeminism has always existed as a part of the historical societies in which it has developed, it has been influenced by the specific social, economic and political traits of its society. As a movement, feminism has a long history of rebellion, more of less organised but always expressing opposition to the social institution that made possible the inferiority of women.

Charles Fourier, the French socialist argued that the degree of women's freedom decided the extent of social progress. Women's emancipation was thus linked to the idea of progressive social reform and historical change.

Feminist theories have been divided into specific ages: Primitive and Modern. Primitive feminism begins with Mary Astell (1666-1731), who has been known as the first English feminist.

Seventeenth century feminism had been inspired mainly by the conservative defender of monarchy at home as well as within the state. According to them, in state, the authority of the King over his people was sanctioned by "God' and by nature in exactly the same way as that of father over his family. This theory of the century justifies social convenience and men's superior strength to justify the continuous subordination of women. It means they saw men as independent and rational individual capable of perceiving and pursuing their own self interest and saw women as wives and mothers and weak creatures.

The shortcomings of radical feminism had given birth to the liberal feminism of eighteenth century, during this time women's rationality became less fashionable than belief in their innate weakness and dependence on men.

But above beliefs were later challenged by Mary Wollstonecrafts in her Vindication of the Rights of Women (1792), and by the French writer Condorect that women were capable of reason and should be educated accordingly, that they had therefore the same political right as men, and to deny this was an unacceptable tyranny.

According to Wollstonecrafts women are not less capable of reason than men, but vanity, weakness and frivolity were the natural attributions of her sex. She argued that if men and women equally possessed reason, they must be equally educated in its use. To her, as men's and women's common humanity based on their shared and God given possession of reason, then virtue must be the same for the both sexes. She argued forcefully that a woman taught only passive obedience to her husband could never be fit to bring up children, women must be given education so that they can make rational choice.

Wollstonecraft insisted that women had an independent right to education, employment, property and the protection of the civil laws; this argument was needed to ensure that women were not forced into marriage through economic necessities and that wives were not entirely dependent on the goodwill of their husbands. Women, therefore, needed legal rights in order to make independent rational choice and achieve virtue.

Apart from the radical and liberal school one more school is there, i.e., Utopian Socialist school; the earliest socialist thinker St. Simon, Fourier and Robert Owen who saw relationships between the sexes and within the family as central issue. Changes in society were not seen as simply the by-product of social change or class struggle but were themselves a necessary precondition for the transformation of society. The feminist aspects of their thought were developed by their followers.

Ideas of Owen and Fourier has been more explicit in the writing of William Thompson, who was an ardent follower of Owen and Fourier.

Thompson was not simply a liberal feminist, but a socialist also. He favoured the equal rights for men and women, and he asserted that the rights of women only can rest in the cooperative, socialist societies, where women would get full worth of their contribution. He was not in favour for capitalist system of society, where laws are made unequal.

Thompson did not support the separation between men and women rather he believed that the true interest of sexes could be reconciled.

During the nineteenth century a new turn took in the feminist conception. They inspired the movement for the total social, legal, educational, moral, etc. reformation. The feminists of this period claim the moral superiority of women over men that is why the feminists of the nineteenth century were considered more radical, and the feminist writers of this period were considered as reformist because they did not make any attack on the existing socio-economic system rather wanted the extension of legal protection and right to women.

Gradually organised feminism shifted from America to England and the thinking and discussion of feminism in the mid 19th century tended to concentrate in the writing of John Stuart Mill, his Subjection of Women (1861) was the most important writing on women's position by him.

According to his Subjection, he is in favour to give men and women equal political rights. There must be no bar to women's education and employment. To him, sexes play very different role in the society, he is in favour of giving the women free will to follow the career of their choice and they should not be forced into marriage through economic necessity.

Mill was always in favour of mass education, legal, political power to women, plus he wanted their employment also because he had a panic of male sexual violence over female.

Mill's conception regarding the tackling of domestic tyranny and granting of legal political freedom to women, are same as of Stanton, both of them were emphasised on legal and political reformation rather than economic dependency within the marriage, nor sexual division of labour.

One more aspect remains in the field of feminism that is Marxist Feminism, most interesting thing is that Marx himself had not produced or propagated any feminist theory, but the worker on feminism applied the theory of Marx on feminine question and stand up a theory as Marxist feminism or Marx's view on feminism.

According to Angel, women were defeated firstly when men decided to overthrow the private property to their son and not to his wife. This system made women slaves. She became only a possessor of her husband, son and became economically dependent on men. It also means that female oppression had no other material cause, it is a part of class society, but not a necessary or permanent feature of human relationship.

From the above discussion, though in nutshell, we can come to the conclusion that all the theories, either radical, liberal, socialist or Marxist feminism, all of them believed on the emancipation of women from the exploitation either sexual, physical or mental, may be their way of thinking is different. In fact, on certain points, they oppose each other, but the ultimate views is the same, out of four, liberalism is the most expanded one.

By the end of the nineteenth century, most of demands made by the liberalist feminist had been granted by America and Britain. Women were granted education, middle class women could now own her property and keep her own earnings. She had now rights concerning the custody and welfare of children, and she had some degree of protection against physical abuse from her husband, though the divorce law still was not clear or remained of double moral standard. Women also started to enter into public life on an unprecedented scale. Working women themselves also began to organise both independent and mixed organisations. In spite of the domestic work responsibility, organisation of labour also involved women in strike and trade union activities.

Taking into consideration the status of women and discrimination against women, a well documented book, The Feminist Mystique' was published by Kenndy Commission in 1963.

After the publication of the book, the effect started in the same year (1963) the Equal Pay Act was passed in 1964 a clause prohibiting discrimination by sex was added to the Civil Right Act. But the subsequent failure of the authorities to implement the sexual aspects of the Act, gave birth to the strongest women organization in the world known as National Organization of Women (NOW) in 1966.

However, it must be understood that gender inequality is not only the root cause in inequality between men and women but race, class etc., also have very much significant role to unite women within themselves against men domination, of course, the problem and the cause may differ from country to country.

By and large it is felt that the discriminations and inequalities against women might be removed by the women's participation in the political process, people in mass including women only can participate actively in the democratic form of government.

Democracy is the form of government where people's participation, direct or indirect in decision making and decision taking is a remarkable feature. The government takes important decision not only on important issues but also including the matters concerning the life of women. The policies of women upliftment are usually reflected in election manifestoes of political parties. In our sociopolitical feature women are not only deprived and by-passed but also marginalised in decision making. It has accentuated of gender injustice, naturally the real objectives of attaining equality had been defected. To solve the problem of gender injustice, it is desirable that women should get enough power to influence the government. It is possible when women actively participate in the political process.

By political process, we mean exercise of power, naturally, participation in politics means participation in exercise of power, which has an active role in changing the society and the existing social system.

Participation of women in politics and decision making process is essential because policy making and their implementation are the basic functions of the government, in this regard women can create pressure on the government and women's involvement in politics means collective endeavor for social transformation. Though involving themselves in politics women can raise voice against oppression, exploitation, injustice, degradation, etc. Collective involvement of women in politics can shake all the departments of government and can raise the question against gender blindness.

So far, Indian womanhood is concerned, a long gap is found in the standard and status of them. During the Vedic period women enjoyed a status and prestige in the society, husband and wife together constituted a unit in the society. Women were treated as the embodiment of goddess of wealth, strength, and wisdom. Women had the freedom in different activities of the social and political life. But gradual changes took place during the later ages, as the period advanced, there was a gradual decline in female education. Consequently, there arose a tendency to curtail religious rights and privileges of average women.

Women of the Aryan's time were crude hardy camp dweller who did not know urban luxuries. In the inter racial marriage, men were Aryan and women were non-Aryans. Since the Aryans held the view that woman marrying below her caste or status demeans herself and family, no such stigma was there for men. This rule is valid even today to a large extent.

Gradually, women were completely detached from the public life and the outer society. But because of women excellence in music, dance and poetry they began to appear on the scene to entertain men, woman became an object of men's pleasure, gradually the social evils like prostitution came into existence. Modern system of Devdasi or Murly which has been long practised in South India is also a means of sexual exploitation of women. Position of Hindu women had deteriorated in whole. They lost their ground both economically and socially due to lack of vigilance. Politically too they were isolated, so they became powerless. Being illiterate, they were unable to challenge the system and therefore, submitted to it, and the system of child marriage, purdah pratha (system), sati pratha, restriction on widow remarriage etc., all social evils came into existence. The oppressive conditions of women were contributed by the advent of Muslim in India too.

During the later part of the 19th century, several enlightened individuals and groups sprang up they were Raja Rammohun Roy, Dayanand Saraswati, Iswar Chandra Vidyasagar, etc., who were mortified by the miserable plight of women. The Brahma Samaj (1828) and Arya Samaj, Ramkrishna Mission, Theosophical Society, etc. were formed. Men provided leadership to these associations, while many heroic women worked hard to achieve social gains. The ultimate aim of the reform movement was to secure equal rights for women as human beings. As a result of these movements the Hindu society gradually started realising the need for giving a better deal to women. Consequently, legislations were passed validating the widow remarriage and the minimum age of a girl to marry was also increased. The conception of women upliftment or equal rights was advocated by Annie Besant, Sarojini Naidu, Maharani of Baroda, Rameshwari Nehru etc. too. Women" movement in India achieved success in the field of their political representation first in 1917, the female enfranchisement were issued in 1923 and by 1928 they were declared eligible for legislature also.

After the independence a new chapter began, the framers of the Constitution acted on the principle, to provide every citizen justice in social, economic and political field, liberty of self expression and belief, equality of status and of opportunity irrespective of caste, class and gender, and also signifies the dignity of each individual. Thus the constitution of India granted to the women the right to vote and be elected and thereby govern a right which was traditionally denied to her throughout the history of India.

In spite of the constitutional and legal provisions, women have not been able to get adequate and proportionate representation in the Lok Sabha, the top legislative body. The table given below is the evidence of it.

Women Member in Lok Sabha

Lok Sabha	*Duration*	*Total Seats*	*Seat contested by women*	*% of women contested*	*Seats won by women*	*% of women member*
1st	1952	499	51	13%	22	4.4%
2nd	1957	500	70	14%	27	5.4%
3rd	1962	503	68	13%	31	5.9%
4th	1967	523	66	13%	31	5.9%
5th	1971	521	86	17%	22	4.2%
6th	1977	544	70	13%	19	3.4%
7th	1980	544	142	26%	28	5.1%
8th	1984	544	159	29%	44	8.1%
9th	1989	528	89	17%	28	5.3%
10th	1991	531	55	10%	39	7.9%
11th	1996	545	NA	NA	40	7.3%
12th	1997	545	NA	NA	44	8%
13th	1999	545	NA	NA	45	9%

Parliament is the highest legislative body in India, while formulating the constitution of India the framers made the reservation of seats on the basis of caste, but, forget to reserve seats for them, who constituted the 50% of the total population as well 50% of total electorate too. They were no body but "WOMEN" in Society.

To uplift the condition of women different social legislations were enacted as The Dowry Prohibition Act was passed in the sixties was amended a few years ago. The suppression of informal Trafficking Act was also amended, making the man equally guilty in commercialised prostitution. More teeth have been provided to the Rape Law concerning Indecent Exhibition of Women in Advertisement. In the labour front, there is the Equal Remuneration Act and the Maternity Benefit Act. But inspite of that the violence against women have not reduced.

In the economic sector a majority of women are to be found in the vast rural and urban unorganised sector. According to an estimate by the National Commission on Self Employment Women, 94 per cent of the total female workforce operates within this highly exploited sector. Employment in this sector is characterised by low pay, long hours of work, low productivity, low skill and lack of job security.

A recent United Nation report says- Two out of every three people who cannot read or write are women. Women who make up around 50 per cent of the World's population, work twice as hard as men, but receives merely 10% of the world's income and own 1% of the world's property.

Subject to note that taking into consideration the factors, purpose and process of violence against women, Government appointed the Committee on the Status of Women in India to make a study on above subject. Consequently, a National Perspective Plan for Women was prepared in 1998, but the ever-increasing crimes against women have proved the failure of the plan. Actually plan needs policies, policies are needed for actual implementation which of course depends upon the desire of the Government machineries. Though few recommendation have been implemented such as Family Courts Reservation at Panchayat level, setting up of National Commission for Women, etc.

One more interesting thing is that women who form almost 50% of the country's population are not even 10% of the total members of the National Parliament. It was not better earlier, inspite of all the constitutional and legal guarantees and a galaxy of outstanding women leaders including Prime Minister for 16 years. Women have not been able to get adequate and proportionate representation in the Lok Sabha, the highest representative body in the country. Being the minority in the parliament women were not successful in the legislative functioning also, the following table shows the list of bills introduced by Women parliamentarians in India during last 45 years.

Bill Introduced by Women Parliamentarian

Duration	*No. of Bills introduced*	*Passed*	*Lapsed*	*Not known*	*Bills on Women*	*passed*
1950-51	3	1	2	—	2	—
1952-57	26	6	17	3	17	1
1958-62	14	3	10	1	4	—
1963-67	16	6	5	5	—	—
1968-70	3	—	3	—	2	—
1971-77	26	17	9	—	2	—
1978-79	4	—	2	2	—	—
1980-84	37	3	31	3	14	—
1985-89	43	9	16	18	13	4
1990-91	14	—	11	3	5	—
1991-91	23	—	—	23	7	—
Total	209	45	106	58	66/209	5/66
		21.5%	50.75%	27.75%	31.5%	7.5%

The table shows that there were almost 209 Bills introduced by the women in the parliament from 1950 to 1996. Out of all 66 Bills were on women problem which could be divided into 26 categories. Ten categories were there on which Bill introduced only ones, but on the other categories Bills were introduced time and again. As it has already been mentioned that the laws of women in India are boldest in the world, but the position of Indian Women perhaps worst also in the universe.

According to need and changing phenomenon and time the bill had been introduced but only 5 bills were passed and the fate of other 61 bills of 20 categories were either lapsed or not known.

Not the non-passing but the non-discussion of the bills shows the dominating character of male society, because all of the above written subjects were important and related to effective matter in the society. Only 19 or 44 women among 544, what can they do or capable of doing anything! The representation seems few drops of waters in the ocean or may be said a hut of papers which cannot exist in a violent storm.

Point to note that maximum of the Bills which had lapsed were introduced in connection of CSWI's report.

The findings show that one type of Feminist movement in India is successful to uplift the women's condition and to reduce the women's questions of violences, and therefore perhaps the reservation for women in every sphere and more education to male section is the only answer to women's question.

A system of reservation may also increase the women legislator's sense of responsibility and concern for the problem affecting women, thus ensuring the presence of a body of spokesmen of the women's cause in the representative bodies of the States. Such a system would also help to increase the degree of political mobilisation of women both in the electorate and within the parties.

Therefore, perhaps, this (Reservation) is the most and only important path for the proper emancipation of women, even if economic source plays an important role in the life of women, but they are the subject to be exploited through the unequal distribution of wages in different working sectors. Different laws and acts have been made by the Government of India, but all of them are full of loopholes, which is one of the cause of ever-increasing of violences and crimes against women in India.

Thus reservation of 33% for women in Lok Sabha might replace the theoretical words of preambles of the Constitution of India, into reality the words are—

"Justice-Social, Economic and Political;

Liberty of Thoughts Expression, Belief, Faith and Worship;

Equality of status and of opportunity;........"

Sangh Mittra

4

Lesser Known Women in Ramayana

I

It is irony of history and unfortunate for historians giving more attention to characters having a deep bearing on their role as rulers, conquerors, exploiters and administrators. Their theme may, however, revolve around a big country or a small one, even a tiny village, the name of the 'Head' is very often mentioned with much emphasis on his success or defeat. If we browse through the pages of historical narration of any country, this kind of style is found to be a glaring phenomenon—teachers in the classrooms do lay emphasis on this style and the reality is forgotten, rather frozen for all time to come.

What is that reality? It is evidently true that a common man or woman is a part and parcel of our society and his or her contribution, big or small, cannot be ignored, as it is effective in one way or the other. One would call them the essential and significant factors in strengthening or weakening the administrative setup at the state level or at the local level. Sometimes there could be stupendous gains from these small characters or there could be havoc in the whole set up. But their contribution, as will be emphasized with the foregoing examples, would not be negligible as it is often thought to be. To prove my point, I may recall that a few years ago, the TV serials of *Ramayana* were shown to the people of India and elsewhere by Ramanand Sagar and he was very keen, of course, after consulting different versions of *Ramayana* in various languages, not to ignore even a smallest character of this Great Epic. Accolades were showered on him for giving due emphasis to this significant aspect in his serials.

The *Ramayana* is one of the two great Indian epics. It tells us about life in India around 1000 BC and offers models in dharma. The hero of this epic is Rama who lived his whole life obeying the laws of dharma. The concised story of *Ramayana* is placed here for the benefit of readers:

1. Dashratha, King of Ayodhya, has three wives and four sons. Rama is the eldest. His mother is Kaushalya. Bharata is the son of his second and favourite wife, Queen Kaikeyi. The other two— Lakshman and Shatrughana are twins. Rama and Bharata are depicted as blue, perhaps indicating they were dark skinned or originally south Indian deities.
2. A sage takes the boys to train them in archery. Rama succeeds in hiting an apple hanging from a string.
3. In a neighbouring city the ruler's daughter is named Sita. When it was time for Sita to choose her bridegroom, at a ceremony called a *swayamvara*, the princes were asked to string a giant bow. No one else can even lift the bow, but as Rama bends it, he not only strings it but also breaks it into two. Sita indicates she has chosen Rama as her husband by putting a garland around his neck. The disappointed suitors watch.
4. King Dasharatha, Rama's father, decides it is time to give his throne to his eldest son Rama and retire to the forest to seek *moksha*. Everyone seems pleased. This plan fulfils the rules of dharma which enjoins that the eldest son should rule and, if a son can take over one's responsibilities, one's last years may be spent in a search for *moksha*. In addition, everyone loves Rama. However, Rama's step-mother, the king's second wife, is not pleased. She wants her son, Bharata, to rule. Because of an oath Dashratha had made to her years

before, she gets the king to agree to banish Rama for fourteen years and to crown Bharata, even though the king, on bended knee, begs her not to demand such things. Broken-hearted, the devastated king cannot face Rama with the news and Kaikeyi must tell him.

5. Rama, always obedient, is as content to go into banishment in the forest as to be crowned king. Sita manages to convince Rama by virtue of her being his life partner, the ought to be with .... both in good or bad times him.............. that, she belongs to his side. His brother Lakshman to .... on begs to accompany them. Rama, Sita and Lakshman their set out for the forest. Bharata, whose mother's evil plot has won him the throne, is very upset when he discuss out truth. Not for a moment does he consider proper beat the rules of dharma and becoming king in Rama's place. He goes to the forest and begs of Rama to return and rule, but Rama refuses. "We must obey father." Rama says. Bharata then takes Rama's sandals saying: "I will put these on the throne, and every day I shall place the fruits of my work at the feet of my Lord." Embracing Rama, he takes the sandals and returns to Ayodhya.
6. Years pass and Rama, Sita and Lakshman are very happy in the forest. Rama and Lakshman destroy the rakshasas (evil creatures) who disturb the sages in their meditations. One day a rakshasa princess tries to seduce Rama, and Lakshmana inflicts a nasty blow open her injuring her beg. She returns to her brother Ravana, the ten-headed ruler of Lanka (Sri Lanka, formerly Ceylon), and tells her brother (who has a weakness for beautiful women) about lovely Sita.

   Ravana devises a plan to abduct Sita. He sends a magical golden deer which Sita desires. Rama and Lakshmana go off hunt the deer, first drawing a protective circle around Sita and warning her she will be safe as long as she does not step outside the circle. As they go off, Ravana (who can change his shape) appears as a holy man begging alms. The moment Sita steps outside the circle to give him food, Ravana grabs her and carries her off to his kingdom in Lanks.

7. Rama is broken-hearted when he returns to the empty hut and cannot find Sita. A band of monkeys offer to help him find Sita. Ravana has carried Sita to his palace in Lanka, but he cannot make her his wife so he puts her in a grove and alternately sweet-talks her and threatens her in an attempt to get her to agree to marry him. Sita will not even look at him but thinks only of her beloved Rama. Hanuman, the general of the monkey band can fly since his father is the wind, and Hanuman flies to Lanka and, finding Sita in the grove. Comforts her and tells her, Rama will soon come and Save her.
8. Ravana's men capture Hanuman, and Ravana orders them to Wrap Hanuman's tail in cloth and to set it on fire. With his tail burning, Hanuman hops from house-top to house-top, setting Lankas afire. He then flies back to Rama to tell him where Sita is.
9. Rama, Lakshmana and the monkey army build a causeway from the tip of India to Lanka and cross over to lanka. A mighty battle ensues. Rama kills several of Ravana's brothers and then Rama confronts ten-headed Ravana. (Ravana is known for his wisdom as well as for his weakness for women which may explain why he is pictured as very brainy). Rama finally kills Ravana.
10. Rama frees Sita. After Sita proves her purity, they return to Ayodhya and Rama becomes king. His rule, Ram-rajya, is an ideal time when everyone does his or her dharma and "fathers never have to light the funeral pyres for their sons." Mahatma Gandhi dreamed that one day modern India would become a Ram-rajya.

The Ramayana also focuses on the social structure, which was at that time in a nascent stage of development. Ram who was the symbol of morality tried to go against the established norms and the case in point is the character of Shabri.

The Ramayana tells us about the importance of morality in life. It has both positive and negative characters. It shows that characters with a positive disposition every victorious in the end.

In this paper, an effort has been made to strengthen the Epic story by weaving it with lesser known characters. Spread emphasis has been given to women from some of the main races of that time who have played a significant role in Ramayana. The races are the Aryan race, the Asura race, the Bheel race, the Vanar race, the Yaksha race, the Nagas race and the Apsaras. In the Aryans, I have taken the characters of Kaikeyi, Sumitra, Kaushalya, Ahilya, Mandavi, Shuthkriti, Sunayana and Sulabha; in the Assures the characters of Mandodori, Trijata, Suparnakha, Saramaand and Kaikasi; in the Bheels the character of Shabri; in the Varnas the characters of Anjana and Tara; in the Yakshas the characters of Taraka and Surasa. And in the Nagas I have taken the character of Sulcohana.

II

THE ARYAN WOMEN

I may add to sentence here that Prof. H.D. Sankalia, a reputed historian his written a book on 'Ramayana: Myth or Reality' in 1973 in which he has given scholarly arguments on several aspects of the Great Epic. My argument would not have this kind of bearing, but it would straightway deal with, as I mentioned earlier, less-known women in this romantic epic, read and reread and also interpreted in numerous ways. The religious epic as depicted by Valmiki rishi and later on by Tulsidas and several others in regional languages, clearly depict the doings of numerous women who have deep-rooted role in the long-drawn saga, revered and respected by Hindus all over the globe. Each female character has deep links with the text of Ramayana, Sita being the chief woman, known as Avtar, being the wife of Rama, is surrounded by several women in one way or the other. As analytical study of these characters for a host of historians in the Indian sub-continent and south east Asia. Take for example the birth of four sons from three wives of king Dashratha. They are living peacefully at Ayodhya for a number of years. But when Rama attains the age of 30, and Dashratha felt that he was growing old and must appoint his legal successor, a great obstacle like lightening fell on the horizon of his kingdom in the shape of the role of Kaikeyi.

KAIKEYI AND MANTHARA

Before I take up Kaikeyi in my analysis and assessment, I think it proper to explain, in a few lines, the role of Manthara, who is working as a maid in the royal palace at Ayodhya and a great confidant of Kaikeyi. Manthara is relentless in her effort, and crooked and cunning, the hunchbacked maid-servant of Kaikeyi, infused poison in the mind of Kaikeyi. And for all this, she did deeply allured of princely concessions from the Queenside once her vicious scheme succeeded. Thus having succeeded in persuading her, she gives her all the advice to ensure a hundred per cent success for her.

It was evident to every body that the Dashratha, the ruler of the Kingdom of Ayodhya, was growing old and he made up his mind to hand over the royal powers to his elder and beloved son, Rama. It could not be a secret affair. The royalty was announced and the transfer of power was to be done with much pomp and show.

The auspicious day arrived and now starts something unimaginable which even the old King and his eldest wife, Kaushalya could never think of. To complete the full circle, the most filthy part was played by Manthara who did not leave any stone unturned to poison the ears, mind and heart of Kaikeyi to the fact that if once the royalty was given to Rama, her official position and the status of her son, Bharata would be in jeopardy. Here we find the sense of jealously, unhappiness, anger and ill will crossing all the limits of morality, good will and welfare of the family as well as the state. Had not the seed of jealously been sown by Manthara in the mind of Kaikeyi the latter would not have compelled the old and feeble King to banish his eldest son for long fourteen years. This shows human greed for power and pelf, showing a sense of utter carelessness for dear and near, even the husband as it has been depicted in Ramayana in numerous meaningful verses.

Kaikeyi was the favourite queen of Dashratha and the king spent most of his time in her palace. Hailing from the frontier regions, she possessed charm and grace in a greater measure than the other queens and monopolized the king's love. The character Kaikeyi is utterly devoid of wifely responsibilities. She did not feel that her demand, indeed a 'Filthy' demand, would destroy the whole fabric of the Ayodhya Kingdom. In fact filthy and vicious way in which, the maid. Poisoned Kaikeyi mind was abominable. Vanvas for fourteen years and the royalty for her son, were the two demand which crippled the old king and wife Kausalya. Kaikeyi gained a bad name and I may add that no mother would name her daughter as Kaikeyi. It is also evident from reliable records that young girls were not barred from even military training, as is clear from the fact that Kaikeyi accompanied King Dashratha to the Devasura battle. When the King was rendered unconscious by wounds received in the battle, Kaikeyi, by her pluck and resourcefulness, removed him from the battlefield and saved his life. The implies knowledge of driving was chariots and rendering first-aid and physically strong women were not a rarity in those days.

KAUSHALYA

It is a perfect statement about Kaushalya that the greatness consisted in her having been the bother of Rama. As the chief queen she had no commanding on a influential voice like Kaikeyi. She was neglected by the king and insulted by Kaikeyi. Kaushalya devoted her time in performing religious rites and austerities for the welfare of her son. The sacrificial house of Dashratha's Asvamedha was decapitated by his eldest queen, Kaushalya, by her own hand with three strokes of the sword. It shows that women were physically strong.

SUMITRA

Sumitra's marriage was a politically motivated one. She was Karani, daughter of Dashratha's minister, Vamadeva. Badar, quoting Monier Williams, says that Lakshmana and Satrughana were born earlier, but as their mother was born as a Vaisya, Bharata is considered the elder brother. Nowhere in the

Ramayana do we got such a reference. Bharata was infact the elder. But the fact that Sumitra was not a princess did not effect the position of her sons as Anumola marriages were prevalent and princes born of such marriages were not only considered as true Kshatriyas but if their mothers were ambitious there was nothing to debar them from the Throne also, except the law of primogeniture, which does not seem to have been very much respected. All this discussion is to prove that it was due to Sumitra's character and her upbringing that her sons had nothing to do with the throne and kingly ambitions. Had she got the ambition of Kaikeyi there was no social bar to check her, as Badar and Monier Williams wrongly think. Her character is truly Spartian. She remains calm and is a source of strength to all when the great tragedy hits their family. To her the path of righteousness and duty was far more important than the kingdom. She can be well compared to Ghandhari, but as her sons were of like opinion, she does not suffer like Ghandhari.

It may be that king Dashratha respected her for qualities and calmness and therefore gave her double share of 'payasa' after deliberation. He had such respect for her that he is afraid of losing her confidence in case he banishes Ram. She had no fear of Kausalya or Kaikeyi nor she had nothing to lose in case either Rama or Bharata was installed on the throne.

URMILA, MANDAVI AND SHUTHKRITI

Urmila is the illustrious wife of Lakshman. Who is devoted not only to her husband, but also to the welfare of the royalty of Ayodhya. Indeed she is the true embodiment of sacrifice and selflessness. In fact she is the only woman in the earth great epic who has been kept away from the company of her husband from beginning to the end. Yet she is calm, patient and enduring in her temperament. Is it not something like injustice to this great leady who does not utter a single world in anger or unhappiness.

Urmila was the daughter of Janaka. Mandavi and Shuthkriti were the daughters of Janaka's elder brother. Along with Sita, Mandavi was married to Bharata, Urmila with Lakshmana and Shuthkriti's with Shatrughan. These three sisters had an intense bond of love with Sita. They created a tranquil atmosphere in their household. They won everyone's heart with their behaviour. They were struck and felt bad when they heard about the exile of Rama and Sita.

Urmila was the worst hit by this tragic incident because she had to stay away from Lakshmana for fourteen years. Bharata and Shatrughan too started living like sages in their respective palaces. The three sister were despondent sulk in pangs had to suffer the blow of destiny. Mandavi gave birth to Taksha and Pushkal. Urmila begot Angad and Chadraketu and Shruthkriti gave birth to Subahu and Shatrughati. All three of the sisters submerged themselves with their husbands in Saryu after Rama died in a similar way.

The decision of Lakshmana to accompany his brother Rama and Sita to exile for fourteen years was indeed .... hard decision for his young wife Urmila, who was to stay back at Ayodhya. One could not *ignore* the great sacrifice, to remain a celibate for 14 years, of Urmila whose heroic endurance and unwavering love for her husband are remarkable. She bore patiently her agonies and performed husband, the members of her family as well as the state of Ayodhya. indeed, she was a source of consolation and moral support to her in-laws and thus tried her best not let them feel the pangs of agony with the announcement of exile for Rama and Sita. All these qualities of her head and heart made her the embodiment of the ideal wife who waited and waited for days, weeks and long years of fourteen years. It is indeed a lesson-giving example that the great lady Urmila set up for posterity.

AHILYA

She was the daughter of Brahma who was brought up by sage Gautam in accordance with the instructions of Brahma. She grew up to become a very beautiful lady. Brahma decided to choose an appropriate husband for her. He invited all Devas, Asuras, Danavas, Yakshas, Kinnars, Gandhravas and the sages for his daughter's *Swaimvara*. On seeing such a beautiful, young damsel, each one of the prospective grooms was keen to win her lord in marriage. Even Rishi Gautam, his foster father, could not .... and joined the others in the fray. To get our of this situation and to find the best person in the assembly for his daughter, he told all who were present that whatsoever takes a round of the earth and comes back first will get his daughter in marriage. A massive race was started. Gautam saw a cow named Surabhi, which was in the process of giving birth to her calf and a shivalinga and came back to Brahma before the others did. Brahma said that a round of the cow and the shivlinga is equivalent to taking a round of the earth. So Ahilya was given to Gautama as his wife. She served him well but Indra had an evil eye on her. He disguised himself as Gautama and corrupted her. Gautama blamed it all on Ahilya. She was cursed to become a stone pillar. She was later revived by Rama.

This sad tale of Ahilya tells us of the sick social pattern of the Vedic civilization where even a foster father becomes attracted to his daughter and marries her. From birth onwards she is exchanged like property. She has no say in her defence when fingers are pointer of her and all her pleas of justice fall on defences. She is made to lie as stone for ages for a crime that she committed out sheer ignorance and in good faith.

SULABHA

She was a great sage and yogi of her times. She was probably the only lady yogi in her times. She was born in a royal family of Pradhans but became a sage when she could not find a suitable match for herself. She was the first woman sage who was an expert in the theory of metapysics. Among the few people who opposed her sect was Janaka, the King of Vidharba.

She decided to meet him. So she disguised herself as a beautiful lady with the help of her mystical powers and went to Janaka who was a disciple of the great sage Panchshikhika saw through her disguise and recognized her. A philosophical and intellectual discussion started between the two. She told him about metaphysics. She was able to change his perception about her sect.

SUNAYANA

She was the wife of King Janaka and the mother of Sita and Urmila. But she is not well known today and her character had not been highlighted in the Ramayana. When she heard that Rama had been exiled from his kingdom, she went to Chitrakoot with Janaka.

As the Epic moves on towards the forest-sometime green and sometime dry-the trio Rama, Sita and Lakshmana meet several people on the way. People recognize them vividly as members of the royal family of Ayodhya. They receive special treatment for humble people living in the remote villages. One such welcome was received by an insignificant Bheelni lady named Shabri belonging to the Bheel clan in the deep forest regions.

III

THE BHEEL WOMEN

Shabri

Shabri was a trial woman. She was Bheel by caste. She had a deep desire to serve the rishis and sages. She wanted to learn everything that they preached. She was especially influenced by sage Matanga. She went to him to seek knowledge. Matanga gave permission to her to build her hut near his abod. He was delighted to have her as his disciple. He considered her as his daughter. But the other sages in his ashram were not happy that a low-caste woman was living with them. Hence they avoided her. One day by accidentally in focused in garment of a sage. As a result, a lot of the rishis complained to Matanga. But Matanga was sure that it was not Shabri's fault .... The complaining tights left the ashrama as a result of displeasure— but Shabri remained with Matanga self till his death. Before dying, Matanga told Shabri that she would meet Rama one day and then attain salvation. Even after his death, she differently sewed his ashrama and waited for Rama.

It is evident that she is an ardent Ram Bhakta, a devotee who was told that Rama would pass through that region. She began to wait to have a full glimpse of Rama at any cost. She wished to entertain Rama with something sweet in the contents. Therefore she begins to collect plums (Ber) from the forest. She waited and waited and sometime she was disappointed but at last Rama, Sita and Lakshman appeared on the scene, the place where Bheelni lived. Bheelni received them with much love, respect and reverence and offered them rustic plums which she had gathered from the forest. The trio was very happy to eat them and how Bheelni was happy at this point time, his been explained in a few verses in Ramayana.

IV

THE ASURA WOMEN

Rama's stay in the forest posed no problem in the initial stage of his exile. As time passed, certain events occurred which led to difficult situations leading to a 'big' war between him and Ravana. As I explained earlier, each known or unknown character has contributed towards the making of this great epic, now a difficult situation posing a most complex problem arose in the jungle. Rama, Sita and Lakshman had encamped near Panchvati, incidentally, on the scene, the sister of Ravana, Surpanakha appeared.

SURPANAKHA

In her amorous passion she resembles somehow her brother, Ravana. The absurdity and ridiculous frivolity of her passion is marvelously sketched by the poet and made the center of a whole character-study. Surpanakha's love at the first sight, coarseness and vice incarnate for a "prince" who is an embodiment of beauty, refinement and virtuousness. She was a widow trying to get a husband.

A Rakshni by birth, she had complete sway over a part of the forest in which the royal prince had encamped. And being sister of Ravana, the king of Lanka, she was supported and respected by the tribal living in the forest, and while moving about she saw Sita and Lakshman–The latter being a handsome young man. She came near them and expressed her desire to marry Lakshman. It was an odd situation. Lakshman was a married man and secondly, who should be marry a Rakshni? She insisted time and again with the hope that possibly, Lakshman might agree. At this point of time, as it is evident in the verse of the Great Epic, Lakshman got very angry at her behaviour and cut her nose.

This was the beginning of a great epic, which followed after his episode. Suparnakha, in revenge for her own humiliation and insult and chastisement in the hands of Lakshman, succeeded in poisoning the mind of her brother Ravana on false statement.

She could insinuate her brother, who is a victim of pride and passion, to invite his opponent in a brawl. Ultimately, she proves to be the cause of the ruin of her own family and race and indirectly aids Rama spread the culture of the Aryans to the territory beyond the Vindhya, Had she not been present in the Panchavati and experienced the sad plight, the story of the Ramayana would perhaps be different as there would be no war between Rama and Ravana and the spread of the Aryan culture would have been retarded, so far as the idea of the composer of the Great Epic is concerned.

MANDODARI

Next comes the role of Mandodari, the chief queen of Ravana, the King of Lanka. She was the beautiful and majestic queen of Lanka proud of her lineage, husband and sons, had also to suffer on account of her husband's obstinacy. She is sober, intelligent and appears to be quite helpful to her husband. Mandodari: the queen wide of Ravana has been depicted as a devoted wife who is very much worried about the moral behaviour of her husband. She feels much offended by her husband's passion for Sita to the neglect of her, who is "Far superior to Sita in rank, beauty and kindness." (V, 16) When Sita landed in Lanka and made a captive and Ravana began to show his ambition to have indecent advances towards her, Mandodari did not like this kind of indecent behaviour of her husband. To her thinking, Sita was not her equal in any respect. Time and again she exhorted Ravana to correct her behaviour in order to save his family and the race. She was aware of the fact that Sita as a captive in Lanka would prove disastrous for Ravana, as he was no match for Great Rama. The verses in Ramayana are full of Mandodari's entreaty to Ravana. She, very wisely, reminded him of the colossal loss, which Lanka would sustain in a war with Rama, the Avtara. But Ravana was obstinate and nobody could challenge his obstinacy, pride and strength. Time and again, he used to say that he was invincible and nobody cold kill him, in a way he could be right on account of the bounty of several powerful and prominent deities on him, but how he was killed is very clear from several verses of Ramayana. Thus I may say that Mandodari, a pavitra wife, failed to bring round her husband to her point of view and ultimately the consequences were disastrous for Ravan and his race.

KAIKESI

This Asura damsel was the wife of sage Visharva. (son of Pulastya rishi) She bore him four sons and a daughter. The eldest son was named Kuber who later became the king of Lanka. Visharva did not like Kuber from the very beginning. Then she gave birth to Ravana and Kumbhakarna. Later she gave birth to twins who were named Khar and Suparnakha. In the end she gave birth to Vibhishana who later turned his back on his own brothers and helped Rama against them.

SARAMA

Vibhisana conspired against his brother Ravana and joined Rama against him. Ravana exiled him for his betrayal. Sarama was the wife of Bibhisana. She was not able to accompany her husband in his exile as women were prohibited from goes to the battlefield. She understood the pain of solitude, and gave Sita company when Sita was kept in the Ashoka Vatika. She was a source of strength to Sita during her gloomy days. Later, when Rama won the war, Sarama's husband Vibhisana was proclaimed the ruler of Lanka.

TRIJATA

Trijata was one of Ravana's maid servants. She was kept in Ashoka Vatika with some other Rakshashis to take care of Sita. She consoled Sita whenever in latter was gloomy. She was a source of strength to Sita. She often prayed to for Rama's victory. Lord Shiva for Rama's victory. When Rama won the battle, Sita told him about her. Rama gave Trijata the blessing that her descendants would rule the earth till the ed of the earth and that the sun shall never set in their empire. The British people are said to be the descendants of Trijata. In Bhagwata Purana, the English are referred to as 'GURANDS'. Trijata being a woman understood the plight of Sita.

RAVANA'S HAREM

Women in Ravana's harem were said to endowed with radiant beauty, charm and royal splendour. Through this amorous passion and of Ravana's concubines is intimately linked with and expressed in sexual revelry, they do manifest a deep psychic attachment to Ravana, as the poet indicates at several places, which is confirmed by their heart rending lamentations of grief over the dead body of their lord.

V

THE VANAR WOMEN

In continuation of this theme, the list of several less known women could be exhaustive. The other women which could be mentioned here are Tara, the wife of Vali, Anjana, the mother of Hanuman.

TARA

Tara has been depicted as an educated woman, particularly in religious books and she was one of the most intelligent and influential ladies. Due to the obstinacy of her husband, her attempts to make peace with Sugriva by giving him back his wife, Ruma and making him heir failed. However, Vali did recognize her sagacity and recommends her counsel to Sugriva, for Vali must have realized later the soundness of her advoce. Indeed her reasoning and argument were perfect in contents, and her resourcefulness, later on, saves Sugriva from Lakshmana's wrath.

Her queenly majesty is evident even when she is grieved at the death of her husband and very intelligently he musters the vanaras who were fleeing from the presence of Rama. She is also bold and fearless and does not hesitate in blaming Rama for killing Vali. Although she felt much grieved at the death of Vali, Yet she gathers strength and marries Sugriva for widow remarriage was probably a custom among the vanaras.

ANJANA

She was the mother of Hanumana and wife of Vanar King Kesri. Kesri was given a blessing by Rishi Bhardwaj that he will have a son who was to be the bravest and strongest amongst the vanaras and that no one could defeat him in war. Thus Hanuman was born.

YAKSAS AND NAGA WOMEN

Taraka

An important women character in Ramayana is that of Taraka. She was the daughter of Suketu who was a Yaksha. Taraka was granted the strength of 1000 elephants. Later she was cursed by Rishi Agastya and she and her son Marich became Rakshas. All her beauty was taken away by the divine powers of Agastya and she became an ugly, man-eating woman. She was killed by Rama who was directed by Viswamittra.

Sulochana

She was the wife the great Asura warrior Meghnath (son of Ravana). She was a naga princess. When Ravana attacked Naglok, the abode of the nagas, Sulochana's father, the naga King Takshak, gave her as a gift to Ravana so that the war could be stopped. Sulochana was an ardent devotee of Shiva (the Dravidiana lord Shiva Pashupati who is depicted in the seals obtained from the Indus Valley civilization). She was married to Meghnath. When Meghnath was killed in the battlefiled, one of Lakshmana's arrows carried his severed arm to Sulochana's palace. Her love for her husband was so intense that she did not touch the arm last showed her corrupted if it was the arm of sowed other than her husband. She went to Rama's camp claim the head of her husband. Rama praised her and told her that her husband was a great warrior, and that could tell him if there was anything that he could do for her, she could less him which hesitation. She asked to grant him just one wish, which was to stop the war that day as she wished to get sati in the funeral pyre of her husband.

Sursa

She belonged to the Naga race. The King of Devas asked her to test Hanuman's strength when he was going to cross the ocean. She disguised herself as a rakshashi and stood in the way of Hanumana. She asked Hanuman to pass through her mouth else she would not let him pass. Hanumana became angry and asked her to expand her mouth big enough so that he may enter it. Hence Sursa expanded her mouth to 10 Yojanas (an accident unit of length, 1 Yojana = 16 miles, i.e. 16 × 10 = 160 miles). To counter her move Hanuman enlarged his body to 10 Yojanas. She further enlarged her mouth to 20 Yojanas. Then Hanuman shrieked his body to the size of a thumb and quickly went in and came out of her mouth. Sursa was greatly when she was Hanuman's bravery and intelligence. She threw away her disguise and blessed him.

VII

When we analyse these characters, we are placed in a difficulty whether to call them 'known' or less known. If a different lose prevent of the Great Epic reveals that these women were truly remarkable in their invisible own way. Very few were having destructive temperament, but proved helpful in building up the story of Ramayana. The examples of Kaikeyi and Surparnakha are the glaring phenomenon, others are sober intelligent and supportive characters who could help their kith and with the sense of responsibility.

The custom of presenting smart and beautiful women, as a gift, is found time and again in the epic. Beautiful dasis or slave girls were presented to Rama as a tribute. So far so, at Dashrath's Sraddha ceremony, Bharat bestowed maidservants, upon Brahmans for the welfare of the departed spirit. Even king Janak gave away a hundred young maidens at the nuptials of his daughter Sita.

Besides this, the opulence of the age was responsible for the practice of bestowing young mid–servant for men's bathing and toilet services. Indeed princess and nobility were massaged, bathed, rubbed with fragrant sandal paste, dressed and undressed by young maidens. So far so, at the termination of the battle of Lanka, Vibhisana told Rama that lotus-eyed damsels, conversant with the art of declaring, stood ready to perform his bathing. At Bhardwaj's hermitage, each soldier of Bharata was allotted several females who massaged his body with oil, bathed him the lovely banks of the rivers, wiped his body, pressed his legs and offered him heady drink to quaff.

Thus Woman was generally treated as a sort of property, the owner having naturally the authority to do what he liked with her, Ravana considered his wives like his other property such as property as food articles of luxury, cloths, house, city or country. Indeed like property, women had to be constantly protected and guarded; complete independence was never her right as it has been emphasized that, the first refuge of a woman is her husband, second his son, third the reations: no fourth she has.

The attitude towards women was unsympathetic; if a woman has the misfortune of falling into captivity even for a short time, she finds it impossible to get readmission into her family and society. Rama refused to accept back Sita after the overthrow of Ravana. He informed her that all his efforts to kill Ravana were only for the purpose of avenging the wrong done to him, he had no idea whatsoever of accepting back a wife, who had stayed so long in the house of the enemy. Sita points out in reply that being in captivity, she was no longer the master of her person; she could command only her mind and that was always faithful to her husband. A number of Smrities and Puranas declare that women, who had the misfortune of being made prisoners or being assaulted criminality, should be treated with sympathy and not with contempt, and be accepted back by their families after they had performed certain purificatory rituals.

The custom of sati or self-immolation by the widow is the husband's pyre, however has little sanction in the Ramayana; none of the wives of King Dasaratha or Ravana are represented as joining their husbands on the pyre.

Among the Aryans widow the question of their remarriage did not normally arise in view of the solemnity and irrevocability of the marital tie in life as well as in death, here and hereafter, among the Vanaras, however, prevalence of widow remarriage must be accepted as a matter of fact. For example, Tara, at the death of Vali, wailed on her plight but after Vali cremation, the new king Sugriva compelled her to be his wife.

But among the Raksasas of lack of morals, widows generally found another mate, whether through regular marriage or Gandharva marriage. Thus, Suparnakha, Sister of Ravana and widow of Vidujjihva, passionately appealed to Rama to wed her. Ravana, too, had also forcibly introduced into his harem several beautiful women after slaying their husbands.

State etiquette of the period and proverbial Indian foundness for pageantry, necessitated employment of a large retinue and notch girls as escorts of honour. But it is quite Evident that ladies were quite distinct from common prostitutes, and their services were requisitioned in all royal festivities. When Rama was to be consecrated as the crown prince, Vasistha directed preparations to be made for the purpose, among which was a band of well declared dancing girls drawn up within the second apartment of the royal palace.

Indeed with grief, wrath and vengefulness in her spirit of revenge, leaving no stone unturned till her vindictiveness is satisfied.

Undoubtedly women got a thorough education during maidenhood, they were allowed considerable freedom and opportunities for several kinds of recreation, and they were not forced into any seclusion or purdah. With the choicest ornaments on, they used to frequent city gardens, and parks for play and sport in the evening and heartily enjoy music and dancing at such places.

Daughters were given instructions pertaining to their duties and obligations after marriage. Sita, insistent on accompanying Rama to the forest, tells him that she is well instructed by her parents regarding wifely duties. The princesses of the time were also initiated into political rights and duties so that they should prove valuable helpmates to their royal consorts. Besides, many girls were imparted training in some of the fine arts like music and dancing for instance, ladies in Ravana's harem were dexterous at playing all sorts of musical instruments.

Polygamy was almost the order of the day among the kings. Most of them whether Aryan, Vanaras or Rasasa possessed large harems. Dashratha is said to have had 350 wives, besides the four principal queens, Ravana marrried many women and his harem contained a thousand mistresses; Sugriva to had a large harem; and king Janaka had evidently more than two wives as he is said to have handed over the baby Sita to his eldest wife for rearing up.

The main point and my concluding remark would be that there should be more research on these characters so that whereas we are well aware of the Rama, Sita and Ravana, we should also know more details about these less known women as I have mentioned in my paper.

The very fact that we ignore them or accord them less significance, would tantamount to sheer injustice in the sequence of history. In fact our ancient culture and society are deeply indebted to these characters who, in no way, could embark upon a backward trend in the advancement of the Great Epic, Ramayana, let us see therefore who takes the leap in this context and dig out the material hitherto unseen by any academic. Indeed, it could be an arduous academic exercise.

Lesser Known Women in Ramayana

The Aryan Women	*The Asura Women*	*The Bheel Women*	*The Vanara Women*	*The Naga Women*	*The Yaksha Women*
Sita	Suparnakha	Shabri	Tara	Sulochana	Taraka
Kaikeyi	Mandodari		Anjana	Sursa	
Manthara	Kaikesi				
Kaushalya	Sarama				
Sumitra	Trijata				
Urmila	Women in Ravana's Harem				
Mandavi					
Shukriti					
Ahilya					
Sulabha					
Sunayna					

Chitrarekha Gupta

5

Working Women of Ancient India

D. D. Kosambi, "whose was a paradigm shift in early Indian history"[1] showed in his article 'Urvasi and Pururavas', the nature of conflict between the old mother goddess cult and the invading patriarchal domination through the projection of male godheads, and also tried to understand the socio-economic context of the conflict. The relation of narrative to history was also focused by his analysis of the differences in narrations of the same theme in the Vedic literature and in the play of Kalidasa.[2] Paula Webster, a feminist archeologist, on the other hand, has questioned whether the existence of mother goddess can "automatically prove the existence of an entire social status for women".[3] She concludes by saying: "If it is the future that interests us, what is the value of a vision of the past? Whatever past history women think they had, none produces a blue print for the future."[4] Thinking in this line makes the study of history redundant. In a country like India where social structure received its sustenance from deep-rooted tradition, it is necessary to study these traditions in their historical perspective and give analytical understanding of the causes behind the growth of such traditions. In women-studies it is now required to juxtapose the myths, which have haloed round women since ancient days and the reality, which they face even now. It has rightly been pointed out by Uma Chakraborty and Kumkum

Roy that unless women or gender as an analytical category is taken for study from a changed perspective certain ill founded notions about individual woman and woman as group will go unchallenged and will be reinforced through constant reiteration.[5]

The present paper aims to deal with working women of ancient India—a profile which was not taken seriously by Altekar[6]. General perspective of women of ancient India centres round those who lived inside domesticity, and were dominated by brahmanical rules of *varnasramadharma*. Their ideal was to become *pativrata* and goal was to become proud mother of male progeny. A perfect wife, as is known from the autobiography *of Isisasi,* had to leave her bed early in the morning before anyone else and do all household duties including cooking for the whole family and wait upon the comforts for her husband and other members in the in-law family.[7]

The patriarchs harped on inherent sinfulness of *strisvabhava* and suggested that it could be controlled (emphasis added) by their ordained function as wives.[8]

There are, however, scattered references here and there in ancient Indian literature and epigraphic documents about women who worked even outside domesticity, earned their own bread and, thus, did not conform to the norm laid down in didactic texts. Since, for obvious reasons, such references are not many, I have collected materials in a random manner, without emphasising chronological and special connection of the data and have tried to analyse gender in ancient Indian.

The Rig Veda speaks of Vispala, wife of Khela, a tribal chief, who fought battles along with her husband and lost her leg in one such encounter. She was not the only woman of her time to take arms in hand. Women warriors of the *Dasas* and *Dasyus* also find their mention[9]. In course of time through state formation process material role of women was marginalized. Army consisting of *chatas* and *bhatas* were recruited from men. But the amazons could not be completely denied. The Maurya court had female soldiers. It is recorded in the *Arthasastra* of Kautilya that female guards bearing weapons surrounded the king as soon as he had risen from the bed.[10] Megasthenes, as quoted by Strabo, supplies the additional information that when the king went for hunting in fenced enclosure armed women used to stand beside him. In unfenced hunting grounds when the king hunted from an elephant, women guards rode partly in chariots, partly on horses and partly on elephants. They even accompanied men in war field being equipped with all kinds of weapons.[11] In southern India also the custom of keeping women bodyguards for kings prevailed.[12] *Patanjali knew the female spear bearers or saktikis.*[13] If Kalidasa belonged to the Gupta period, the tradition of women guards in courts and palaces continued, as is suggested by the characters like *partihari Vetravati, dvarapalika* Madhavika or the Yavana girl who was ready at hand to supply the king bow and arrow. Kaikeyi is known to have gone to the battlefield with Dasaratha. Thus martial quality of women was utilized by the state: only their role as 'hero' and 'saviour' was marginalized by men. Gradually women came to be projected as 'weaker sex' incapable of even protecting themselves, far less the state.

Women excelled in gymnastics, which required physical strength and courage. Acrobats were popular in India from very ancient days. An interesting account of a woman-acrobat may be gathered from the commentary of the Dhammapada. There was a group of five hundred tumblers who used to visit *Rāgjagriha* once or twice a year to give performance before the king. A description of the show of the tumbler-girl, the central figures of the story may be obtained here. She " climbed a pole, turned somersaults thereon and balancing herself on top of the pole, danced and sang as she trod the air".[14] Had this tradition been kept alive, Olympic medal in gymnastic for girls could not be far off. But as she did not conform to the role model of women, she became insignificant. That the tradition of women acrobat existed is suggested by street shows of acrobatic feats performed by men, women and children belonging to the lower rung of the society. The most important part of the story reflecting on gender is that, the son of wealthy merchant fell in love with this acrobat girl, but her father declined to give her to him and instead asked the lover to travel with them. Obviously, she was the main money earner for the team, but not a free woman.

References to high ranking women administrators are extremly rare;[15] but women working as *dasis* and *dhatris* in the houses of rich men, including kings and nobles, urban and rural elites, are well documented in various sources. Maid-servants were of different categories. The function of the *dhātī* was so important in the upbringing of a child in the family of the rich that Asoka had to take this simile while referring to his appointments of Rājuka-officials for the welfare of the country people.[16] Attention may be drawn to an inscription from Mathura recording the donation of Mitrā, the *dhātrī* of Indragnibhadrā, the daughter of king Visnumitra.[17] From Mathura many records of women donors of the Kushana period have been found. This was the peak period of urban development in India. Most of these women donors, coming from affluent merchantile communities of the urban sector are found to be streotyped as daughters, wives, daughter-in-laws, mothers or grandmothers. They are proud in the reflected glory of the males.[18] Compared to them Mitrā is striking. She donated by her own right out of her own earning, so she needed no reference to her kinship relations. If she was proud of anything that was her royal connection.

Some women took the profession of a teacher. This is suggested by the differences in the terms *upadhyayas* or *upadhyayis* and *upadhyanis*, referring to women teachers and wives of male teachers respectively.[19] Girls of the upper stratum of the society, particularly among the brahamanas and the kshatriyas received education, may be from such women teachers. With the lowering of the marriageable age of girls and marriage taking the place of *upanayana* for them, female education in general suffered and we can not agree with R.C. Majumder when he suggestes that "women teachers were large in number."[20]

Women were intimately associated with production. During the Maurya period, crown land was partly cultivated, under the supervision of the *sitādhyaksha*, by the *ardhasitikas*, who retained half of the produce.[21] These cultivators probably had their own means of production like bullocks, ploughs etc. there was another group of cultivators who received only one fourth or one fifth of the produce. The latter group possibly gave their labour only. There were also agricultural labourers who received one and a quarter *pana* per month over and above food for his family. The same rate was fixed for labourers working in vegetable gardens, fruit orchards, flower gardens and also to herdsmen.[22] If this was the government rate, it may be assumed that the same rule was more or less followed by individual landholders in their private firms. No mention has been made by Kautilya to women workers in agriculture or dairy farming. But a legal clause in his text implicates the women. Kautilya says that a wife shall not be applicable into wives of farmers and cowherds working for half the produce.[23] This suggests women's active participation in these works along with their husbands. I-tsing, during the seventh century A. D., saw in Buddhist monastic lands male and female workers carrying on farming.[24]

Anthropologists are of the oppinion that women were the first agriculturists, but as society advanced from hoe cultivation giving surplus, women labour was marginalized in agriculture. Women were forbidden to touch the plough, but had to do many other works associated with agriculture.

Something happened in case of hunters also. Food providers became more powerful than food processors. In many tribal societies gradually women were not allowed to go for hunting, though we have already seen that fully armed women accompanied the kings in hunting during the Maurya period. An instance at hand for taboo regarding women's participation in hunting is the yearly tribal hunting festival at the Ayodhya hill in the Puruliya district, West Bengal.

Though fishing in the sea was a monopoly of men, women took part in salt water fishing. Selling of fish was usually done by fisher women. There are many references to fisher women in early South Indian literature.[25]

Women showed proficiency in various crafts and earned their breads through these professions. Women during the Vedic period were both spinners and weavers. The *Gobhila Grihya*

Sutra offers prayers to goddesses who spun and wove.[26] The *Panchatimsa Brāhmana* suggests women's participations in different stages of weaving.[27] But because of their skill in spinning women could not be ignored and the rule did not get universal acceptance. Kautilya's *Arthaśāstra* suggests that women coming from different social strata earned their living by spinning. The *sutradhyaksha* or the superintendent of yarns used to get yarn spun out of wool, back fiber, cotton, silk cotton, hemp and flex through women. These women included poor widows and maidens, crippled women, women who were paying off their fine by personal labour, women who had left their homes, mothers of courtesans, female slaves of the king.[29] Payment was made to each worker according to the quality and quantity of the yarn.

Since this was a popular means of earning livelihood to needy women of upper caste also, Kautilya instructed that women who did not stir out could send their maid servants for carrying raw materials and supplying finished products. If such women came personally, the concerned superintendent was enjoined to exchange goods and wages early at dawn.[30]

For looking at the face of the women and conversing with her on trivial matters other than the official business 'a lowest fine for violence' was imposed. For delay in payment of wages and for payment of wages without getting the work done middle fine for violence was imposed. But if a women worker failed to perform the work after receiving the wage or had misappropriated or stolen and ran away, her thumb was cut too.[31] Thus, though some women received legal protection, women in general were harshly treated for their offence.

Women also participated in dyeing cloth and *rajayitri/ rajakini* were terms used for such women. Vijaya Ramaswamy informs on the basis of references in the Sangam literature that women also took part in bleaching and washing of cloth. Such women were called in the south Pulatti.[32]

The Jain texts, the *Bhāgavatisutra* and *Uvasagadasao* speak of Halahala, a women, who had large-scale pot manufacturing centre at Śrāvasti. Many workers worked under her.[33] As she owned a factory it can be assumed that she also had close connection with the trading-nexus of the commodity she produced. Gradually, however, women ceased to be big potters as they were denied that right to touch the potter's wheel. Women remained as assistants in the work of pot making.

Women as basket makers are portrayed in the Vedic literature. With the introduction of metal this craft became less profitables and people associated with this craft were pushed to the lower rung of the social structure. In such families both men and women worked together. A women basket maker was called *bidalakan*.[34]

Women were expert garland makers. The *Gāthāsapatasati* refers to a female flowerist.[35] An eleventh century inscription from Tiruvamattur, Chennai, records that women were employed in the Abhiramesvara temple to pick flowers and make garlands.[36]

Vijaya Ramaswami has referred to association of women with various other crafts like extraction and sale of oil, pith work, production and sale of salt, extraction and sale of toddy. Yajnavalkya mentioned that a husband was not bound to repay the debts incurred by his wife. But milkmen, distillers of wine, washer men etc. were required to pay off the debts of their wives because in such families men earned their livelihood with their help.[38]

Women also took part in many consumer-service-oriented works. The *Gāthāsapatasati* speaks of *prapapalika* (Sanskritized from Prakarit), who supplied water to travellers.[39] Reference to such places for supply of water are found in some Nasik inscriptions and also in the *Mahābhārata*.[40] But it is from Hala's anthology that we came to know about women's association with such *prapas*.

There were not only centres for supply of water to travellers but also small shops from where merchants and other travellers could purchase their necessities en-route. There were also inns for them. The *Samayamatrika* speaks of one such woman innkeeper—*pantha vasatha palika*.[41] South Indian source also refers to small inns run by women.

Women confectioners hawking in the streets, sweets prepared by them were not uncommon scences.[42]

Women are traditionally good cooks and this also became a profession for some of them. A very important information comes from the *Talagunda inscription* of 1158 A.D. It speaks of an *agrahara* where three women were appointed to cook food for the students. It is obvious that these cooks belonged to the brahamana caste. They were paid wages and clothes.[43] *Tirupati Devasthanam* inscriptions show that such women cooks were employed in temples also.[44]

Women showed proficiency in performing arts like paintings, music, dance and acting. *Chitralesha*, the companion of Usha, was a good painter and had drawn a life-like portrait of Aniruddha. There are may references to women musicians, dancers and actresses. There were women vocalists as well as instrumentalists. In temples, courts and houses of nobles there were occasions to appoint paid musicians and dancers. I have excluded from my discourse in paper *devadasis* and prostitutes as they are 'class by themselves' and have received academic importance to some extent. Kautilya has referred to *rangopajivins* and *rangopojivinis*, actors and actresses performing on the stage. He also refers to *stripraksha* along with *purushapreksha* suggesting thereby that some times shows were put up only by women as also only by men.[45] Bharata speaks of groups were men and women performed together.[46] Kalidasa's play *Mālavikāgnimitram* suggest that women were given training in music and dances by male instructors like *natyacharya arya* Ganadasa of the play. The play also shows that women became famous by composing dance dramas. Name of Šarmisthā has been associated with 'Chhalika', a type of drama, difficult to act.[47] Vatsyayana enumerates sixty four arts and says that these should be studied not only by prostitutes but also by ladies of noble birth, because if a wife became separated from her husband and fell into distress, she could support herself easily even in a foreign country by means of her knowledge of these arts.[48] Thus, it is clear that many women earned their bread through these arts and all of them were not prostitutes.

The professions enumerated above may not be exhaustive, but clear enough to indicate that one dimensional perspective of ancient Indian women needs revaluation in the face of strong documentary evidence to the country.

A gender analysis would show that women workers were exploited in varuous ways even in those ancient days. They were exploited as wage earners. For the same work woman received less pay than his male counterpart. A Chola inscription records that when both men and women worked as daily labourers, women received half of what the men got.[49] The *Tiruvamattur* inscription mentions that men received eight *nalis* of rice per day for lifting water, irrigating the fields, gathering flowers and making garlands, women were paid only half of that for the same work.[50]

We have already noted how women workers of the state department of yarn were more severely punished for their offences than the offending officials.

Women workers were sexually harassed in their work place by village headman, royal officers and the like.[51] In the rural sector when a woman came to the house of such a person to fill the granaries, to take things in and out of the house, to clean the house, to work in the field, to purchase cotton, wool, flax, hamp and thread they were sexually exploited. They were entrapped also at the season of purchase, sale and exchange of various articles as well as at the time of other works. Similarly, the superintendent of cow-pens enjoyed women when they came to work in the cow-pens. Officers entrusted to look after the welfare of the widows, supportless women and women who had left their husbands were themselves exploiters of women. Only a small fine was imposed on misbehaviour with menial servant girl and even with wondering women ascetics.

Thus, the state did not provide adequate protection to women who came out of domesticity because of bare necessity or otherwise. On the contrary, the society is found to brand most of these women, not conforming to the role model of women at home, as bad women. Some women took the profession of spies, which required lots of courage and intelligence and which was an important wing of state machinary. Kautilya was in favour of appointing a wondering nun, poor widowed, bold, brahamana by caste and seeking a livelihood as a spy. She could be sent to houses of high officials with the purpose of spying easily because of her respectability in the royal place itself. Nuns of heretic sects could also be used in the same way. Women spies could be in the disguise of female artists, singers and females slaves also. They were expected to convey information obtained through songs recitations, writings concealed in musical instruments or songs.[52]

Nuns, female ascetics and women musicians, dancers and actresses were looked with disdain. Women bodyguards of the kings, otherwise beautiful, courageous and alert were grouped as courtesans.[53] A Perfect wife was enjoined to shun the company of women ascetics.[54] Performing women artists received no status. Sexual misconduct with another man's wife was punishable according to Manu's dictum. But he emphatically said that the rule would not be applicable to the wives of actors and singers because they themselves, overtly or covertly, allowed their women to co-habit with other men.[55] Such a general statement reflects the attitude of society towards these professions, which involve participation of women.

The lawmakers imposed another type of restriction on working women so that they could not become socially powerful and economically potential. Kātyāyana said that income in these working women could not be regarded as their *stridhana*, over which they could have exclusive right.[56] This rule, however, indicated that the number of working women was not negligible and so it became necessary to promulgate laws to put them under domination.

We would like to conclude by references to a passage in the *Yugapurāna*, which relates to women. While speaking of the *Yavana* invasion of Magadha it mentions that after the devastation of war, male population declined. Women outnumbered men, in such a situation, women had to carry on agriculture, including tilling the fields. Women were enlisted as soldiers in the army. Administration of villages and towns was also conducted by them.[57] We have seen that women could do all types of works-physical and managerial. But here we have a confirmation, which goes to show that the patriarchal society had no hesitation in conceiving women in these roles in times of their need. So the imposition of all taboos on women is an implement in the hands of the patriarchal society for marginalizing the roles of women as 'social adults' and to keep them within domesticity and subordination.

What can be more degrading for a women than to worship her husband as a god "even though he might be destitute of virtue or seeking pleasure elsewhere or devoid or good qualities".[58] This fetter imposed by Manu is not yet removed from women. The role model of working women may be an alternative for them as a step towards a goal. Most of the women workers of ancient India were economically constrained and were obliged to earn their livelihood. But it is a known fact that the basic reason of women's subordination is social surplus controlled by men. Women also came to be conceived as 'property' to be used by men at their sweet will.[59] Relation between production process and social stratification being intimate, the toiling *sudras* in India form the lower rung of the social structure, and women, irrespective of their caste, are grouped along with the *sudras*.[60] A woman looking to the past in search of her cannot ignore the social processes and the structures created thereby. So, she feels like holding the hands of working women of the past. Here is a role model, which was never projected and was hardly appreciated by the patriarchal society. On the contrary, the patriarchs tried to marginalize the worth and work value of these women. It is time to project them.

NOTES AND REFERENCES

1. Romila Thapar, *Narratives and the making of history,* OUP, New Delhi, 2000, p.V.
2. Kumkum Roy ed., *Women in Early Indian Societies,* Delhi, 1990, pp. 257-285.
3. Paula Webster, Matriarchy: A Vision of Power in Rayna R. Reiter ed., *Towards an Anthropology of Women,* U.S.A. 1975, p.143.
4. *Ibid.,* p.155.
5. Uma Chakravarti and Kumkum Roy, In Search of Our Past-A Review of the Limitations and Possibilities of the Histriography of Women in Early India, in *economic and Political Weekly,* April 30, 1988.

6. A.S. Altekar, *The Position of Women in Hindu Civilization*, reprint Delhi, 1983, (1st ed. 1938).
7. Bhikshu Silabhadra ed. *Therigatha*, Calcutta, Varga 1357, pp. 148-157.
8. Julia Leslie, *Perfect Wife*, Delhi, 1989, p.272.
9. B.S. Upadhyaya, *Women in Rg. Veda, 3rd ed.*, New Delhi, 1974, p. 149.
10. R.P. Kangle ed., *The Kautilya Arthasastha*, reprint, Delhi, 1988, 1.21.1. p.29.
11. R.C. Majumdar ed., *The Classical Account of India*, Calcutta 1960, p. 271.
12. Kumkum Roy ed., *op. cit., p.164*, T.N. Subramanian, *Sangam Polity*, Bombay, 1966, p. 289.
13. R.C. Majumdar ed., *The Age of Imperical Unity*, Bombay, 1960, pp. 563-564.
14. I.B. Homer, *Homer Under Primitive Buddhism*, Reprint Delhi, 1975 (1st ed. 1930), p. 84.
15. The Nowgong copper-plate inscription of Balavarman III refers to the *mahallaka praudhikas along with rajnis, rajaputras* and other high officials. Ref. M.M. Sharma, *Inscriptions of Ancient Assam, Gauhati*, 1978, o, 146. See also Vijaya Ramaswamy's *Aspects of Women and Work in Early South India*, in Kamkum Roy ed., op. cit, pp. 162-165.
16. D.C. Sircar, *Select Inscriptions Bearing on Indian History and Civilization*, Vol. 1,Calcutta, 1965, p.57.
17. Luders, *Mathura Inscriptions*, p.207.
18. Chitralekha Gupta's 'Rural Urban Dictionary' in the Concept and Status of Women: An Examination (from the Mauryas to the Guptas) in L.K. Tripathi ed. *Position and Status of Women in Ancient India*, Vol. I, Varanasi 1988, pp. 192-193.
19. Katyayana, *Varttika*, IV.1.48.
20. R.C. Majumdar ed., *The Age of Imperical Unity*, Bombay, 1960, p. 563.
21. R.P. Kangle ed., *op.cit.*, 2.24.16 .
22. *Ibid.*, 2.24.28.
23. *Ibid.*, 3.11.23
24. J. A. Takakusu ed., *A Report of the Buddhist Religion as Practised in India and the Malay Archipelago* by I-t sing, Delhi, 1982, p.61.

25. Vijaya Ramaswamy. Aspects of Women and Work and Work in Early south India. in Kamkum Roy ed. Op. cit. Pp. 158-9
26. Gobhila Grihyasutra, Benaras, 1936, IV. 10.10.
27. Vijaya Ramaswamay, *op.cit.*, p.155.
28. *Ibid.*
29. R.P. Kangle ed., *op.cit.*, 2.23.2.
30. *Ibid.*, 2.23. 11-12.
31. *Ibid.*, 2.23. 14-15.
32. Kumkum Roy ed., *op.cit.*, p.155.
33. *The Bhāgavati sutra*, Calcutta ed., 1243 a; Hoernle ed., *Uvasagadasao*, ii, Appendix I., 6-7.
34. A.K. Tyagi, *Women Workers in Ancient India* Upto c.300 A.D., Delhi, 1994, p.48.
35. R.G. Basak ed., *Hala's Gatha-Saptasaati*, Calcutta, 1971, 6.96.
36. Kumkum Roy ed., *op.cit.*, p.159.
37. *Ibid.*, pp.157-9.
38. *Yajnvalkyasmriti*,
39. R.G. Basak ed., *op.cit*, 2.61.
40. *Ibid.* p. 24.
41. L. Gopal: *The Economic Life of Northern India*, (c. 700-1200 AD), p. 98.
42. Kumkum Roy ed. *Op. cit.*, p. 160.
43. *Epigraphia Carnatika*, vol. VII, sk. 185.
44. *Tirumalai—Tirupati Devasthanan Inscriptions*, vol. II, no. 135.
45. R.P. Kangle ed., *op. cit.*, 2.27.28; 3.3.21.
46. Bharat's *Natyasastra* 1.46-47; 36, 71.
47. Kalidasa's *Mālavikāgnimitram*, Act 1.
48. S.C. Upadhyaya ed.: *Kāmaśutra of Vātsyāna*, Reprint 1963, 1st ed 1961, p. 80.
49. *Annual Report of Epigraphy*, 1917, no. 223.
50. *Ibid.*, 1922, no. 18.
51. S. C. Upadhayaya ed., *op. cit.*, p. 194.
52. R.P. Kangla ed., *op. cit.*, 1.12.4-5, 1.12.13.

53. T.N. Subramanian, *Sangam Polity,* Bombay 1966, p. 289.
54. Julia Leslie, The Perfect Wife, Delhi 1987, p. 139.
55. *Manusamhita 8.* 362-363.
56. Subrata Sen, *The Institution of Stridhana in the Dharmāsāstra,* Calcutta, 1995, p. 115-124.
57. *Yugapurāna,* 8. 362-363.
58. *Manusamhitā,* 5. 154.
59. Chitralekha Gupta, Women, Law and the State in Classical India, in H.B. Kolver ed., *Recht, Staat and Verwaltung in klassischen Indien,* 1997, p. 209.
60. R.S. Sharma, Co-reference to Women and Sudra in Early Literature, in *Perspective in Social and Economic History of Early India,* Delhi, 1983, pp. 45-48.

Anita Bagchi

6

Involvement of Women in Some Scientific Activities in Ancient India

The longest period of human history has been spent for the task of gathering food by way of hunting animals and collecting fruits and vegetables from jungles. Arriving at the Neolithic period, the man acquired the skill of polishing stone implements which helped him to establish control over his food supply. He began to cultivate plants and domesticate animals.

The generally accepted view of the scholars[1] is that the women were the first to attain the knowledge of agriculture. It was only after the domestication of cattle and invention of plough, which came much later, that women were liberated from the toil of cultivation.

Bernal[2] regards the invention of the technique of agriculture in the same rank with the discovery and utilization of fire and power. Development of agriculture and thereby consequent increase in food produce necessitated the making of pots for storage of foodgrains. Actually the use of pottery extended the range of cooking operations and improved the diet of man. Making of pots, spinning and weaving are again credited to women.

Bernal observe, "the forms of patterns produced in weaving and the number of threads involved in producing them are essentially of a geometrical nature, leading to a deeper understanding of the relation, between form and number". This may be regarded as the fore-runner of weaving technology.

So, we find that the women from the dawn of human civilization had been playing a very important role in each and every step of its advancement. This is also true in case of India.

We have no literature of the Indus people. Enormous archaeological remains have been unearthed. Still we are not in a position to make an assessment of the role and involvement of the ladies in the process of development of this culture. The degree of women's participation in the scientific and technical activities of the society can not be discerned.

The Vedic Period is rich in literature. From the Rgveda[3] it is know that sewing, the plaiting of mats from grass or reeds and the spinning and weaving of cloth were chiefly done by women. To reconstruct a connected account of women's involvement in the scientific activities and practices during the ancient period is a difficult job because of paucity of informations. The study of plants and plant life ultimately gave birth to the sciences like Agriculture, Medicine, Arobori Horticulture etc. By the post-vedic period, there are enough evidences to show that Botany developed as an independent science on which the sciences of Medicine, Agriculture and Arbori-Horticulture were based. This branch of science came to be known as 'Vrksayurveda of Parasara. By the 4th century B.C. the art of agriculture received a consummate perfection and Arobori-Horticulture developed in ancient India as a distinct branch of Vrksayurveda.[4] It dealt with the construction and maintenance of gardens and public parks. In the Sukraniti[5] though of much later date, we find that parks and pleasure gardens came to be regarded as essential necessities of city social life. These were meant for health and recreation. These were in charge of a Superintendent (Aramadhipati).

It would not be irrelevant to mention here that apart from these public parks and gardens, there were gardens attached to dwelling houses. According to Kamasutra[6] of Vatsayana, "attached to every house there should be a Vrksavatika or Pushpavatika, a garden with wide grounds where flowering plants and fruit trees can grow, as well as vegetables. The garden should be in charge of the mistress of the house. She is to duly procure seeds of kitchen vegetables and medicinal herbs, such as mulaka, trapusa, aluka, palanki, demanda, amrataka, ervaruka, vartaka, kusmanda, alavu, suraha, sukanasa, svayamgupta, tilaparnika, ognimantha, Iasuna, palandu and such others." The direction is also given as to how greens and vegetables are to be reared in specially prepared beds, sugarcane in clumps, stunted shrubs of mustared, jiraka, ajamoda, satapuspa and similar herbs in patches and the dark tamala tree in groves. On the basis of these informations, we can make a comparison between the duties of the state-appointed superintendent of the parks and pleasure gardens and a mistress of the house, shouldering the responsibility of the flower cum kitchen garden of her house. The superintendent had to know the causes of the growth of plants, development of fruits and flowers, the method of planting and curing diseases by selecting proper soil, water and by administering medicinal plant drugs. Likewise the mistress of a house had sufficient knowledge of seeds, soil, water, rearing and caring of plants and their growth characteristics, Kamasutra regards the Vrksayurveda as on one of the sixty-four kalas or arts to be acquired by the ladies.

An interesting corroborative evidence regarding the botanical knowledge of the ladies in ancient period is furnished by the Deopara Inscription of Vijayasena.[7] The translation of the relevant verses runs thus: through his grace the Brahmanas versed in the Vedas have become the possessors of so much wealth that their wives have to be trained by the wives of the town people to recognise pearls, pieces of emerald, silver coins, jewels and gold from their similarity respectively with seeds of cotton, leaves of saka, bottle-gourd flowers, the developed seeds of pomegranates and the blooming flowers of the creepers of pumpkin-gourd. From the above quoted portion of the said inscription, one thing is evident that the women had to bear the responsibility of supervising the kitchen garden attached to their houses and thereby developed practical knowledge in this branch of science.

The aphorisms of Khana[8] provided very strong evidence in favour of women's awareness and profound knowledge in agricultural science. Only a few are quoted here.

The following aphorisms of Khana contain the direction of aerating the soil for different plants.

Translation: For the successful cultivation of cotton one has to plough the land 16 times, for radish 8 times, for paddy 4 times and for betel nil.

In this context I quote the opinion of the well known Botanist Prof. G.P. Majumdar[9], "The Soundness of the directions becomes at once manifest when one takes into consideration that cotton plant has an elaborate root-system, radish is a herb, paddy is a surface feeder, and betel is a climber that produces numerous adventitious aerial roots."

It is well-established now that the food of plant is manufactured in the green leaves. Before the establishment of this great truth in modern science, in the remote past Khana had the perception of this physiological phenomenon of plant. She also realised that the productive output of plant depended on the manufacture of food in the leaves. This is why she advised–

Translation: After you have planted the banana plants, do not cut of their leaves, and this will bring you both bread and clothes.

There are so many other sayings of Khana which are very much striking.

Khana says–

Translation: The paddy develops day by day owing to sunshine by day, and water by night.

The modern scientific explanation of the above quoted maxim of Khana is that during the sunshine food of the plant is manufactured, assimilated and stored; and during the night time the growth of plants takes place and for this water supply is needed.

The number of maxims of Khana, the depository of the wisdom of ages, is too many to be accommodated in this paper. Without going into more we can easily conclude that these aphorisms were very much popular among the people mostly dependent on cultivation and agriculture.

Nihar Ranjan Ray[10] has referred to Dak and Khana whose sayings were very much popular among the agrarian people of Bengal from an earlier period. The form in which these were current in Bengal was medieval in character. Nihar Ranjan Ray expresses his view that these vachans or sayings undoubtedly bear the tradition of a very early period. On the basis of the maxims of this illustrious lady, one can easily think of her wide range of knowledge about soil, ploughing, sowing and planting, reaping and harvesting and above all her meteorological observations.

Prof. Majumdar says "the striking resemblance between some of the aphorisms of Khana relating to agriculture and some of the verses in Krishi-Parasara on the same subject may warrant us in the supposition that the authentic treatise in Sanskrit might have a good deal to do with the mythical author of the aphorisms of Khana who carried the lessons contained in the Krisi-parasara to particular applications in minute details."

The study of plants gave birth to another branch of science i.e. science of Medicine. In ancient India medicinal science is known as Ayurveda. The literal meaning of the Ayurveda is the 'Science of Life'[11]. The beginning of the Ayurveda may be traced first in the *Rgveda* and then in the Atharvaveda. But the contributions of Buddhist Scholars in this field are of great significance. The fundamental perceptions and observations on different subject were collected together under appropriate titles from the 6th century B.C. Our knowledge of this ancient science comes mainly from the surviving written treatises, the oldest of which are the *Samhitas* of Bhela, Charaka and Susruta.

The Buddha prescribed for the religious life in the Samgha the resources like medicine and *Vihara*.[12] The bhikkhus suffered from various ailments and the fellow bhikkhus were asked to nurse the diseased monks. The Buddhist *samgha* had provisions to offer medical services. Even there were sickwards within the compound of the monastery. Evidences show that in this task of medical service, the lay persons were also interested and assistance came not only from the male person but from the lay woman also. A devout woman Suppiya[13] once donated a piece of flesh from her thigh to a bhikkhu who had undergone a fistula operation. Such liberal act of donation of flesh for the purpose of a surgical operation in the remote past should be viewed not only as an example of her philanthropic attitude but also an instance of her earnest involvement and cooperation for the success of medical treatment. Now a days, conscious people and organisations occasionally make appeal to the people for voluntary donation of human organs. So such an act of donation of flesh deserves special mention.

The *Kautilya Arthasastra* (ii. 4-55)[14] recommends for the construction of *bhaisajyagraha* i.e. a hospital within the compound of a fort. The same *Arthasastra* refers to an organisation which would remain equipped with physicians with surgical instruments, machines, remedial oil and bandages, and women in charge of food and beverage etc. Here also my contention is to highlight that in discharging the medical duties the physicians were assisted by the ladies. It is well-known that food and beverage have a great importance in the Ayurvedic system of treatment and the women certainly proved themselves competent enough to bear the responsibility of the diet of the patients.

We may now turn to a story of *Asokavadana.*[15] the story tell us: once *Asoka* fell ill. Tissarakkha, his queen diagnosed the disease and cured her husband. The diagnosis was conducted by finding a similar symptoms in another person and then eliminating various possibilities by a variety of treatment until the proper antedote was identified. Romila Thapar commented that this event throws light on the medical analysis of the time. Tissarkkha's success in curing her husband by following a process of trial and error indicates her profoundness in medicinal science. Her attempt to select the right antedote on the basis of trial and exclusion principle on a man clearly shows that she knew well that experiment and observation are the basic requisites for any success in medical research. If we take this episode to be true, we can hardly deny her intellectual perception.

But it is a matter of regret that inspite of inherent intelligence and talent, most of the women in ancient India could not give expression to their qualities of head and heart owing to the absence of privilege for education. Still, amidst this situation, some of them displayed their promise in various subjects, mostly in literature; and a few among them excelled even in science subjects also. We may refer to the name of Rusa.[16] This lady wrote a medical treatise on the diseases of women which was translated into Arabic in the eighth century. Rusa, certainly was a great authority on Gyneacology and her work probably was of a high order which attracted woven the notice of the Arabic world. The medical scholars of the two lands contributed much to a mutual enrichment of knowledge and in this exchange the contribution of a lady authority is simply fascinating in the history of medical science in ancient India.

Women's privileges for education were being curtailed increasingly during the Smritiage and the male dominated society had little headache for recording the contributions of this large section of the population. The smriti *sastras* by progressively advocating and sanctioning early marriage of girls in fact closed the door of higher education for them. The *smritis* imposed ban on the study of the Vedas by women and threw them to the darkness of ignorance. This is proved by the significant omission of their names in the contemporary lexicographical works.[17] Some of the ladies belonging to higher classes might have enjoyed some facilities.

Poet Rajsekhara (900 A.D.) commented that he met many princesses and poetesses, daughters of Prime Ministers and other dignitaries who were well versed in science i.e. *Sastras.* But it did not reflect the general picture of the prevailing social condition.

Therefore, those few ladies who distinguished themselves going against the social dictum of the day should be regarded as the morning star of women's participation in science.

Inspite of impediments, the scientific pursuit of woman might have continued as a subtle flow through the ages. Coming the 18th century we get the names of some lady Ayurvedic physicians who became very famous for their profound knowledge. We can refer to Yadur Ma[18] of Dorjipara who was consulted even by many British and native doctors. Sonajaru, prepared on her own formula was very effective. Iswargupta's comment in the Sambad prabhakar may be quoted here:

Daktar Kabiraj rane yare hare
Yodur janani giya joy kare tare

Apart from her, Hatividyalankar, Anandamayidevi of Vikrampur and Vaijayanti Devi of Kotalipara were renowned lady Ayurvedic physicians. Among them Hatividyalankar was a child-widow of a Kulin Brahmana family of Radha. Her original name was Rupamanjari. She established an Ayurvedic School and many male as well as female students came from different parts of the country to learn from her. She died in 1810.

All these informations enlighten us about the involvement of women in agricultural and medicinal sciences from the ancient period. We can conclude with the comment of Rajsekhara that "culture is connected with soul and not with sex".

NOTES

1. Randhawa, M. S. (1969), The Quaternary Period-VII, The Neolithic Culture: Invention of polished stone implements, discovery of agriculture and domestication of animals. In *Evolution of Life* (ed. Randhawa *et al.*). Publications and Information Directorate, New Delhi.
2. Bernal, J. D. (1954), *Science in History,* Watts & Co. Let., London.
3. Majumdar, R. C. (1996), *The History and Culture of the Indian People: The Vedic Age*. Bharatiya Vidya Bhavan, Bomabay.
4. Majumbar G. P. (1986), The History of Botany and allied sciences (Agriculture, Medicine, Arbori-Horticulture) in ancient India (c. 2000 B.C. to 100 A.D.). In *The History of Science and Technology in Ancient India: The Beginning* (ed. D.P. Chattopadhyay). Firma KLM Pvt. Ltd., Calcutta.
5. Sarkar, B. K. (1975), *The Sukraniti* (Eng. Trans.), Oriental Books Reprint Corporation, New Delhi.
6. Tarkaratna, P. and Bandopadhyay. M. (Bengali San 1398). *Vatsyayanas Kamasutra* (Bengali trans.). Sanskrit Pustak Bhandar, Calcutta.
7. Majumdar, N. G. (ed.) (1929), *Inscriptions of Bengal,* Vol. III. The Varendra Research Society, Rajshahi, Bengal.

8. *Khanar Bachan* (in Bengali). Vatala edition.
9. Majumdar, G. P. (1927), Vanaspati: *Plants and Plant Life as in Indian Treatises and Traditions.* Calcutta University.
10. Ray, N. R. (1980), *Bangaleer Itihas: Adiparba.* Vol. I. Paschimbanga Nirksharata Durikaran Samiti, Culcutta.
11. Majumdar, R. C. (1989), Medicine. In *A Concise History of Science in India* (Ed. Bose *et al.*). Indian National Science Academy, New Delhi.
12. Ray, K. (1998), Buddhist Monsatic Medicine and Arogya-Vihara. *Indian Museum Bulletin,* Vol. 33.
13. Malalasekera, G. P. *Dictionary of Pali Proper Names* Vol. 2.
14. Bandopadhyay, N. C. (1927), *Kautilya,* Calcutta.
15. Thapar Romila (1998), *Asoka and the Decline of the Mauriyas.* Oxford University Press, New Delhi.
16. Ganguly, D. C. (1975), Some aspects of the position of women in Ancient India. In *The Culture Heritage of India,* Vol. II. The Ramakrishna Mission Institute of Culture, Calcutta.
17. Majumdar, R. C. (1993), *The History and Culture of the Indian People: Vol. IV, The Age of Imperial Kanauj.* Bharatiya Vidya Bhavan. Bombay.
18. Pahari, S. (1997), Kabiraji Chikitsa: Oupanibeshik Bangalay Kabiraj O tar janapriyata. In *Bharater ittibas Vijyan O Prajukti* (ed. A. Basu) Bangiya Viyayan Parishad.

S. L. Baruah

7

State, Patriarchy and Women: A Reappraisal on Phuleswari Konwari

The organised civil society with governmental machinery, called the State, is a creation of males. Its distinguishing feature is force or coercion. Since the males are physically stronger than the females, and since success in politics depends largely on the use and control of force, politics has always been regarded as the domain of males. There are other reasons also, for which, women all over the world had been, by and large, excluded from politics. The main purpose of organising a civil society was defence. Defence meant martial power which depended on the physical strength and wielding power of the soldiers who had to keep themselves away from their family for a considerable length of time for rigorous physical training in times of peace and for fighting in times of war. This was not possible in case of women, as in the absence of family-planning programme, procreation and rearing up of children had been a life-long and sole business for women. However, women in many royal and aristocratic circles, associated with the administrative machinery, received military training and some of them could exhibit their proficiency as warriors. Karnavati of Chitor, Lakshmibai of Jhansi, Mulagabharu, Radha and Rukmini of Assam are examples of some of the famous women warriors. This however, does not indicate the participation of common women in administrative machinery or in the military force organised for the defence of the land.

The state being based on patriarchy with the principle of male domination and female subordinates, women generally play only indirect role in politics either as unofficial advisors or as regents, although this role has been very influential and remarkable. Nongoniak of the Satavahana empire, Tarabai of Kolhapur, Ahalyabai of Indore and Lakshmibai of Jhansi are some of the very well known queen regents of Indian history. Nurjahan played a dominant role in the Mughal Court politics since her marriage with Jahangir (1605-27) in 1611 till 1628, when Shahjahan (1628-58 AD) fixed a settlement for her, where she lived a retired life till her death in 1646. In the history of our state, Chaoching, the queen of Suklenmung Garhgayan Raja (1939-52 AD)[1], Numali Rajmou, the queen-mother of Kamaleswar Singha (1795-1811 AD) and Chandrakanta Singha (1811-18 AD) played important role.[2]

Examples of women becoming *de-jure* sovereigns of large and powerful countries are, however, very few and far between despite their efficiency, the problem of their sex had been working on them as Sophocles' sword, sometimes affecting the life of the subject population and compelling the women—rules either to enter into political marriages or not to marry at all. We can refer in this context to Queen Elizabeth I (1558-1603 AD) of England who remained a spinster, because, if she were to accept a husband, the only choice would have been Philip II of Spain as subjugation of Spain was a must for the ascendancy of England during her time. The most important problem for Sultana Razia (1236-40 AD), the first and the only women-sovereign of India was her sex. Although endowed with all the admirable attributes and qualifications necessary for a kirulvegs,[3] she had to accept an ignominious end of her career as 'the proud Turkish nobles could not reconcile themselves to the rule of a woman'.[4]

In the light of these precedents, if the career of Phuleswari Konwari of Assam is assessed, the image generally drawn about her appears to be somewhat distorted. S.K. Bhuyan calls her an Assamese Nurjahan. In captivating the mind of king Siva

Singh (1714-44), by physical charm and winning for herself the office of the Chief queen by qualities of head and heart and conferring important officers on her kith and kin, she resembles the great Mughal queen but although the latter was not the de-jure sovereign, she was exercising tremendous influence in court politics during a long period of nineteen years, whereas in spite of being entitled as Bar-Raja (Great King), Phuleswari's power was controlled and regulated by her hen-hearted husband and she was exploited only as a weapon to realise the objectives of her husband's power-loving shrewd Sakta preceptor.

It is generally opined that Phuleswari's persecution of the Vaishnava Mahantas was the most important cause of the Moamariya Rebellion, which paved the way for the fall of the Ahom kingdom. Hence, historiographers show no mercy to her. They often describe Siva Singha as a 'henpecked' husband and Phuleswari as a proud and arrogant queen, who was abusing the power conferred on her. Harakanta Sarma Barua Sadar Amon while describing the activities of Phuleswari writes in a tone as if pride is a natural trait of a young beautiful women.[5] Dutiram Hazarika through the mouth of Siva Singha states that women by nature are evil-minded.[6] In fact, almost all scholars are very critical about this lady. No one was ever deemed it necessary to analyse the facts and examine the reality in which she had to work as an agent of a state policy and understand that she was a victim of patriarchal social structure.

Siva Singha became king in 1714 AD and it was eight years after his accession to the throne that the prediction was made that he was under evil influence of stars *(chatra bhanga yoga)* which might cause an end of his rule.[7] One year earlier to this event, he married Phuleswari (Phulmati), the daughter of a professional Koch dancer of China tali and made her the Parvatiya Konwari (second queen). The Ahom nobles could not reconcile to this, as Phuleswari was not only from a non-Ahom family but had also a very humble origin. The other court ladies were also jealous of the king's fascination for her. In this situation, Krishnaram Nyayavagish, the Sakta priest from Bengal who was accepted as Guru by Siva Singha, became her friend, philosopher and guide. Krishnaram was gifted with large estates of land and put in charge of the Kamakhya temple on the Nilachala hill at Guwahati, for which he came to be known as the Parvatiya Gosain. Krishnaram calculated that this young beautiful damsel could be used as the most effective weapon to realise his goal of making Saktism the state religion and thereby becoming the prime religious preceptor in the Ahom kingdom. He exploited the young queen Phuleswari's devotion to him and allured her to perform some ignominious jobs by calling her an embodiment of the goddess Durga. She was renamed by him as Pramathewari (a name of the goddess), when she was made the Chief Queen and declared 'Bar-Raja'.[8]

Krishnaram was well aware of the fact that the Ahom nobels were critical of his religious policy and of the special favour shown to him by the king. It was also known to him that earlier one Paramananda Bairagi of Gakulpur in Brindavan coming to Assam, attempted to make the Ahom nobles and the Vaisnava preceptors his disciples through the patronage of king Udayaditya Singha (1670-73). But this had cost the lives of both the king and the Bairagi. However, things by the time of Siva Singha had greately changed. Not only the socio-religious scenario of the land underwent a transition, Assam's diplomatic relations with the neighbouring Bengal guided by policy of alienation had also got transformed to one of free mix-up.

Krishnaram knew when and how to strike. He caught hold of the prediction of the astrologers that the king was going to have an end of his rule and advised him to hand over his regalia to his favourite queen.[10] Siva Singha could visualise that the Parvatiya Gosain's policy would be sowing seeds of dissension not only among the Ahom nobles but also among the native Sakta priests and Vaishnava *Satradhikars* making him highly unpopular. True to the male psyche befitting an irresolute sovereign, he wanted to keep his image high by performing work of dignity and grace like making land-grants, constructing temples, patronising learning and literature and doing works of public welfare, whereas, those involving the sentiment of the nobles and the subject population, he tactfully left to his queen.

It was certainly at the instance of the Parvatiya Gosain that Phuleswari ordered the Vaishnava Mahantas to worship the goddess Durga and forbade worship of other deities and personally supervised the act of desecration encamping at Sonarijan. Learning that the Sudra Mahantas were strong monotheists, she held the Durga puja in the capital at Rangpur and forced the Mahantas to offer obligations to the goddess and have their foreheads besmeared with the blood of sacrificial animals.[11] This act of the queen had injured the religious sentiments of the Vaisnava preceptors, the Mayamara Mahanta in particular.

But, what would she gain by doing all these ignominious works? There is no denying the fact that she was merely acting as an agent of the Parvatiya Gosain and on behalf of her feeble husband, and as a reward for this she secured the concurrence of the king in appointing her kith and kins to high offices in administration. Thus her brother Harinath was made Barpatra Gosain (one of the three guest councillors of the state) and later Rajamantri and her uncles, both of paternal and maternal lines were made Baruas of different departments.[12] Her mother was allotted establishment called Purani Mel and granted the privilege of using a special kind of sedan called *Kekora dola*, an insignia of royalty.[13]

Despite Phuleswari being the *Bar-Raja* or de-jure sovereign, during the period 1722-31 AD, coins were not minted in her name alone, but in the joint names of her and her husband where the Persian legend was used, the first of its kind in Assam. During the period, Siva Singha continued to issue land-grants to engrave inscriptions in his own name. Of the five rock and copperplate inscriptions of the period, three, namely, landgrant copperplate inscription of the Siddeswar Temple of 1723 AD[14], Rock inscriptions of Mandakata Rampart of 1723 AD[15] and the copperplate inscription of the Garaimari Satra of 1724 AD[16] bear the name of Siva Singha alone with epithets like Swarga-nripa, Saumareswara Rajadhiraj, etc. In the fourth, namely that of the Rock inscription on the Kamaleswar temple on the Nilachal Hill, dated 1724 AD the name of Phuleswari occurs. It is recorded in the inscription that it was caused to be engraved at the orders of Sri Sri Phuleswari but its *prasasti* is for Sri Sri Siva Singha and Phuleswari is mentioned only as the accomplished and Jewel-like consort of the king.[17]

Phuleswari definitely tried her best to assert her position, as evidenced by the fifth inscription of the period. By this inscription dated 1726 AD, she made a *Brahmottara* grant of 10 *puras* of land as dowry to a Brahmana of Kamrup named Vidyabhatta and his newly wedded wife, where her name occurs first and Siva Singha next, who is called her beloved.[18] Three things relating to the text of this copperplate inscription and its significance may be noted: (i) Although Siva Singha is given here a junior status, Phuleswari is also simply called a young lady devoted to the worship of Hari and Gauri. She is not mentioned as *Bara-Raja*. (ii) This is for the first time that a wife's joint right to landed property along with her husband has been recognised by the state (Assam). A very radical step indeed. (iii) The *Brahmottara* land grant was made as dowry and dowry is always given to a bride. It is understandable that Phuleswari wanted to give the benefit of the grant to the bride alone, but a state based on patriarchal structure was not prepared to accept a land-grant in the name of a woman of humble origin because, this would make other women conscious of their property rights and individual identity.

Intelligent and strong-willed Phuleswari then looked for other means to leave the record that she had once been the de-jure sovereign. In an inscription engraved on a cannon made of bell-metal dated 1729 AD, she assumes the title Sri Sri Svarganarayani as well as *Brihatratta*[19], Sanskrit form of the Assamese epithet *Bar-Raja*. Cannon inscription was a media confined to a very limited circle and hence somewhat insignificant, although as a source of history it has its own importance. Phuleswari might have done the job without taking concurrence of the king or even if she did, the king probably did not object, considering it a petty matter.

Phuleswari started a Sanskrit school in the capital for the sons of the Ahom nobles.[20] This was definitely a very bold step aimed at sanskritising the society on a profound basis. Under the patronage, the *Gaurisagar tank* was excavated on its bank.[21]

But so much focus has been given on Phuleswari as a persecutor of Vaishnavism that her radical steps involving benevolent works of great value seem to be ignored.

Phuleswari remained as *Bar-Raja* for only nine years (1722-31). She died at the threshold of her youth as a result of miscarriage. Judged from the marriageable age for girls in those days, she was at best in late twenties at the time of her death. As a young and immature lady of humble birth, brought up in an environment not acquainted with statecraft, it was natural that she would be used as a tool to realise the selfish ends of the king-maker. Her Vaishnava persecution was, therefore, not promoted by the zeal of a neophyte but backed by the ambition of a power-loving religious preceptor.

The *Tungkhungiya Buranji* records that Phuleswari suppressed the age-old Ahom custom of burying their dead and compelled the Ahoms to take the Hindu custom of cremation.[22] But it is difficult to say how far this command was carried out in practice. Because when Phuleswari died, she was not cremated but buried in a *maidan* near Charaideo according to Ahom rites.[23] There is no record to prove that the royal priest uttered a single word to get the death rites of the *Bar-Raja*, who was a devout Hindu, performed according to Hindu rites, and her beloved "hen-pecked" husband did not hesitate to throat to the wind her command even while performing her own death rites.

It is said that the rivulet called *Dijay-Khana* that flowed near the place where Phuleswari Konwari was buried, obnoxious smell came out for several days.[24] It is interrupted by some that Phuleswari Konwari was so gross a sinner that even the earth refused to accept her dead body. But religious persecution was not done by Phuleswari. It is a fact that she took away the freedom of worship of the Vaishnava preceptors but she did not take the life of anyone to fulfill her religious zeal. On the other hand, there were many Ahom Kings who killed Vaishnava disciples and preceptors on the ground of religion. During the period of Moamariya rebellion both Lakshmi Singha (1769-80) and Gaurinath Singha (1780-95) put thousands and thousands of Moamariya rebels to death but for this genocide, their bodies were not considered impure. Viewed from male psyche, Phuleswari was a fundamentalist and a power-living tyrant but an in-depth study reveals that actually she was not so as it appears to be. She was only used as an agent by a power-loving religious head and a weak but cunning husband.

NOTES AND REFERENCES

1. At the instance of this queen, ramparts were raised around the Ahom capital for which it came to be known as Garhgaon. The office of the third great councillor of the Ahom state called Barpatra Gohain was also created at her suggestion. See *Assam Buranji*, obtained from the family of Sukumar Mahanta, (ed) S.K. Bhuyan, Department of Historical and Antiquarian Studies, (DHAS) Gauhati, 1960, p. 27.
2. She played the leading role in getting Bidhan Chandra Borphukan, the Governor of Lower Assam, who brought the Burmese to Assam in 1817 killed by a mercenary soldier Rup Singh by name- See *Assam Buranji* by Harakanta Barua Sadar Amin, DHAS, Gauhati, 1962, p. 88; *Asamar Padya Bauranji*, Two metrical cronicles of Assam by Dutiram Hazarika and Biseswar Baidadhip (ed.), S.K. Bhuyan, DHAS, Gauhati, 1938, pp. 141-2.
3. Minhazuddin Siraj: *Tabaquat-i-Nasiri*, Quoted in R.C. Majimdar *et al., An Advance History of India*, Calcutta, 1967, p. 279.
4. Majumdar *et al., op. cit.* p. 279.
5. *Asam Buranji* by Harakanta Barua Sadar Amin, p. 41.
6. *Asamar Padya Buranji*, p. 68.
7. K.N. Tamuli Phukan, *Asam Buranji Sar*, (ed.) P.C. Choudhury, DHAS, Gauhati, 1964, p. 43; *Asamar Padya Buranji*, p.65.
8. Tamuli, *op. cit.*, p. 43; *Asamar Padya Buranji*, P. 65.
9. *Asam Buranji*, obtained from the family of the Sukumar Mahanta, pp. 104-6; *Asam Buranji* (1648-81), (ed), S.K. Dutta, DHAS, Gauhati, 1938, p. 33.
10. *Asamar Padya Buranji*, p. 35; K. N. Tamuli Phukan, *op. cit.* p. 43.
11. *Ibid.*, p. 66.
12. *Ibid.*, *Tungkhungia Buranji* (trans and ed), S.K. Bhuyan, DHAS, Gauhati, 1968, p. 41; K. N. Tamuli Phukan, *op. cit.*, p. 43; *Asamar Padya Buranji*, pp. 63-4.

13. Gogoi, *Bali Mar Gal*, Dibrugarh, 1983, p. 30; Hiteswar Barbarua, *Ahomar Lila Din, Gauhati*, 1981, p. 244.
14. For text of the Inscription see *Prachya Sasanavali* (ed) Maheswar Nego, Gauhati, 1974, serial no. 24, p. 16.
15. *Ibid.*, Sl. No. 25, p. 17f.
16. *Ibid.*, Sl. No. 128, p.114.
17. *Ibid.*, Sl. No. 26, p. 18.
18. *Ibid.*, Sl. No. 130, p. 115.
19. *Ibid.*, Sl. No. 125, p. 110f.
20. Hiteswar Barbarua, *op. cit.* p. 245.
21. K.N. Tamuli Phukan, *op. cit.* p. 43.
22. *Tungkhungia Buranji*, p. 41.
23. Hiteswar Barbarua, *op. cit.*, p. 246.
24. Lila Gogoi, *op. cit.*, p. 36.

Sutapa Bhattacharya

8

Liberation to Emancipation-Through the Eyes of Women

"Behind the Bakuls and Paruls of Bengal lies a long history of struggle. It is the story of Bakul-Parul's mothers, grandmothers and great grandmothers. They were not large in number; they were individuals in a crowd. They walked alone ahead of others-over puddles and marshes, decimating stone hurdles and uprooting thorn bushes. Probably, they were often confused in their task of cutting pathways, perhaps had often been trapped in their self-made excavations. Yet others followed in the pioneer's footsteps, took up the former's self-appointed task. This is how the highway (to freedom) was constructed". *Prothom Protishruti* begins with these words of Ashapurna Devi and makes it evident that what she wanted to express through her trilogy was the story of such path-making. That history, can of course, be constructed from various external evidence. However, such is to not my intention here. I would like to capture the essence of such history, which is the evolution of women's thoughts over time. For this, I search women's prose and the one dominant idea found in such writing-the seeds of women's *liberation* or its sister word-*emancipation*. Throughout the nineteenth century the word describing freedom of thought and action in the context of women's issues in the works of both male and female writers is *Female liberation* (stree-swadhinata) not *women's emancipation* (narimukti). Women's emancipation is a product of the twentieth century. Absence of freedom or bondage has often been bewailed in the writings of nineteenth century women. The earliest aspect of female subjugation to be noted was that of confinement to the interiors- and exclusion from public life. Bamasundari's complaint in *Somprakash* (1862) published as an 'open letter', is particularly poignant: "You now enjoy the various beauties of the town Munger and gloat over your pleasures.... We will never be able to see such objects; men might have some hope but we (women) have none... we are so enslaved that we cannot even hope..." The reasons behind Bamasundari's complaints is the male adherence to the age old concept of deserting women while travelling, which takes away from women the right to perambulation.

The line that demarcates the home world boundaries of male-female codes of habitation is responsible for such feelings of female deprivation. It has to do with the pains of being denied a public life, which is great in itself. A bridge is built over the Ganga at Howrah, all flock to see it, but female interns have no hope of ever seeing it, although they are all citizens of city of Calcutta, because "women have no right to see (view outside the house) anything". These words of Mayasundari's clearly make audible the repressed cries of women caged in within the wall of their households Confinement creates restriction; it also petrifies existence between the four walls of a house. Women writers show their consciousness about such spiritual mummification which confinement induces. In *Bama bodhini* (1871) an anonymous woman writer from Boalia rued this fact about women's existence. She complained that women in our country "spent their days as inanimate objects" in the absence of true freedom. Women cannot go where their "mortal and after life" can be bettered. They cannot meet any person who might have given them good advice. Bengali girls are from birth imprisoned like "beasts in a cage". This is why, she reasons, girls become fearful by nature. To put foot outside their hearths or to talk freely to friend of relative is regarded as a task 'that is death bringing'. This lady regrets the fact that men do not give a thought to freeing women from this mental "prison".

In Bamabodhini again (1872) Prasannabala Gupta voiced not regret or resentment, but the demands for equal rights for women. She could proclaim that God had created both men and women "free in nature". Which is why, one's domination over the other was going against the laws of God. If one disobeys such a law it makes him or her an offender in the eyes of God. This offence the writer sees to be rampant in society. Men are as largely free as women are enslaved. This bondage is not merely the deprivation of public ambulation; Prasannabala emphasizes the suffering women undergo when they are not allowed to undertake "good projects" in society. Their masters may not allow the women to indulge in harmful activities but they do not sanction female participation in good work either. In Bamabodhini again, at about the same time, Laksmimani Devi in her "Subjugation-What a pain!" did not merely identify lack of freedom with confinement. She stressed women's demeaning toil of supplying the master's wants all the working hours of the day, on the disgrace of accepting false praise as the ultimate goal of life. She showed the hollowness of such belief and lamented the lack of judgement in women in general. She put the blame for such mental slavery squarely on social norms. In Laksmimani's writing we find the same animal analogy as is found in the words of the Boalia writer. Women are "encaged beasts", she says. "What can I do? I'm a bird in cage"-This is from Rasasundari. When her mother died she could not attend the funeral because she was a woman and not a man. This subject was "a cause for no petty grief" to her. The married woman with her face demurely covered is compared in her writing to the beast of labour-the ox, which turns the mustard mill and similarly has its eyes covered. The tearful bride as she leaves her paternal home is like the sacrificial goat whose fearful cries sound like a child's cry for its mother, "maa maa..." A husband's house to her was only a "glorified prison". That absence of female freedom is not only a matter of external confinement, of restricted peripheries of movement-that the woman's spirit is also hemmed in by walls patriarchy sets up within relationships, is an awareness fully exposed in such writings.

However the question of this absence of inner space, the question of male love of domination, were issues that seldom troubled women writers of the time. The obstacles of social confinement, the suffocating lack of space, were aspects of women's live more easily visible and was hence the main preoccupation of writers of this time. Some women tried to rationalize such bondage by going back to the history of Hindu nationalism. "From the time of the Muslims who hated their Hindu subjects, Hindu men kept their women behind the purdah in order to protect their honour... the cause of female freedom suffered a great setback from this time onwards. Cooking and other subsidiary household work was defined as being the right and only work for women. As the Muslims went from power to power the issues of female liberation and female education became weaker and weaker." This is from Kamini Kumari Gupta who was not only troubled by the phenomenon of servility of Hindu women but expressed rage-"if the Hindu women are not liberated now, the whole of Hindus society will be destroyed by their curse."

Those who were expressing their desire to enjoy freedom as "men" did not think that the wall dividing interior and exterior was irremovable. But conservatives believed in the immobility of the divide; they would not agree to a insignificant factor of public life. Therefore it is not surprising that such an attitude is also present in women's writings of this time. This attitude is reflected in the recognition of validity/legitimacy of this divide. The editorial of the women's journal *Banga Mahila* states, "Bengali women do enjoy proper freedom, but a few regard it as servitude and demand the right to liberty for women. We cannot permit such sentiments". According to *Banga Mahila* the ability to transact household chores is freedom enough for women. To one who considers the peripheries of the home to be the true limits of a woman's life the restricted and forced inferiority of a woman will hardly seem to resemble captivity. Nagendrabala Mustafi, in 1895 wrote in a similar conservative vein. "Where we ever like caged beasts?

Is the household hearth a prison? That we are slave to our husbands or Hindu women lead a slave like existence is a fable created by materialist social thinkers from abroad".

However, she who dismisses such allegations as "foreign fabulation" had herself proclaimed the same a few months back. She wrote, "we are caged birds imprisoned by social obstacles". It is evident that in the ancient-modern debate "foreign" was one weapon in the hands on the ancients. But some, like Mayasundari, could draw the analogy between political subjugation and women's enslavement. "As you are under the rule of the British, so are we under you. Men are free at home, slaves outside it; we are enslaved both inside the house and out of it". That there are two circles of domination-colonial and patriarchal-is an awareness that is specifically women's and of not foreign origin as was preached by the orthodox thinkers.

The second phase in women's thinking begins with the writing of Krishna Bhavini Das. Her essay on women "Women and men" (1889) was published in *Bharati* can be recorded as revolutionary in the context of contemporary thought. She pointed out the domination of ideology in the lives of women. She said that it was the enslavement to particular ideas that was the chief impediment to women's emancipation, the essence of such ideology being: "women have been created for the use of men and there is no other reason for their existence". Krishna Bhavani condemned this as an "uncultured and hateful" idea. In another article she replies to Tagore proudly, "women have not been created brainless creatures to act as slaves; nor are they mere playthings. To be of service to others and to live for others is a woman's aim in life but she also lives for herself". When she begins to live for herself, a woman develops a true self, she attains freedom. This particular idea of freedom is not to be found in earlier writings.

Begum Rokea presents a picture of such fulfillment of a woman's wish to attain freedom through symbolic fiction at the turn of the new century. The narrator reaches a land in dreams where women lord it over their men who reconfined to their homes. The inside-outside divide is implemented very stringently but of course in a topsy-turvy fashion. The female narrator related the problems of her own country where society frames cruel laws to chain, to enjoy an "elevated" peer status with men, to win social rights for women signified freedom for Begum Rokea. This may be called a "liberal outlook". Like other liberals she also laid great emphasis on individual liberty. Likewise she emphasized the importance of economic liberty without which personal liberty becomes meaningless and equality with men a farce. For this, pursuing a professional career becomes all important. "If necessary, we will become lady clerks, lady magistrates, lady barristers and lady judges..."

Perhaps Rokea formed such ideas under the influence of western liberal feminists but she was very well aware of the distinctions between conditions in the west and conditions in the east. "In the east, men dominate over women in the name of religion; he burns her alive and keeps her fasting without food and water on Ekadashi (eleventh day after the new/full moon)-all in the name of religion". Rokea also observed that where religions slackens its stranglehold in society "women are relatively freer".

Another women writer of eminence who began her career with reflective prose protesting against traditional norms was Jyotirmoyee Devi. In an article published in 1921 she says it is extremely "contemptible/condemnable" that religion preaches ever-enslavement of women. All the heroines of her novels are different in the realization of self-hood. In her *Baisakher Niruddesh Megh*, dark-skinned Bina cannot be married off because of her complexion but Bina suffers not because she has to remain unmarried but because she realizes that the worth of a girl is be measured in terms of man's need of her, as if, above all by relationships. A girl can never be judged as an individual human being. Tagore's Mrinal, of *Streer Patra* had sought to liberate herself from the familial role she plays within the household. Jyotirmoyee Devi's heroines often crave for the same emancipation although "liberty" (mukti) is a word they never use. Jyotirmoyee introduced women's issues in her novels. In *Chhaya Path* the heroine Supriya longs for a woman leader who will show the world that woman is not merely a toy a commodity but a complete individual. Women are identified in society by their relationship/non-relationship with men by the roles imposed on them by patriarchy-the questionable glory that attaches to them as stereotypes as Sati, Sita and Savitri or as Urvashi, Vasantasena and Cleopatra. The way Jyotirmoyee exposes the meaninglessness of their lives also reveals the latent urge in such souls to attain freedom.

Probably after *Streer Patra*, emancipation becomes the key idea rather than liberation in women's writings. Anindita Devi even says woman is no longer a construct of male ideology-"She has now achieved self-realization. Today a woman is aware of her of own identity in a major way".

This claim is perhaps true for a small number of women in society. But a woman with a full realization of her 'selfhood' has exited from sentimentalized romance, from repressive household chores. She now needs a field of activity proper to her identified 'self'. We now begin to see the heroines of women's novels become politically conscious. They are not now only concerned with discrimination between peoples but with lack of political liberty. Jyotirmoyee's Bina takes part in the Dundee march, Ashapurna's Subarnalata burns foreign goods inspired by the Non-cooperation movement, Sulekha Sanyal's youthful heroine Chabi joins relief work for famine starved people even after she is beaten up by her grandfather. Sabitri Roy's "Swarbalipi" or "Paka Dhaner Gaan" are stories of political struggle, a conflict seen through the eyes of women. These writers point the women's situation within the political movement from a sociological point of view. In Mahasweta Devi's novels heroines are often very politically conscious. It is not only the educated middle class woman who is so but the tribal Draupadi or the prostitute Kanchana is able to transcend the society (-) directed roles to share in the work of rebellion or revolt.

But the prime confinement of women's power is her body. What has the Bengali woman thought about physical emancipation? Even Jyotirmoyee Devi with her razor sharp intelligence did not perhaps understand the significance of such corporeal emancipation. In one of her writings she quotes H.G. Wells and poses a few questions. "Not until you gain mastery over your body can you be free". Jyotirmoyee asks, "Does this indicate perversion like the prostitutes? Or promiscuity like the man?". Her questions tell us that she could not fathom the deeper implication of the issue, because she believed that women cannot shirk off accountability for their bodies. This was a burden they would continue to bear, a burden imposed on them by nature and God. Which is why her fiction carries the weight of women's conflicts, women's problems, but no sense of shame regarding lack of freedom of their sexuality. That is to be found in Ashapurna's 'Subarnalata' and "Bakulkatha". Parul in *Bakulkatha* prefers widowhood (read: freedom from male sexual domination) to the married state. Parul's God had shown a slight kindness to her. He had relieved Parul from the lingering pain of being a victim to unrefined male's desire, the desire which is sticky like a salivation covering all (facets of a woman's personality), the desire which does not allow windows to open on freedom".

That mastery of the body is related to the idea of woman's emancipation is a recognition of truth that is proclaimed boldly by the women writers of Bangladesh. In 1992, one of the slogans on Women's day read, "my body is mine, no one else has a right over it". In Taslima Nasreen's "Charkanya" we see the picture of sexual emancipation of woman. Purabi Bose from Bangladesh, paints a terrifying picture of a woman's desire for mastery of her own body. In "Salehar iccha-aniccha", the lover and not the husband wishes to enter Saleha without her consent. In protest Saleha cuts off his genitals. Patriarchy has tried to erase the question of female consent in matters of sexual union. It is not only a man who is so hurt by the act but the whole construct of patriarchy itself. For this Purabi Bose's Saleha had to undergo terrible punishment. This kind of protest has generally been absent, however, from the women writing in West Bengal. But many other heroines besides Parul have often been seen to welcome widowhood as freedom in their lives. The heroine of Sulekha Dasgupta's novel "Mitra" thanks her husband for dying early and so gifting her liberty. Suchismita Bandopadhaya celebrates such liberating death of the husband in a story she calls "Mukti" (freedom). In both "Mitra" and

"Mukti", the widowed state is seen as a portal through which the souls of the heroines pass through to attain fulfillment of artistic selfhood. To seek liberty in widowhood may be seen as the ultimate form of freedom from a relationship with males-a movement that gained momentum in the West quite a while ago. Homoeroticism, however, has not found a place in the writings of women, with the exception of a few lesbian poems. This proves that ideology of female emancipation is not imported and has evolved within the context of indigenous problems of existence.

There are two main facets of such existence. One, where economic instability is the signifier, poverty chains in both men and women. Within this, there is another ring of oppression, which enslaves women-namely, male domination. We sometimes find pictures of struggle against this double bondage in the fiction of Maheswari Devi; in *Giribala,* Giribala's husband sells their daughters in the name of marriage, and builds a house with the proceeds of the sale. After her first two daughters are sold in this way Giribala rebels and leaves homes with her third daughter. This is the picture of desperate struggle for freedom. *Jhukku jhakku jhuk jhuk ab gila gadi,*is about the Kolati community of Maharastra. Men of this community sell the first-born daughter at a high price and live off the money as long as it lasts. If the girl flies from her creditor and returns to her parents, she is promptly sold off again. Chhabu protests against this. After being sold twice she refuses to be sold for the third time. She leaves home to set up a *tamasha* group and is joined in her endeavour by other girls from the community. The story shows how, girls from social strata lower to which we educated women belong, are in constant rebellion against the oppressions of patriarchy.

The other aspect refers to the lifestyles of girls belonging to a more affluent section of society. If a married woman satisfies a husband's every wish and accepts a consumerist way of life, she generally faces few problems. But if a woman seeks to establish her selfhood, she is in deep trouble. The 'caged bird' analogy is still true for such girls although the cage is not glided-it is a cage of security, a cage of comfort. In Mahasweta Devi's

Hazar Chaurisir Maa we see the terrible suffering of such a caged woman, although the 'cage' as metaphor is absent in the novel. This image is used boldly in Suchitra Bhattacharya's *Hemanter Pakhi.* If a girl wishes to write, paint, sing, she will realize that she is imprisoned in an invisible cage. The heroine of *Hemanter Pakhi* was happy in leading the life of fulfilled housewife when Hemenmama of her childhood acquaintance comes and incites her into writing. Her husband and son were at first rather indifferent in their careless praise. But as soon as her lifestyle assumes a character of her own, her husband becomes every inch the master and she feels, as surely as her pet parrot is, she herself a bird in a cage. Today, the external divide no longer keeps the woman in and male domination is not always overtly present in various walks of life. Yet to the family and society at large a woman's selfhood is of no value whatsoever. The desire for emancipation is even now, in the 21st century, often taken as a by-word for self-indulgence and the woman who desires to be 'free' intellectually and spiritually- is often rebuked and shamed. Yet when an intellectual like Kamini Roy talks about the woman's right to be free she also says "freedom is not anarchy, not the right to do whatever one wishes whenever possible! But the right to one's own happiness and well-being while maintaining discipline at home, in society and happiness and well-being for men and women irrespective of differences". Any self-conscious woman of today has no hesitation in echoing Kamini Roy when she says "an individual's happiness and well-being is inextricably linked to the happiness and well-being of others". As there are indisciplined men in society, there are indisciplined women and yet society does not make examples of the former. They do so only with wayward women. Which is why, even after we have reached the 21st century, and women have earned a respectable amount of economic independence, the family and society in general are still happy only to see the woman in the role of homemaker.

Tahmina Alam

9

Bengali Muslim Women in Post-Rokeya Period: Samsun Nahar Mahmud and Fazilatunnesa

The wave of 19th century reawakening was largely restricted within the Hindu society. The Muslim society of Bengal was not affected by this new cultural movement and as a fallout of this partial influence of the regeneration in Bengal the condition of Muslim women was miserable as it had been ever. The society was corrosive to any possibility of women emancipation and women as a class did not have any voice in the society. In a situation, as if, within a prison on the so-called society, the Muslim women were without the invigorating light of education.[2]

Begum Rokeya Shakhawat Hussain (1880-1932) appeared as a harbinger of hope breaking the tortuous silence of centuries. She initiated a new age when women in general and Muslims in particular got an opportunity to liberate themselves from the shackles of age-old bondage. She combined in herself the spirit of a writer the tenacity of an educationist and devotion of a social reformer.[3] But she was not alone in such a mission and was joined by Samsun Nahar and Fazilatunnesa who sallied out for a new dawn for the Muslim women perishing in silence. Samsun Nahar was in fact the perfect disciple of Begum Rokeya.

She was an educationist, writer and a crusader combined in one and devoted herself to brave through all difficulties and thereby facilitated a new era of women liberation.

Samsun Nahar was born in 1908 at Noakhali District (now in Bangladesh) and was from an aristocratic lineage. Having passed an eventful life of about 56 years she breathed her last in 1964. From available sources it appears that her great grandfather Munshi Tamizuddin was a Government pleader while her grandfather Maulavi Fazlul Karim was a Munsif and he was the first Muslim graduate from Noakhali. Nahar's father was also an enlightened man with a background of higher education – but he died young at the age of 25 only much before starting his career. Mother of Samsun Nahar was Ashiya Khatun Chaudurani. She knew Bengali language well and had sufficient command over Urdu and Arabic.[4] Ashiya Khatun thus became a widow in her teens and had no alternative but to return back to her father's house. Samsun Nahar's maternal grandfather Khan Bahadur Abdul Aziz was a Divisional School Inspector. Despite congenial academic atmosphere in the family, Samsun Nahar was allowed to study upto Six standard - and her further study was postponed as her parents were succumbed to the social pressure.

But Samsun Nahar was not a lady to compromise with such a situation and accordingly continued her studies with the active support and favour of her maternal grandfather Abdul Aziz. In course of time, she passed Matriculation in 1st Division with a distinction in 4 subjects. But Samsun Nahar was a victim of circumstances and she had to overcome many blocks of trouble before she achieved her academic excellence.

Samsun Nahar was married to Dr. Wahiduddin Muhammad who earned his reputation in the society as a liberal and progressive man. She got inspiration from such a person like her husband and she was enormously inspired to pursue her career further and in the year 1928, she passed I.A. Examination. Her domestic compulsions stymied her literary pursuits for the time being–but in leisure she continued her literary endeavour. She wrote about women liberation and obviously she was influenced by Begum Rokeya. She was an avid reader of Begum Rokeya's tirades on women oppression published in the contemporary journals. Samsun Nahar herself commented: "I got myself introduced with Begum Rokeya through monthly journals. I was fascinated by her easy but vitriolic writings from my early childhood. I was touched deeply by the lines of her emmaculate expressions which spoke about life's journey towards a new horizon."[5] Samsun Nahar was deeply expressive of herself while commenting on her first visit with Begum Rokeya . She says, "I saw the enigmatic women of my dream world in 1925 in Calcutta. It seemed to me that I have become expanded and I have a new birth."[6]

The relentless inspiration of Begum Rokeya worked as booster and she passed B.A. in 1932 from Bethun College, Calcutta and completed M.A. from the Calcutta University in 1942. Under the initiative of Begum Roekya, she was felicitated on the occasion of her graduation on behalf of *Anjumane Khawatine Islam*.[7] The felicitation function was attended by the headmistress of Gokhale Memorial High School Mrs. P.K.Roy and also Mrs. Gajnavi, lady Farooqui and others among three hundred famous women personalities.[8]

In her speech Begum Rokeya said: "We are assembled today to celebrate Nahar's achievement in academic field-she has passed B.A.; but this glory is not of her own alone. We all women share the spectrum of the splendour. Nahar stands apart from the rest of the graduates—she had to achieve all these besides being involved as a wife paying attention to her husband, her children and the total family household which are not mean achievements. I hope the girls in our society will follow Nahar's footsteps."[9]

Samsun Nahar started her career as a lecturer in Bengali in Lady Brabourne College, Calcutta. She worked for creating facilities so that women could persue higher studies. Many women were later placed in higher services and they were all inspired by Samsun Nahar. At that time the Principal of the College was Catherine Grace—she was a Briton. In the governance of the College she used to take suggestion from Samsun Nahar and used to give much importance to Nahar's valuable directions in decision making. Samsun Nahar was very sincere in her duties and very shortly she was recognized amongst all. The college soon became a center of excellence. Lots of women enrolled as students and they ended up by and large with satisfactory results. Samsun Nahar had to resign from her service in 1947 owing to ill-health.

Begum Rokeya was the first Bengali Muslim women who tried to unite the marginalized Muslim women and established *Anjumane Khawatine Islam in 1916* . It was aimed at to shape up the women's lot and make them free from the fetters of age long social bondage. Samsun Nahar was a member of this organization. Begum Rokeya died in 1932 and after her death Samsun Nahar took the responsibility to scuttle the sparks of the enlightenment among the Muslim women. Samsun Nahar was attached to most of the women welfare institution like *Nikhil Bharat Mahila Samiti, All India Women's Conference, National Council of Women in India, Bengal women's Education League and Bengal provincial Council of Women.* She made full use of these institutions to achieve milestones in the sphere of women liberation.

During the 30's of the 20th century the Indian women did not have voting right. Samsun Nahar joined the movement in support of women's franchise and strongly represented the women lot before the Indian Delimitation Committee in Calcutta.[10] The event had a tremendous impact and the literate women were granted voting right.[11] Beside this, the movement achieved another milestone—a few seats were kept reserved for women in the Legislative Assembly.[12]

Samsun Nahar represented the Muslim women from Bengal in the International Women Conference held in Calcutta in 1936 under the auspices of the International Council of Women. The Conference was attended by the delegates from Ireland, Great Britain, Belgium, Rumania, Switzerland, France, Denmark, Greece, Holland, Australlia, New Zealand and China . Samsun Nahar drew the attention of all participants through her impressive speeches in the said conference. She worked as a member of the *Bangiya Prodeshik Stree Siksha Board*. She was also a member of a few other educational institutions–namely, *Girls' Schools and Colleges* and helped in spreading women education all over. She was an examiner of Calcutta University in the Department of Bengali. And in the year 1939 Nahar joined in Bengal Educational Service. In 1944, the British Government appreciated her contributions and offered her M.B.E. Degree.[13]

After the Partition of India 1947, she took over many responsible posts in different organizations like *"Nikhil Pakistan Shiksha Updeshta Board"*, *"Jatisangha Shiksha"*, *"Bigyan O Sanskritik Parishad"*, *"Pradeshik Red Cross Society"*, *"Bangla Bhasha Sanskar Committee"* etc. Nahar was very much associated with "Begum" a journal[14] from its very inceptions. She was the President of 'Begum-Club'[15], the first culture oriented institution, meant for women in East Pakistan.

In the year 1952, she went to Turkey and traveled many places in the Middle East. In 1956, she headed a six member delegation to represent Pakistan in the Golden Jubilee Celebration of International Council of Women held in Colombo. She was elected Director of this international women unity representing the Asian sub-continent. In 1956, Samsun Nahar travelled across many places in America and Europe and visited many Schools, Colleges, Universities, Hospitals and women organisations.

While travelling around the European countries, she gathered knowledge about the educational institutions. She visited the old *Yun Public School* and the Oxford University. She addressed people in many occasions, including women conferences. During that time, she visited Paris and Rome. She met many distinguished women from different countries. She got in touch with lady Md. Safi, lady Abdul Qadir, Begum Shanewaj from India, Madam Halida, Edib Hanum from Turkey and Mrs. Elinor Roosevelt of the United States of America.

All Pakistan Women's Association (APWA) was organized under the patronage of Begum *Rana* Liyakat Ali (wife of the then Prime Munister of Pakistan).[16] The eastern branch of this organization was set up in Dacca. Begum Narul Amin (wife of Bangladesh Premier) and Samsun Nahar were the Joint Secretaries of this organization. APWA was a powerful women's Forum. The Pakistan Government was forced to set up a commission in 1955 to reform the Marriage Act and Domestic

Act. In 1961, the Muslim Family Law was passed which banned whimsical Talaq system and Polygamy. This revolutionary act brought down the marriage age to 18 and 21 for girls and boys respectively.[17]

Samsun Nahar was a tireless crusader for social justice and women liberation. Her ceaseless effort paved a new way for the advancement of women in Bengal.

'Fazilatunnesa' was an exceptional women figure. She contributed substantially for the advancement of higher education in the Bengal Muslim society. She was born in 1905 in Mymensingh and died in 1976. Her father Wazed Ali Khan was a small employee of very moderate income in the family of the zamindar of Karatiya, Maymensing(now in Bangladesh). Though Wazed Ali Khan was not much educated but had a wide vision on women education. Fazilatunnesa pursued higher education with her own initiative and inspiration from her father. She did her matriculation from the Eden School, Dacca in 1921 and passed her inter-mediate examination with distinction from Bethune College under Calcutta University. In the year 1937, she showed the flare of her academic excellence by completing post-graduation in mixed Mathematics as the exceptional degree of excellence—she was first class first—an achievement without match by any Indian women at that time. She was the first Muslim woman student in the Dacca University. She had to tide over a series of difficulties but she stood like a rigid mile-post defying all oppositional currents. In 1928, she went abroad with State's scholarship which paved a new era of women liberation.

Fazilatunnesa was helped by Md. Nasiruddin, editor of the Saugat, a popular periodical and then Khan Bahadar Latif, ADPI of Mahamedan Education. But, at the top of everything she was a self propelled genius and there was exceptionally something new in her transcendental mission at the beginning of 20th century.[18] She wrote to Nasiruddin:

"You must have heard the extent of torture I had to withstand during the course of my mission to complete my post graduation. Now I wish to go abroad for higher education. But I have no capital other than my gritty determination. The

Dacca University has declined to send me abroad as I am a Muslim woman. They fear the Muslim society will react to this, with violence as it is against religion".[19]

In 1928, Md. Nasiruddin arranged a felicitation function on behalf of the *Saugat*. A renowned educationist and retired school inspector Maulvi Abdul Karim told in his address:

"She is the only Muslim women in Bengal so far to cross the geographical boundary and go abroad with such huge felicitation. I'm amazed to see the exceptional bravery of this Muslim girl shining like an angel from this other darkness of ignorance and resistance."[20]

Kazi Nazrul Islam presented a self composed song in the felicitation ceremony:

"Are you the girl responding to
the call of the seven seas ?
the moon from the maze of dark cloud....
Traveling the foaming sea beel–
into the ecstatic land of beauty
where the flowers bloom
in the green branches ......
thousand of stars revet their eyes
on the window of darkness.......
the radical *Eves* are reaching out
to break the lock!
the Heaven should not
blind your vision .....
and forget the lot at this side of the shore ...... !
Touch the end of the golden boat
again ..... here we wait
without motion."[21]

The folk poet Jasimuddin was eloquent in his spontaneous appreciation:

We are on this part of the streaming river ....
dark prejudices cover up the
faces of the millions ....
on the other side the golden boat
is in a voyage out ......
Oh! The morning star–

female voices regrouping
You move .... and they run after.[22]

Fazilutnnessa returned home in 1930 to attend her ailing father. She was married to Mr. Samsuz-Zoha, the son of renowned educationist Khan Bahadur Ahsanullah. Incidentally Mr. Zoha was the first Bengali solicitor.

Fazilatunnesa joined the Eden College in 1923 and also worked in Bethune College. In 1947, after the partition she joined as the Principal of Eden College and retired from the same college in 1956. When Fazilatennesa took over as the Principal of Eden College, the College had only Arts stream in the intermediate level. She introduced science and opened Humanities departments at graduation level. Staff strength was increased. Afia Khatun the English teacher, Khodja Khatun teaching Bengali, Jahanara Khatoon in Economics, Mrs. Zebunessa was in History, Akhtar Iman taught Logic and Philosophy.[24] Thus, the first woman degree college was established in East Pakistan.

During the fifties the original building of the college started at Ajimpur along with hostel. Fazilatunnesa served the Eden College from 1947 to 1956 and set a new trend in women education. Eden College under her patronage was one of the frontline colleges in Bengal.

Fazilatunnesa worked ceaselessly for women liberation. She was a born fighter and showed her right and spirit through her forceful writings in the form of essays published in the contemporary journals. She followed the footsteps of Begum Rokeya and in her writings there is a deep imprint of her (i.e. Rokeya's) influence.

What is unique about Fazilatunnesa is that she was ever vitriolic in her attack against woman oppression which she believed had been based on false façade of scripture and religion. She argued in the *Jagaran:*

"Islam does not direct women to stay cocooned. It rather directs women to acquire knowledge. The system of purdah under false pretention of religion is the best of the worst weapons to kill women. It is a strong deterrent against women enlightenment and employment. Such social blockages and lack of education are pushing the women to the doorway of death."[26] She was against the male—centric society. She rebelled against arbitrary male domination. In this matter her voice was forceful and she says:

"This society cannot improve without the proper shaping up of the women lot. Women cannot be at the receiving end at the mercy of the male folks. She has to take the responsibility to educate a human being in the society. She has to establish herself as a human being in this society. She cannot be like the beggars and slaves sinking under the male propelled social system. The time is to de-shackle and assert womanhood with pride. Only education can make women courageous to take on the social oppression."[27]

Bengal has seen the worst fall out of autocratic male domination—they have deprived the women from due rights. Thus Fazilatunnesa asserts through the *Jagaran* and draws the attention by saying:

"the first thing to question—who have deprived women from their due hold on their own rights ? Is it society ? Society is a formation of a handful of human beings and their will. Their arbitrary imposition has already done enough damage and bit by bit it is dragging the whole society to the pit of destruction—and the situation will take worst turn unless women get her rights offered by Islam."[28] She further states:

"There are many who are sensitive to the question of women education. They fear that education will destroy the sanctity of women. What is the meaning of sanctity, if it is to be preserved inside the domestic prison ? Women understand the value of life—they are capable of regrouping themselves and do the rescue work. The sparks of enlightenment will have glowing effect on women and she will learn to win over difficulties. And she will never do anything which could bring her down and thus failing to honour her conscience."[29]

It is a fact that Begum Rokeya was the 'morning star' of women liberation movement at the advent of the 20th century in Bengal. The Bengali Muslim society found a new direction and hope and women formed their own opinion and front challenging the male centric domination . Samsun Nahar and Fazilatunnsa accelerated the momentum and women could at least learn about their due rights to work shoulder to shoulder with their male counterparts in every spheres namely, in teaching, politics medicine, science, adminis-tration, industries—everywhere in terms of progress. In legal profession and in armed forces women are no less capable of. Women have a new skyline of hope and the time of brightness shows a new direction—the yellow pages of history will ever remember these soldiers of women liberation.

NOTES AND REFERENCES

1. Far details about Bengal Renaissance or Reawakening—see Nimai Sadhan Bose, *Indian Awakening in Bengal*, Calcutta, 1976; also Susobhan Sarkar, *Bengal Renaissance* and other Essays, New Delhi, 1981; Davidkopf et al. *Reflection on The Bengal Renaissance*, Dacca, 1977.
2. Far a detail information about the condition of Muslims women of Bengal the following articles are worth-mentioning. These are: a) Mrs. R.S. Hussain—Abarodhbasini; monthly *Muhammadi, Mahila Mahafil*, 3rd year, issue 10, 1337 (B.S.), p.751; Collected Works of Abul Fazal, Chittagong, 1967.
3. Far details Tahmina Alam, *Begum Rokeya Shakhawat Hussain: Chinta Chetanar Dhara O Samaj Karma*. (Bengali), Dhaka, 1992.
4. Anwara Bahar Chaudhury, *Samsun Nahar Mahmud*, Dhaka, 1987, p. 13.
5. Samsun Nahar, *Rokeya Jibani* (Life of Rokeya), Dacca, 1958, p. 102.
6. Samsun Nahar, *op.cit.* p. 104.
7. It may be noted that Begum Rokeya was the first Muslim lady to realize to inspire and unite the Muslim women for the cause of the motherland and the nation as a whole and also convinced them about the importance of an united effort to organize through an institution. This was the background for her efforts to establish the *Anjuman-e-Khawatine-Islam* in 1916. For details see Tahmina Alam, *Pratham Bengali Muslim Mahila Pratisthan : Anjuman-e-Khawatine Islam*, Bangla Academy Patrika, Magh-Chaitra issue, 1398 (B.S), p. 45.
8. *The Musalman*, Vol. xxv, T.W. Edition Vol. viii, July, 5, 1932, No. 76, p. 3.

9. Anwara Bahar Chaudhury, *op.cit.* p. 20.
10. The chairman of this committee was Sir Larry Hamold, Governor of Assam and Subba Narayan, Justice of Madras High Court and also Din Muhammad, Justice of Punjab High Court.
11. The Proceeding of the Anjuman-e-Khawatine Islam Bangala (Nikhil Banga Muslim Mahila Samiti) from April 1933 to 1936, pp. 9-10.
12. Samsun Nahar, op.cit. p. 72.
13. Anwara Bahar Chaudhury, op.cit. p.34; also Muhammad Nasiruddin, *Bangla Sahitya Saugat Yug*, Published by Nirjahan Begum. Dhaka, 1985, p. 599.
14. A weekly Magazine, published from Calcutta on July, 20, 1947. After the partition of India 1947, this Magazine was being published from Dhaka , dated May, 1950.
15. The Begum Club was established on 15th December, 1954.
16. The main objective of this institution was to inspire the women for progress and also to convince them the importance of the progress of the motherland and the nation.
17. The 'Order' relating to the Muslim Family Law, 1961.
18. *Jenana Mahfil* : a collection of articles of the Muslim women writers edited by Shalin Akhtar and Mausumi Bjhowmik, Calcutta 1998, p.159.
19. Muhammad Nasiruddin, *op.cit.* p. 585.
20. Muhammad Nasiruddin, *op.cit.*, p. 589.
21. Sayed Ali Ashraf, *Nazrul Jibane Premer Ek Adhyay*, published from Karachi University, 1967, p. 13.
22. Muhammad Nasiruddin, *op.cit.* p. 590.
23. The students of Salimullah Hall, Dacca University, established an organization named *Parda-Birodhi Sangha* in 1927. It was a bold step to protest the existing *Purdah* system during in the second decade of the 20th century.
24. Akhtar Imam, *Fazilatunnesa Ebang Bangladeshe Narir Uchcha Siksha O Agragati* (Fazilatunnesa and the Higher Education and Progress of Women of Bangladesh) published in *Begum Rokeya and Nari Jagaran* ed. by Farida Pradhan, Dhaka University, Rokeya Hall, Dhaka, 1995, p. 94.
25. Akhtar Imam, *op.cit.* p. 95.

26. M.A.Fazilatunnesa *'Muslim Narir Jagaran'*, published in *Jagaran*, First year, First issue, Vaishak, 1335 (B.S.), p. 22.
27. Miss. M.A.Fazilatunnesa, *Muslim Narimukti*, Published in the *Saugat*, 7th year, First issue, Bhadra, 1336 (B.S.), p. 2.
28. Miss M.A. Fazilatunnesa, *Muslim Narir Jagaran*, Published in *Jagaran*, First year, First issue, Vaishak, 1335 (B.S.), p. 20.
29. Miss M.A.Fazilatunnesa, *op.cit.*, p. 22.

I. Sarkar

10

The Role of Women in the Tebhaga Movement of North Bengal (1946-47)

The Agrarian movements of India traverses a wide range which includes the economic legacy that British colonialism bequeathed to India, and occupies a prominent position in modern Indian historiography. India had been underdeveloped by two centuries of colonial rule and subordination to British economy. Indian agriculture had entered a prolonged period of stagnation both in production and productivity from the beginning of the 20th century—and this very backdrop led to a violent movement from 1946-47 with a popular slogan *"Adhi nay Tebhaga chai"* (we want two thirds share of the harvest instead of half) and entered a period of prolonged intensity in the districts of North Bengal notably Dinajpur, Jalpaiguri, Rangpur and Malda. Although every part of Bengal was touched by this movement and the spontaneity was a conscious one, a striking feature of it in North Bengal was large scale participation of the people from Rajbansis, Oraons, Santals and Muslim communities. Once this movement entered its main phase, an interesting phenomenon was the active participation and role of the peasant Women of these communities who demonstrated their reaction side by side with their male counterparts.

Recent researches, however, have practically redefined this aspect of Indian history. Apart from a number of articles,[1] we have in our disposal a few well-researched information on this problem.[2] All these works have attempted to explore different aspects of this multi-dimensional movement . But surprisingly enough most of these studies have either overlooked or ignored a pertinent issue namely- the role of women of North Bengal in the Tebhaga movement of the concerned region. Incidentally over the decades, a few books have drawn out notice which provide us an insight as to the quality and approach of the study. We may refer here Sunil Sen's *"The working women and popular movements in Bengal"* (Calcutta. 1985) and Peter Custer's *Women in the Tehbaga Uprising* (Calcutta, 1987) which highlight the historic role of the Indian women in various popular and working class movements of India. Of them, Sunil Sen's attempts to deal with women's participation in these movements, is a praiseworthy work but in terms of throwing light in narrating the women activities in the Tebhaga of North Bengal it hardly satisfy our queries. Likewise, Custer's work, although a pioneer of its kind, has got a broader perspective of the women's activities but does not focus on the women participants of North Bengal. Furthermore, in both these works, we do not see much attention to pinpoint and explore the background where such a large scale agrarian based but backward and rural womenfolk might come forward to challenge the existing social system.

Linking my analysis with all the relevant structures, mentioned above, this paper intends to represent the nature and involvement of women in the North Bengal Tebhaga Movement. The questions under consideration investi-gate how far and in what ways did these women take part in this agrarian movement? What provoked the participation of these movement? What was the nature of the socio-economic forces working behind the scenes? and what factors promoted these women to come forward and face the oppression of the Government and their fellowmen? It is here that the paper seeks to explore the answers of these questions and will look carefully and meticulously the contemporary writings, essays, memories, autobiographies, interviews of living participants, further supplemented by other contemporary literature, published works and newspapers.

The one positive feature of this movement was that a number of peoples' organizations namely the Communits Party of India, *Kishan Sabha etc.* had offered the guiding line of this *Tebhaga Movement of Bengal.* We may recall here in he background that in September 1946, the Bengal Provincial *Kishan Sabha* (BPKS) gave an open call to launch a *Tebhaga* movement in the harvesting season.[3] The *Kishan Sabha* held meetings in the villages, enrolled volunteers, distributed leaflets calling upon the *bargadars* to store paddy in their Khamars (nijkholane dhan tolo) and to demand Tebhaga (tebhaga chai*).* It is said that between December 1946 and January 1947, the Tebhaga movement spread to at least nineteen districts of undivided Bengal. In all the regions women of poor and middle peasants families took part—although those of richer were not rate.

One of the striking features of North Bengal *Tebhata* movement was that the women activists belonged mostly to the Rajbansi community. The early starting phase of the movement in 1946 was complex and by December 1946 it had become exceptionally intense.[5] In most of the districts, the communists[5a] and local leaders (also sharecroppers) organized the movement. Initially there were introductions from the leaders to take the paddy for threshing to their own home instead of the house of the landlords. However, the large landowners, despite significant erosion of their influence opposed the method of the peasant leaders and thereafter under the pressure of the movement womenfolk challenged the oppression. As to the case of Dinajpur ways for example at Chirir Bandar, the situation became grave when two local leaders, named, Samiruddin, a peasant labour, and Sibram Manjhi, a tribal peasant, were murdered by the Police on 4.1.1947.[6] The subsequent development was the 'reign of terror' in the area and unwanted police atrocities. It was perhaps the right moment when a young married girl named 'Bhandani' appeared in the scene. During February 1947, when a group of police came on at Ranisankail of Thakurgaon (Dinajpur) to arrest the peasant leaders. Incidentally, this area was under the organization of the peasant leaders Postaram Singh and his wife Jaymani.[7] The Police are said to have faced a strong resistance from the peasant women.[8] Here, it is said, 'Bhandani' snatched away the gun from the *Daroga* who was overpowered and confined to a house.[9] Afterwards, she released him (i.e. *Daroga*) having been advised so by the leader Gurudas Talukdar.[10] It is interesting to note that Bhandani and Jaymani joined hands with Rani Mitra, a Community leader of Dinajpur for their common programmes. Rani Mitra and Jaymani, thereafter tried to mobilize peasant women in west Thakurgaon where a landlord was beaten up. The Police surrounded the village out and they had to leave the place and take shelter at a village in Bihar.[10a] In the same way we may refer to another incident of the eastern part of Thakurgaon. It has been reported that in Birgenj P.S. (5 No. Union) a group of police along with a the *Daroga* came to save the *jotedars* but the women of the locality were so arrogant that they challenged the Daroga and his police force with broomsticks and confined them afterwards. In this incident, the *Daroga* and the police got released after the intervention of Binod Ghosh, a local leader.[11] In the same way at Atoari village of Thakurgaon, a group of women under the leadership of widow Dipasri Sing stood against the barbarous attack of the police and saved the situation in favour of the peasants.[12]

The year 1947 marked another transition in Dinajpur where in Khanpur near Balurghat (at present South Dinajpur) the volume of barbarism and level of police atrocities were rampant on the peasants. Here the *jotedars* under the leadership of one Asitmohan Singh Roy offered tough resistance to the movement of *Tebhaga*. On the morning 20 Feb. 1947, a group of police personnel suddenly appeared at Khanpur.[13] The police are said to have arrested six local peasant leaders on that date.[14] But the peasants made barricades on the road, and demanded immediate release of their leaders.[15] At this juncture a renowned women personality Jasoda Rani Sarkar, mother of two children, came forward to lead the masses. Jasoda along with her women volunteers (*Nari bahini*) condemned the illegal arrest and appealed for release of the leaders.[16] Soon a large number of peasants under the leadership of Chiyarsai Sekh started demonstration. The police prefered firing and it resulted in the loss of lives of at least 22 peasants including Jasoda Rani and Chiyarsai Sekh.[17]

After the Khanpur massacre, a similar incident occurred Thumnia of Thakurgaon. Here on 21 February 1947, police came to arrest peasant leaders namely Kamparam Sing and Doma Sing. The resistance that followed led to the death of Sukur Chand and his wife.[18]

The *Tebhaga* movement also spread to the adjoining district of Jalpaiguri. Rangpur, Malda and Bogra of the then North Bengal. It is noteworthly that the nature of the movement in those areas was the same. In Jalpaugiri the movement was concentrated to four police stations. Deviganj, Boda, Kotwali and Pachagarh; later it crossed to Mal and Metelli.[19] The movement had been intensified at Pachagarh where Charu Majumder, the Naxalite leader of the subsequent time had organized the masses.[20] In no time, the womenfolk came forward to lead the movement. We are informed that at Debiganj of Jalpaiguri, a Ranbanshi widow affectionately called 'Old Mother' (originally named Purneswari Debba) took up the leadership.[21] A good number of male and female peasant including the Muslims joined her and brought the movement to an extreme point.[22]

Under the leadership of 'Old Mother', the wave of the movement swept over other parts of the district, and peasant women like Ujani Barmani (Panchpir), Lila Sen (later on Lila Majumder, wife of Charu Majumder), Kalti Barmani (Haribhassa), Buri Barmani (Maidandighi) and Maili Majhin (Denguajhar), spontaneously responded to the call of 'Old Mother' and joined the movement.[22a] The sole contribution of the 'Old Mother' may be attributed to her role during the police firing at Metelli (Mangalbari) on 4.4.1947. We come to know from an eye witness (i.e. late Dr. Sachin Dasgupta of Jalpaiguri town), that the role of the 'Old Mother' was commendable in terms of her caliber to organize the movement.[23] He is reported to have remembered her tenacity referring to the firing slogan *"Jan devo to dhan debo na"* (We would sacrifice our life but not rice).[24]

The Oraon women of Duars area of Jalpaiguri equally contributed to the movement of *Tebhaga*. According to participants, there was a "massive participation of Oraon women in the Duars region who accompanied the menfolk in raiding *jotedars'* stacks and facing the armed policemen."[25] Four women are said to have lost their lives by police firing."[26] Mention may be made of Mangro Oraoni who tried to snatch away the gun from a police and was shot dead.[27] Likewise we come to know the name of Poko Oraoni who took part in the movement along with her brother. Poko was a militant woman and is said to have chased the police who was ultimately tied to a tree."[28] She had the credit to mobilize a large number of tribal women in the movement."[29]

The *Tebhaga* movement also touched almost every part of the Rangpur district. Although it intensely concentrated at places like Nilfamari and Dimla, the firing wave of the movement covered other areas namely Domar, Atiabari, Harichanda and so on. The movement was led by Dinesh Lahiri, Kalipada Dey, Narayan Banerjee, Tarani Barman and a few others.[30] After the oppression by the *jotedars* on a local peasant leader of Dimla, Mani Krishna Sen, the peasants possibly got frightened.[31] But gradually with the spontaneous response from different people, they became active and brought the movement to a volcanic form. Here we may refer to the dynamic leadership of one Rani Mukherjee, who was a local school mistress but had mobilized the mass admirably and perfectly to the main direction.[32]

So far as the movement at Dimla was concerned, we may refer to a "womens' voluntary organization", which people called *'Gain Bahini'* (organization of the pestlers).[33] It is said that the moment of *Jotedar's* oppression, this *Gain Bahini* used to come forward with their billhooks, brooms and pestles. The leader of this organization was commonly known as *Gain Masi*, (Pestler Aunt).[34] Some of the outstanding figures are reported to be Mohini and Niroda who joined hands with Rani

Mukherjee in different situations and devoted much to make the movement a success.[35] Incidentally, here one may remember a Rajbansi widow, aged 70 years, who is said to have beaten a Marwari *jotedar* Koramal Daga, who used to torture the peasants of the area on various excuses.[36] This widow, popularly known as "mother of Baburi Barman"[37] had , in fact, created a terror for the *jotedars* and is again said to have compelled the said Marwari *jotedar* to leave the village with Police escorts.[38]

The militant spirit of the *Tebhaga* movement also passed over to the sister district of Malda. Evidences are there to show the participation of Rajbansi and Santhal women of Gajole, Old Malda, Habibpur etc. But as per our present information we have not yet come across the names of any women participats who might have taken part in the *Tebhaga* movement of the 1940s.

Clearly the complex, and immense theoretical effort taken to asses women participation of North Bengal *Tebhaga* movement demands critical evaluation of the practice of social forces. In other words what we can learn from such an uprising is the participation of a large scale mobilization of women who faced immense opposition and torture from the government, and still made an attempt for social justice. However, short lived their upsurge was the movement is no less significant from the fact that the participation of women was something spontaneous and that too without political backing. This naturally leads us to explain as to why these women did take part in this movement and this is the concluding part of the present study.

Dhanagare says in one of his articles that "the weakness of the *Tebhaga* revolt was not inherent in the class position and structural dependence of *bargadars*– the poor peasant in the agrarian social structure of Bengal. Rather, a communal politics and the general political development in the country turned out to be overwhelmingly decisive".[39] He, however, lays emphasis upon the 'particularistic nature' of the movement which had definitely circumscribed the scope of the cleavages within the *Kishan Sabha*, viz. cadres (mostly middle peasants) and ranks (*bargadars*, poor peasants).[40] Hence Dhanagare concludes, this factor had weakened the resistance movement. But it is quite interesting that the *Tebhaga* movement was spontaneous one and this propensity was at least reflected in the participation of a large number of women, both tribal and in some cases from higher castes as well. The nature of spontaneous response can, however, be experienced for the first part of the present discussion. All the more, the womenfolk, who came forward to such a democratic call, wanted to negate the so-called tradition of oppression existed in the feudalistic structure of Indian society. Although this section of women could not tune up the wave of the movement to a mass struggle, yet their wholehearted participation and daring efforts brought the whole phase of the *Tebhaga* in North Bengal to a forceful dimension.

So far as the factors working behind the participation of the peasant women are concerned, it seems that they as a part of Indian socio-economic system, might have nurtured a kind of hatred which had spontaneous outbursts in their participation in the *Tebhaga* movement. A few explanations may be presented to justify such proposition.

It may be instructive to note that each and every peasant movement, by and large, appears to be an outburst of protest against oppression and exploitation of the landlords. Here, too, the protest of the women cannot be isolated from the existing land system and production relation of North Bengal even that of contemporary India. Apart from this, the peasant women were victims of the existing social evils which definitely generated a feeling of united protest. What the peasant women needed was an excuse and the issue Tebhaga gave them the opportunity. In this protest, surprisingly enough, there was no political inspiration as such nor any, so called ideology and, if any, not of much significance.

It is, perhaps, admissible here to conclude that the beginning of the British rule in India represented a transitional phase where the feudalistic society was rapidly entering into the grip of capitalism. In this trend, the peasants of India, as a whole, were losing their right of independences and consequently the power of controlling the production system was being centred to the landed aristocrats (*zamindars/ jotedars*) or their middlemen. This turn over in the society of India as well as North Bengal again represented a condition where the peasantry as a producing class became helpless victims of the society. Furthermore, the society (i.e. peasantry) used to provide greater opportunity to the men of high caste and landowning classes, who from all practical purposes, were their superbosses in the society. This higher society had also an opportunity to dictate or mobilize the existing socio-economic or political system within their control. The peasants had to serve this class virtually in different manner and in numerous occasions whenever they (i.e. landed class) needed. A recent study shows that, apart from payment of heavy taxes and tributes, the peasants had to experience the kidnapping of their wives, excessive flogging in their lots and even the use of their wives to fulfill sexual needs by the *zamindars*.[41] It is also reported that in some occasions, the *zamindars* or the *jotedars* themselves were overall charges (including expenses) or marriage of the peasant family and in lieu of this sacrifice (?), the respective *jotedar/ zamindar* was allowed to enjoy the newly married wife sexually in the first night of the marriage held.[42]

Poverty as a curse to the peasants is nothing new in Indian tradition and the so called landowning classes were ever ready to take advantages of it at any cost. Here in North Bengal the peasants are reported to have sold out their children (preferably girl) in order to meet essential needs of life.[43] It has also been informed that in utter economic crises and indebtedness, the peasants were sometimes compelled to mortgage their teen-aged daughter in exchange of money.[44] These poor girls were subsequently turned into maid servants for serving the family of the *jotedars*. Besides, the *jotedars* had the facility to get married daughters of the peasant one after another and this was made possible by alluring the poor father for dowries.[45]

It, thus becomes clear that the peasant women had a genuine hatred to the existing Indian society and in their sensitive mind they cultivated a sense of protest against the evils whereby their dignity as women was severely wounded. In the 1940s, these women were provided with a rare opportunity to express themselves through the *Tebhaga* Movement and they utilized it. They needed social prestige which they had lost. They sought a way out to regain safety and security and when they could realize the root of such injustice, they organized semi militant agitation and took every defensive and offensive actions to redress their demands. Incidentally, we may refer to a few political organizations like *Kishan Sabha* of Bengal, the *Mahila Atmaraksha Samiti, Krishak Nari Bahini* etc., which had some role to ignite the peasant women for movement. But here one may bear in mind that they did not in any considerable way stand as the only factor for the outbreak of the *Tebhaga*. It has already been said that the *Tebhaga* Movement could not become a popular movement but due to the participation of the tribal and non-tribal women and also a spontaneous response of the peasants of Bengal,[46] it could really reach to a culminating point. This was an open challenge to the agelong torture and injustice of the *jotedars* and their fellow men and a large scale participation of the peasant women only goes to signify their importance as a part and parcel of the socio-economic structure of the then rural Bengal.

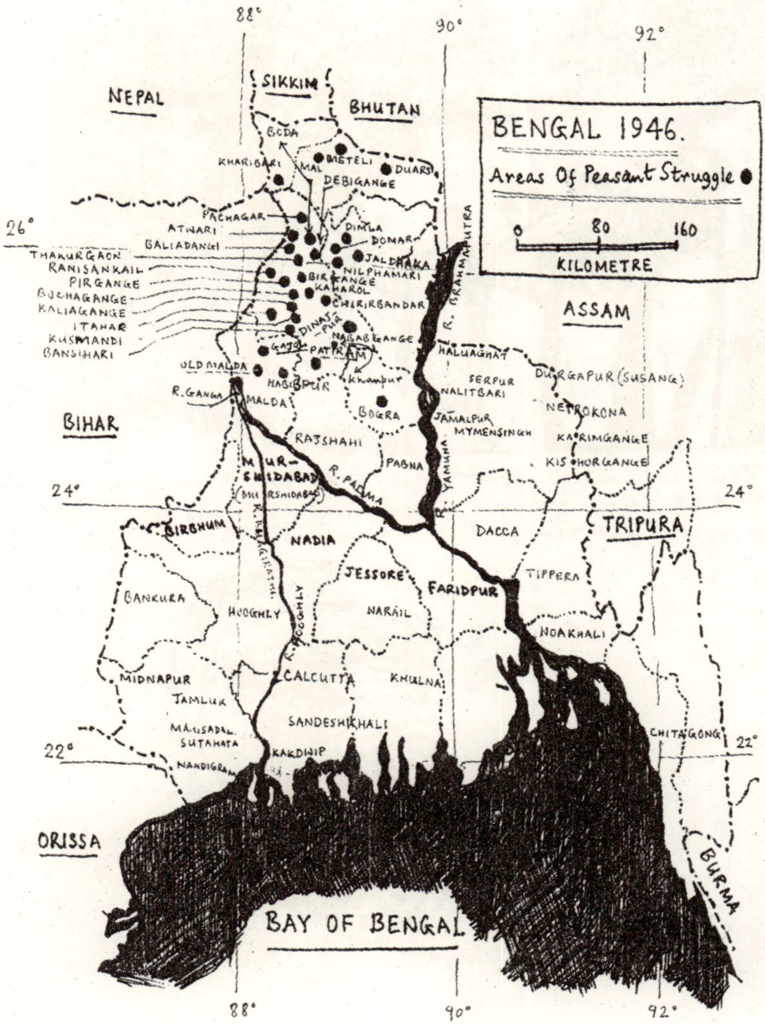

● ⇒ Indicating Areas of Tebhaga Movement of North-Bengal (1946-47).

Courtesy : (a) The Working Women & Popular Movements In Bengal, by Sunil Sen, Cal, 1985.
(b) Sharecropping & Sharecroppers' Struggle In Bengal 1930-50, A. Cooper, Cal, 1988

The "Women Battalion" of the Tebhaga Movement (Courtesy - Tebhaga Samgram, 40th commemorium Vol. Dhaka, 1987)

Mother of Baburi Barmon

Sketch by Somnath Hore

(Courtesy, Tebhagar Diary by Somnath Hore, p.45, Published by Subarnarekha, Cal, 1991)

This is the famous tree where Monuments of the 'First Rebels' of the Tebhaga Movement were erected.

Photo: March, 1988

Courtesy: Tebhaga Samgram, 40th year Commemorium Vol. Dhaka- 1988

(Courtesy- Tebhaga Samgram, 40th year commemorium Vol. Dhaka, 1988)

Gathering of a few veteran Tebhaga participants in the holy site of Samiruddin, the first martyr in the Tebhaga movement at Chirir Bandar (Dinajpur). Photo March, 1988, Courtesy Tebhaga Samgram. Dhaka-1988.

NOTES AND REFERENCES

1. B. B. Chaudhury, *Peasant Movement in Bengal* (1850-1900) in 19th Century Studies, ed. by Alok Roy, Calcutta, 1973.

   ———The Process of Depeasantisation in Bengal and Bihar in Indian Historical Review, 1975.

   ———Organised Politics and Peasant Insurgency ; the Bengal Provincial Krishak Sabha and the Share Croppers' Struggle in Bengal, 1946-47 in the Calcutta Historical Journal , vol. XIII, July, 1988-June 1989.

   ———*Tushkhalir Krishak Bidraha* (Bengali).

   Ratanlal Chakraborty – *Rangpurer Krishak Bidraha* (Bengali).

   Mesbah Kamal— *Nacholer Krishak Bidraha* (Bengali).

   N B. The last three articles are compiled in the *Bangladeshe Sasastra Pratirodh Andolan* (Bengali), Dhaka, 1986. The *Tebhaga* Movement in Bengal, 1946-47 by S. Dasgupta (Occasional Paper No. 89, Centre for studies in Social Sciences, Calcutta, 1986) is another outstanding article with many new information.

2. ———Like Sunil Sen's– *Agrarian Struggle in Bengal* (1972; *Peasant Movement in India* (1982) : K.K.Sengupta, *Pubna Disturbances and the politics of Rent, 1873-85 (1976) : M.H.Siddiqui ; Agrarian Unrest in North India etc. 1918-1922 (1978); P. Sundaryya,* The Telengana Peoples' Struggle (1972) ; E. Stokes, Peasant Raj to Swaraj (1978); Suprakash Roy, *peasant Revolts and Democratic Struggle in India (Bengali) ; Badruddin Umar, Permanent Settlement and the Peasant of Bengal* (Bengali); D.N. Dhanagare, *Peasant Movement in India 1920-50 (OUP);* Adrienne Cooper, *Share Cropping and Share-croppers' Struggles in Bengal 1930-1950, Calcutta 1988.*

   Banglar Tebhaga—Tebhagar Sangram by Jayanta Bhattacharyya, Calcutta, 1996; Women in Peasant Movements, Tebhaga, Naxalite and After by Debal K. Singha Roy, New Delhi, 1992; Peasant movements in post-colonial India-Debal K. Singha Roy, etc.

3. Sunil Sen—*Peasant Movement in India*, Calcutta, 1982, p. 106.

4. Sunil Sen—*The Working women and Popular Movement in Bengal, Calcutta 1985, p. 35, also Rangpur Jelar Krishak Andolaner Itihas O Party,* by Sudhir Mukherjee etc. Sree Rampur, Hooghly 1985, p.93.

5. Sunil Sen—*Peasant Movement in India*, Calcutta, 1982, pp. 106-107.

5a. As in Dinajpur we may refer to a number of Political leaders. They were Rupnarayan Roy, the then Communist M.L.A., Gurudas Talukdar, Sachindra Chakraborty, Barada Chakraborty, Sunil Sen, Haji Md. Damesh, Basanta Chattopadhya, Bibhutti Guha, Janardhan Chakraborty etc. *See Bartika*, a Bengali Journal, (Special issue on *Tebhaga*, July-December, 1978), p. 80.

6. Sunil Sen, *The Working Women and Popular Movement in Bengal*, p. 35.

   For details see *Tebhaga Andolaner Itihas*, (Bengali), by Kunal Chattopadhyay, Cal—1987, p. 40-41.

7. Dhananjay Roy (ed) *Uttarbanger Adhiar Bidroha O Tebhaga Andolan* (Bengali), 1984, p. 65.

8. Amrita Bazar Patrika, January 21, 1997.

9. Sunil Sen, *The working Women and Popular Movement in Bengal*, p. 40

10. Dhananjay Roy, *op.cit.* p. 70.

10a. Sunil Sen, *The Working Women and Popular Movement in Bengal*, p. 45.

11. Dhananjay roy, *op.cit.* p. 70.

12. Dhananjay Roy, *op.cit*, p. 65.

13. *Bartika, Special issue on Tebhaga*, p. 89 also Dhananjay Roy, *op.cit.* p. 25, sunil Sen, *The working Women and Popular Movement in Bengal*, p. 38.

14. Abdullah Rasul, *Krisak Sabhar Itihas* (Bengali), Calcutta, 1982, p. 170. Although Manabesh Chaudhury in his *Khanpurer Tebhaga in Atiter Kahini* (Bengali), Calcutta-1985, p. 5, says that the proposed number would be five.

15. Abdullah Rasul, *op. cit.* p. 170.

16. Manabesh Chaudhury, *op.cit.*, p. 5.

17. The Amrita Bazar Patrika , February 21, 1947, Desh, Falgun 17, 1353, B.S. : Abdullah Rasul *op. cit.* p. 171.

18. Dhananjay Roy, *op.cit.*, p. 5.

19. Sunil Sen, *Peasant Movement of India*, Cal 1982, p. 107.

20. *Loc. Cit.*

21. Nirmal Chandra Chaudhury, *Swadhinata Andolane Rajbansi Sampraday*, (Bengali), Jalpaiguri, 1985, p. 30, also sunil Sen, *The working women ....* p. 40.

22. Nirmal Chandra Chaudhury, *op.cit.*, p. 30f.

22a. Nirmal Chandra Chaudhury, *op.cit.*, p. 30.

23. Cited in Nirmal Chandra Chaudhury, *op.cit.*, p. 30.

24. *Janamat* (A Bengali weekly on Jalpaiguri), 12, 278, Ref. Nirmal Chandra Chaudhury, *op.cit.*, p. 30-31.

25. Sunil Sen, *The Working Women* .... p. 41.

26. *Loc.cit.*

27. *Loc.cit.*

28. *Loc.cit.*

29. *Loc.cit.*

30. Sudhir Mukherjee etc. *Rangpur Jelar Krishak Andolaner Itihas O Party*, Sreerampur, Hoogly, 1985, p. 108.

31. *Loc.cit.*

32. Sudhir Mukherjee, *op.cit.*, p. 109.

33. Sudhir Mukherjee, *op.cit.*, p. 110.

34. *Loc.cit.*

35. *Loc.cit.*

36. For details see Nirmal Chandra Chaudhury, *op.cit.*, p. 93.

37. *Loc.cit.*

38. *Loc.cit.*, also Somnath Hore, *Tebhagar Diary in Ekashan, Shardiya issue, 1388 (BS)*, p. 45; *Tebhaga Sangram ed*. by Nurul Alam Lenin, p. 108 ; *Tebhagar Diary*, Somnath Hore (Bengali, Calcutta, 1991) p. 45.

39. D. N. Dhanagare – *Peasant Protest and Politics l- The Tebhaga Movement in Bengal (India) 1945-47 in the Journal of Peasant Studies* , Vol. 3, No.3, 1976, p. 375.

40. *Loc.cit.*

41. *Tebhaga Andolan O Gramin Nari Jagaran* (Tebhaga Movement and the consciousness of the village women) by Maleka Begum in *Tebhaga Sangram (Tebhaga Movement)* 40th year commemoration vol. Edited by Noor-ul-Alam Lenin, Dhaka, 1988, p. 63. Andrienne Cooper also admits it (vide, *Share Cropping and. Sharecroppers' Struggle in Bengal* 1930-1950), Calcutta 1988, pp. 120f.

42. *Loc.cit.*

43. Maleka Begum, *op.cit.* p. 3f.

44. Maleka Begum, *op.cit.* p. 64.
45. *Loc. cit.*
46. D. N. Dhanagare states "The natural calamities of floods famine and disease were so enormous from 1941 to 1945 that any follow-up on the Land Revenue Commissioner's recommendations was unthinkable. The conditions of *Bargadars*, however, went on steadily worsening, since, despite the famine, the share croppers' obligation to surrender half of their produce to *jotedars* remained unchanged" (Vide D.N. Dhanagare *Peasant Protest and Politics* etc.) in the *Journal of Peasant Studies* (Vol. 3 : No. 3; 1970), p. 368.

Satyadeo Poddar

11

Participation of Women in the Police Administration of Tripura

This present paper deals with the nature of Police administration of Tripura during the Princely days and traces the problems and prospects of women participation after the merger of this State to the Indian Union in 1948. The paper is based on the reports collected from the Administrative Reports of Tripura and personal interviews of Sri Salim Ali (Inspector General of Police); Smt. Roma Rakshit (Additional SP, Tripura West); Sri Khatrajoy Reang (Commandant, Second Battalion of Tripura Police), Mrs. Tapati Debnath (Lady Sub-Inspector, Tripura West); Smt. Lipika Das (Lady Sub-Inspector, Tripura West) and Pranab Sengupta (O/C, Amtali Police Station, Agartala). The interviews of the above police personnel were taken on 2.3.2000 AD in their respective offices.

The general administration of the whole State during Princely days was conducted at Agartala, the capital and residence of the King, but for the administration of justice and other purposes, the north-western and south-western portion of Tripura were placed in charge of two Officers, who had jurisdiction within the sub-division assigned to them. The north-eastern sub-division of Kailashahar was opened at the close of the year 1872 and the south-western sub-division of Udaipur was opened in the year 1874-75 and later on at Sonamura. For fiscal administration Tripura was again divided into several sub-divisions, which varied from seven to ten different times. Each of these sub-divisions was presided over by an Officer ordinarily styled Magistrate-Collector. The tribal chiefs were in all in their respective areas and ruled according to their own system. The kings of Tripura ruled the hills through these chiefs. It was through these chiefs that the government officials collected tributes and other requirements. The village disputes were settled in community trials where the chief of the village presided. In political and administrative matters, the chief acted as link between the king and the tribes.

There were in 1874-75, five police stations and eight outposts in the state. The police stations were situated at Agartala, Bishalgarh, Rishyamukh, Madhabnagar and Sabroon-Magrum. The Police force consisted of three Darogas or Sub-Inspectors, two clerks, one officer called Hazari, five Jamadars or Head Constables, three Dafadars and eighty six constables[1] Radha Kishore Manikya[2] reorganized the police system and separated it from the revenue department. The post of Superintendent of Police was also created in the meantime. In the year 1908 the police force under the Superintendent of Police consisted of 8 Inspectors, 26 Darogas, 33 Naibdarogas, 40 Head Constables and 200 Constables posted at 22 police stations and 34 outposts[3]. There was a jail at Agartala and a Lock up at each of the divisional headquarters.

Apart from ordinary police created accordance with the British Police system, the king of Tripura had a special type of police known as Bininidias. Besides carrying out the king's order, they used to guard the Royal House and had to go into the deep hills and could arrest persons wanted by the king. They had to collect Taithung or free labourers and had a duty of informing the chiefs in hills of the orders by the king. The chiefs of all bininidias was called Along Hazari. They carried a royal insignia made of iron called 'Foorai'. Whatever one could give by presenting the 'Foorai' reached the village, the villagers would themselves carry the same from village to village to announce the proclamation. In the past the 'Foorai' was sent to the hills to mobilize the tribal warriors in the battlefield. Honorary Lt. J.C. Dutta, B.A. continued as Superintendent of Police till 30th Aswin, when he was succeeded by Rai Saheb Akshey Kumar Gupta, late of Bengali Police who held charge for the rest of the year. Rai Saheb A.C. Gupta reired in 1938 and after that Rai G.R. Dutt joined as Superintendent of Police and held charge during the rest of the triennium, the designation of the Office having been subsequently been changed to "Commissioner of Police"[4].

The total numerical strength of the police force during the year 1931-32 was 493; 1932-33, 499; 1933-34, 512; 1934-35, 515 which became 612 in the year 1942-43.[5] The number of village choukidars from 1931 to 1942 remained 176 and became 177 in 1942-43 AD. There were 4 Inspectors of Police throughout the period and their main duties being to exercise control over and maintain discipline amongst the subordinate staff, besides supervision of cases and inspection of Police Stations and Courts. Regarding investigating and intelligence staff, there were 24 Sub-Inspectors including one Probationary Sub-Inspector and 25 Naib Darogas in 1932-33. Good detective work had been done by some of the Sub-Inspectors in tracking and prosecuting several gangs of dacoits and burglars-one in Sabroom where 12 prominent of Makku Palwan's gang were successfully prosecuted, another in Radhakishorepur P.S. where 14 members of another group were prosecuted and another in Khowai.[6]

There were Arms Act cases every year. During 1933-34, 20 Arms Act cases were instituted against 21 persons of whom 12 were convicted, 2 discharged and 7 were awaiting trial as the year closed.[7] During 1933-34 the total value of property stolen, amounted to Rs. 14,675-4-9 against Rs. 12,868-9-9 of the previous year. Seventy-three cases of unnatural deaths were reported during the year 1934-45. In the same period two Inspectors, 8 Sub-Inspectors, 3 Naib-Darogas, 1 Writer Naib Daroga, 1 Jamadar, 1 Armed Constable, 5 Constables (Civil) and 1 Choukidar were fined or degraded and 1 Writer Naib Daroga,

1 Naik, 6 Constables (Civil) and 4 Choukidars were dismissed.[8] The following table depicts the nature of Police activities in the princely days.

Crime Cases Reported

Year	*No. of Cases reported*	*No. of Cases registered*	*True Cases*	*Charge sheet*	*Final reported*
1932-33	1,198	1,094	760	432	328
1933-34	1,009	945	738	363	375
1934-35	894	845	703	404	299
1937-40	2,245	2,117	1,682	858	824
1940-43	2,576	2,509	1,973	1,875	898

Source: Administrative Reports of Tripura from 1932 to 1943.

There was not even a single case of woman participation in the police administration during the Princely days in Tripura but the crime case reported were increasing every year but the charge sheet finally reported were decreasing which indicates that the police administration was to a great extent successful in minimizing the rates of convicts and the participation of women are found in different segments of its administration, despite the reflection of gender biasness during the regime of kingship.

It is difficult to tell exactly when the work of male police ends and the work of female police begins in the existing system of police administration. At present, there are 44 nos. of Police Stations[10] in the State but there exists no Women Police Station in the State. In 1995 a special Women Cell have been formed in Tripura in every district with a view to protect freedom and to give justice, safety from torture (family and social) and to detect the women retaliated cases as well as to prevent the crimes. Thus a woman police should have a working knowledge of the functions and governing principles of police force, as she will be called to assist the other uniform force if situation permits. Likely women, in Tripura participated in the police administration in 1961. The structural strength and vacancy position of Women police in Tripura is as on 2.3.2000 is as follows:

Structural Strength and Vacancy Position of Women Police as on 2.3.2000

Sl. No.	*Rank*	*Sanctioned Strength*	*Present Strength*	*Total Vacancy*
1.	Sub-Inspector	19	17	2
2.	Assistant Sub-Inspector	21	21	0
3.	Constable	175	154	21
	Total	215	192	23

Source: Police Headquarters of Tripura.

The above table reflects that there is meager participation of women police force in the administration of Tripura. Except Roma Rakshit, who is at present holding the post of Additional SP, no women of Tripura are holding the post more than Sub-Inspectors, which indicate lesser participation of women of police in the higher layer of decision making process of police administration. As per the interview from the Tapati Debnath, Sub-Inspector, "there is no scope of promotion, the women police who have joined as Sub-Inspector, are bound to retire as Sub-Inspector".

The changing profile of socio-political culture of Tripura, has given outlets of various forms of administrative problems, wherein the police administration is in dire need of women police forces. In order to dispel the crowds, where presence of women are evident, the deployment of women police have earnestly felt by the administration. The women constables are seen to lead the procession of women organization and they are also helping the police administration to arrest the women culprits and to collect evidences against women law-breakers. In order to find the lost women and missing women, women police are required. Their help is also needed when there is large public meeting of women participants. The women police of Tripura are helping to trace the women miscreants and saboteurs particularly at the entrance area where arrival of distinguished personage are expected. In order to prevent the crime, where women are involved, possession of specific plan of action, rapidity of its execution, firmness in its persecution is required to solve and to prevent the crime for which trained women in Police force is required for bigger interest of the state administration. There are so many women related offences in the Indian Penal Code 498 (A) IPC deals with a cases of husband or relative of husband of a woman subjecting to her cruelty.[11] The women police of Tripura are used in solving the women related crimes particularly in the court and by the Women Commission of Tripura. The total Home Guards in the State are 2504 in which women Home Guards are 202 and male Home Guards are 2302. Home Guards are doing law and order duties, night duties, traffic control (both male and female). The total Gazetted Women Police Officer in Tripura are two.[12] There are no female O/C in the State of Tripura where the number of male O/C is 45, to meet the need of 45 police stations in the State.

The women police of Tripura have witnessed some problems; there is no infrastructure for women police in any Police Station of Tripura. In order to change the dress and use of toilets, etc., there is no clear demarcation in the PS. They prefer to work on easy sector (Special Branch, Security Check-up) and do not seem to take the challenging jobs, as per the narration of Assistant general of Police. They even did not prefer to use police uniform despite lots of enforcement, which virtually hampers the discipline of the system. For better functioning of police administration in the state, there should be women police stations and more vacancies of women force be enhanced and chances of promotion should also be made rational.

In short, participation of women in the police administration of Tripura, is in a state of naive position, but certainly it shows a bold step in order to remove the gender biasness, which were prevailing during the Princely days.

NOTES AND REFERENCES

1. W.W. Hunter, *A Statistical Account of Bengal.* Vol. VI. P. 517.
2. Radha Kishore Manikya, the son of Bir Chandra Manikya was a ruler of Tripura deom 1897 to 1909 AD.
3. *Imperial Gazetteer of India,* Vol. XIII, 1908, p. 122.
4. *Report on the Administration of the Tripura State for the 1932-33, 1933-34, 1934-35, 1940-43.*

5. *Ibid.*
6. *Ibid.*
7. Mahadev Chakravarti, *Administrative Reports of Tripura State*, Vo. IV, Gyan Publishing House, New Delhi, 1994, p. 1754.
8. *Ibid.*
9. It has been found after analyzing the various administrative reports of Princely Tripura.
10. There are 15 Police Stations in West Tripura; 9 in North Tripura; 12 in South Tripura and 8 in Dhalai Districts in the State. West Tripura District (East Agartala PS, West Agartala, Air Port, Amtali, Bishlgarh, Takarjala, Jirania, Sonamura, Melagarh, Kalamchowrah, Jatrapur, Khowai, Kalyan, Teliamura); North Tripura District (Kailasahar, Dharamanagar, Fatikray, Churaibari, Pacherthal, Kanchanpur, Vangmoon, Dhamchara, Panisagar); South Tripura District (R.K. pur, Killa, Belonia, Santibazar, Sabroom, Manobazar, Bikhora, Birganj, Ompi, Taidu, Natunbazar); Dhalai District (Manu, Chamanu, Kamalpur, Saalema, Ambasa, Raisyabari, Gandacharra, Gnaganagar).
11. 304 (B) IPC deals with dowry death; 497 IPC deals with adultery; 306 IPC deals with abetment or suicide; 366 IPC deals with kidnappings, abducting or inducing women to compel formarriage; 373 IPC deals with buying minor for purposes of prosecution etc; 509 IPC deals with words gesture or act intended of insulting the modesty of women; 372 IPC deals with selling minor for purposes of prostitution etc.
12. Additional SP: Roma Rakshit (1 No.) and Dy. Sp.: Hela Datta (1 No.)

Shirin Akhtar

12

Towards Gender Justice in Bangladesh

The widely known stereotype of the submissive, obedient, graceful and gentle women belonging to the upper and emerging middle class in the 19th century Indian families has been the construct mainly of the 'European inspired' historians. The Indian writings also portrayed the women as self-sacrificing, though assertive and rebellious women were occasionally referred to. The achievements of the female members outside the four walls of the family found place in the texts only when such accomplishments were considered 'significant by male standards'.[1] In societies characterized by gender asymmetry or the segregation of male and female social roles, women's contribution to contemporary socio-political processes failed to get proper attention. Since the conventional documentary sources until recently were typically male-authoured and dealt largely with male concerns, topics like household, marriage, divorce, widowhood etc., which were intimately interwoven with women's lives were generally absent or very lightly dealt with.

In the 20th century nationalist upsurge and anti-colonial movement, the nationalist males seemed to favour the agenda of women's liberation from the age-old socio-economic bondage. However, the anti-modernist approach towards Western radicalism and liberalism including the emancipation of women, halted the process of women's progress. Even some liberal nationalist men in the subcontinent were inclined to argue that although they needed to take from the West certain elements of modernization in order to oppose colonial rule, it was essential for them to safeguard the national tradition.[2] Such an attitude perhaps explains the androcentric biases of politics and women" 'exclusion' from spheres of political power and decision-making. In such a perspective, prejudice against women going for higher education, technical courses and paid jobs ran high. In the patriarchal family, the proper place of women was still regarded to be in home, working as unpaid members of the family labour force. Only poverty would force middle class girls or widows to take up selective jobs like nursing or teaching. And even when the limited number of females with higher educational backgrounds took up jobs that required intellectual skills, they were referred derogatority to as 'professional women', modernization failed to stop the spread of institutional education among the women.

If education was the visible hallmark of the *bhadramahila* (as the elite women were given the epithet of), literature became the main medium of self-expression. In fact, these were the two fields where the Bengali women participated, outside the realm of the domestic. And however limited and fragmented were their contribution compared to their male counterpart's endeavour to social reform, the 20th century was marked by a significant shift of mentality of the women which warranted the label, *nari jagaran* (Women awakening).[3]

Like her Brahmin/Hindu predecessor, the Muslim *bhadramahila* was quite prolific in literary output and there were many references by contemporary writers to the *nari jagaran*. Following Begum Rokeya's tradition, Fazilatunnessa and Nurjahan categorically spoke of "Muslim Narir Mukti" through the publication of articles in popular periodicals and went so far as to raise the issues of seclusion and employment.[4] Another prolific writer Shamsun Nahar Mahmud termed the 1920s to 1940s 'as a definite period of stir and activity and heightened consciousness' among the Muslim women.[5] Thus 1940s saw the Muslim women, long disadvantaged by the barries of seclusion coming forward for even higher education.

Post-Colonial national upsurge provided impetus to the socio-economic upliftment among the middle class urban women in the region now forming Bangladesh. The national pride of man urged him to actively support the cause of women's education. Moreover, urbanization was breaking the joint-family system and in a relatively small nuclear family, husbands had to rely on their spouse more than in the previous generation. Though the slowly increasing number of educated women did not give rise to any organized feminist movement in Bangladesh, the changed perception of modern women's attitude towards what they were capable of doing often emboldened some individual women to challenge the discretionary practices in the patriarchal family structure. The need for changes in the legal and social status of women in an independent modern state was felt by some socio-politically conscious women in both the wings of the then Pakistan (1950s). The promulgation of the Family Laws Ordinance (1961)[6] which entitles the children of the deceased parent, who pre-deceased his father, to inherit the property was the outcome of severe criticism and prolonged movements carried out by the feminist organization, All Pakistan Women's Association. The women's representation in the law-making bodies through separate electorate has also been credited to it.

The raising of women's status as an essential part of modernizing process and later on 'integration of women in development as an equal partners of men' have been the avowed principles of Bangladesh ruling elite. The heroic efforts put up by the Bengali women in the War of Liberation and their unique sacrifices, did away with the many prejudices against them. However, the androcentric biases of politics also led to the virtual invisibility of women in the political arena. Though the number of women participation in politics has increased over the years, yet until recently, women's issues did not feature prominently in the mainfestoes of any of the political parties. Women who were active in political parties were used by them mainly to mobilize women's electoral support.[7] In the 1950s, the women's representatives in the parliament were elected directly by a separate female electorate, but in the 1970s this concept of direct election for women's seats was dropped and women representatives were elected by the male members of the Parliament. 15 seats were reserved for women which was raised to 30 in 1979. A few women's organizations raised feeble protests against the provision of indirect election for women but they failed to make a national issue.[8] In recent years the women of Bangladesh in general have become very vocal about this issue, and also about an increased number of seats in the Parliament. Bangladesh Mahila Sangstha the fore-runner of other women's organizations has yet to achieve its political goal of meaningful representation of the women, who constitute 50% of the population of the country. However, the country-wide branches of the organization and the numerous NGOs concerning women's welfare have been contributing in no less degree to the upliftment of rural women and to make them conscious of their rights and privileges. Women's organizations have also been demanding reforms in Muslim Personal Laws, i.e., prohibition of polygamy, restriction on men's arbitrary divorce rights, and guarantee of women's inheritance. But in the absence of a social structural change, legal reforms and establishment of girls' schools would only benefit a small number of middle class women because only they will have the resources to the take advantage of the legal reforms and educational facilities.

In most cases of physical and mental brutality, a woman is forced further to submit to social humiliation. Monetary demands for dowry which have commodified women tend to be extorted through physical violence. The license for polygamy though circumscribed by law, easily dispensed by the clergy has merely facilitated a source of financial gain through marriage.

In Bangladesh a high level of tolerance may have legitimated violence commonly associated with practices such as fatwa, dowry demands and domestic conflicts. In fact, the community's silence and tolerance of such violence could have contributed to an increase in incidents of such violations in recent years.[9] In repression of women, Bangladesh now stands second (next to Papua Guinea) in the whole of the world.[10]

A decade ago, women demonstrated outside state institutions. They have now begun to engage in the legal process through legal aid and as intervenors in landmark cases or in prosecutions relating to violence against women. But this critical engagement necessitates far greater mobilization to ensure gender justice from the courts and to ensure a gender sensitive social response to violence against women.

The State is expected to act as an arbiter with overarching responsibilities, enshrined in several articles of Bangladesh Constitution to establish a balance in rights and responsibilities, as well as equality of opportunities and protection of women. In spite of the state's commitments to women's advancement under the Beijing Plan of Action and to their rights under CEDAW (1979, came into effect from 3 Sept. 1981) state machinery has been slow to address the cause of such violations.

Even when laws are in place, their enforcement is obstructed by conflicting interests. It has been relatively easy to elude justice because of influence, social and political, or when violence is justified in the name of religion, moral codes or family loyalty. One example is that of the garment industry, which, as a major earner of foreign exchange, exercises inordinate influence on policy makers. There is no lobby to protect the interests and safety (personal and sexual) of women workers whose hard labour contributes to such earnings. Thus laws relating to minimum wages or safety regulations are often ignored.

Women's personal relations are subject to glaring inequalities, because matters of inheritance, marriage, divorce etc., are determined by personal laws that are based on outmoded principles. This ambivalence is exacerbated by the persistence of conservative and archaic customary practices. For example, the use of punitive fatwas of control women's autonomy clearly violates criminal laws and the constitution as well as international rights recognized under CEDAW and VDHR (1993). Yet both the police and the lower courts have failed to hold the fatwa givers and their followers responsible for instigating violence and criminal activities.

As seen in most countries, there is a marked distinction between the 'legal status' and the 'socio-economic status' of women. Some argue that economic independence of women is the answer to recognition of the woman as a human person enjoying equal rights and status as that of men. Women enjoying financial independence are still under control of their male counter-parts and cannot even enjoy the basic right of independent opinions and actions. Those women spend all their income on their families unlike their male counter-parts who for the most part reserve a portion of their income for their own personal use. From the money given to them for spending, irrespective of whether it is their own hard-earned money or otherwise, these women manage to save something for rainy days. Most countries in today's world have modified their age-old traditions, laws and customs and usages to end discriminations in keeping with the current Conventions and Treaties as ratified by them. Bangladesh should be no exception as it has publicly committed to end all discrimination between citizens, especially on grounds of gender and religion.

While examining the issue of gender justice, it is to be in mind that-the socio-economic changes via given country have had its impact-on the paradigm of the agenda since its inception. In the past, it was thought-that-education would ensure economic independence which in its twin would strengthen the hands of women in getting recognition as a human being eventually enjoying equal rights and status with menfolk. Standing in the threshold of women's empowerment-in public life, it is still a far cry even for the wage-earning women to the accord and equal status within the family still dominated by the age-old patriarchal ego. Their position in the society is determined by the laws governing the family lives since as the laws of inheritance, marriage, divorce, maintenance, dowry, guardianship and custody.

D. N. Dhangare states "The natural calamities of floods famine and disease were so enormous from 1941 to 1945 that any follow-up on the Land Revenue Commissioner's recommendations was unthinkable. The conditions of *bargadars*, however, went on steadily worsening, since, despite the famine, the share corppers' obligation to surrender half of their produce to *jotedars* remained unchanged" (vide D.N. Dhanagare *Peasant protest and politics* etc.) in the *Journal of Peasant Studies* (Vol. 3; No. 3; 1976) p. 368.

Anuradha Dutta

13

Women and Violance

While powerful elements in a society engineer a conflict, the victims are innocent citizens, children are orphaned, women widowed, citizens are deprived of health care, education and employment. An environment that maintains peace promotes and protects human right, democracy and peaceful settlement of dispute is an important factor for advancement of women. Peace is linked with equality between man and woman and development. Armed and other type of conflicts, terrorism, kidnapping are a common problem in different parts of our country. At the conceptual level considerable progress has been made on women's right as human rights and violence against women is a violation of their human rights. But in a situation of ongoing struggle women's needs and rights are either grossly violated or marginalized. Armed conflict situations are increasing day by day. The UN Department of Disarmament Affair has recorded over 150-armed conflicts in developing countries since 1945. There are, of course many more unrecorded conflicts. While the entire community suffers the consequence of armed conflict and terrorism, women and girls are particularly affected because of their status in the society and their sex. The impact of violence against women and violation of human rights in such a situation is experienced by women of all age groups. Women suffer in various ways such as displacement, loss of home and property, loss or voluntary disappearance of close relatives, torture, sexual abuse etc. Women's lack of social and economic security has compounded their vulnerability to violence and sex discrimination. Women and children constitute 80% of the world's millions of refugees and other displaced persons including internally displaced persons.

The link between militarism and violence against women is explicit. Militarism create and perpetuate on entire culture of violence where solving of dispute through violent means is accepted. Violence serves the function of maintaining unequal power relations between men and women in society. It must be seen as a reflection of deeper socio-economic process, which is patriarchal in nature. The state targets women and use violence against them as means of suppression. On the other hand a community does not pay attention to the special problems faced by women. In such a situation there is violation of human rights for women. As women are viewed as objects in general society in times of peace this point of view will be reflected and heightened at a time of social strife. Women are seen as property of the enemy thus justifying the acts of plunder, forced possession and destruction. At the time of conflict women are often harassed with impunity sometimes using systematic rape as a tactic of war and terrorism. This has far-reaching psychological impact on the victims. "When rape is perceived as a crime against honour or mortality, shame commonly ensues for the victim who is often viewed by the community as "dirty" or "spoiled" (Coomarswamy). As a result many women or their family members never like to inform or discuss the matter.

In a situation like that of North East India there is gross violation of civil and political rights. Like all societies in North East India Women have limited opportunities to contribute to the political process. Assam for the last three decades has been witnessing various forms of unrest, conflict and violence mainly due to the following reasons:

(*a*) Movements like language movement, anti-foreigner movement, ethnic identity;

(*b*) Problems of Demography;
(*c*) Lack of strong civil society to *mediate socially* and politically;
(*d*) Communal disharmony;
(*e*) Lack of overall development of the region.

"Due to ethnological and geographical reasons the state has not been into political economy of the present Indian state nor has it evolved any stable political, cultural or social identity of its own that can be characterized as truly national which could bring to a close the ethnic or socio-political conflict of the post independence period". The conflicts in the various constituent units of North-East have different origin and goals but each one of them is mainly owing to the general lack of development in the state.

Due to more egalitarian tribal culture of the North-East region and absence of some rigid practice such as "*purdah*" and "*dowry*", women of this region are supposed to be in a better position and mobility. But sex ratio in the region does not give us a picture of "Empowered Women". Women's role in decision-making is minimum. On the other hand despite official claims regarding restoration of peace in Assam the state continues to be disturbed. Women suffer due to unimaginative handling of the situation pertaining here for the last several years. In a situation of armed conflict the civilian population, specially women, children, the elderly and the disabled are particularly affected.

The Beijing Platform for Action defines situation of armed conflict as that which brings about "gross and systematic violation and situation that constitutes serious obstacles to the full enjoyment of human right continue to occur in different parts of the world. Such violation and obstacles include, as well as torture and cruelty, inhuman and degrading treatment or punishment, summary and arbitrary execution, disappearances, arbitrary detention, all form of racism and racial discrimination, foreign occupation and alien domination, xenophobia, poverty, hunger and other denials of economic, social and cultural rights, religious intolerance terrorism, discrimination against women and the lack of rule of law...." In North East India conflict in the form of "low intensity silent war" has gone on for decades. There is conflict between the state and more marginalized community within the geographical location of the state which refuses to accept the state governance and fights for self-determination. Assam that was seemingly a stable democratic system suddenly becomes a cauldron of unrest at a specific socio-political reason. After five decades of independence Indian democratic state formation has not been able to fulfill the objective laid down in the constitution. Ours is a multi ethnic and multi cultural state. In such democracies there is continuous effort to create homogenized identity of citizenship that support the central role of the ruling state. In the North-East this has contributed to the growth of cleavages based on language, ethnicity, caste and gender and transform them into newer inequities. According to an observer of South Asian democracies, state ideology is "designed primarily to legitimize control" over diversities either local or regional.

We belong to a border state; borders are not merely lines. "They are zones that are situated in the gray areas where the jurisdiction of one state ends and the other state begins" (Benerjee P.). In South Asia borderlands are people by groups that have linkage to both sides of the border. Border of democratic states emerges as a conflict zone. Despite official claim regarding restoration of peace the states emerges as a conflict zone. Since national borders have become firmly established it is difficult for any minority movement seeking self-determination to achieve a negotiative settlement. Thus there is sheer desperation which goads them to the path of violence, insurgency and political terrorism. Secondly relative deprivation psychology, feeling of injustice by a particular group of community has enhanced alienation. Precious little has been done to end and even lessen this sense of isolation, thus resolve the executive community of the Congress party operating in the North East. Offering much any relief to the people grounding under various stresses and strains has done nothing tangible. This process of isolation began soon after independence and is gradually increasing. Anti-state movements are defined as anti-national, terrorist and disruptive. Assam has been declared as "disturbed area" and a number of acts like TADA (Terrorist and Disruptive Prevention Act) 1985 and 1987 and Armed Forces Special Power Act etc. were introduced.

Women in conflict situations can be playing different roles and within any region can be categorized as follows:

1. Women relative of armed activist-mothers, wives, sisters, daughters and partners of armed activists who are in the struggle by choice or without choice but impacted upon the same way and specially targeted by the state.
2. Women relatives of state armed forces-mothers, wives, daughters, sisters, partners of police, armed personnel and targeted state officials and others—who have no choice in being a part of the conflict and who often remain the 'forgotten' and 'invisible' category.
3. Women militant or combatant-women who are actively involved in the struggle (a) by choice (b) through coercion (c) who have become a part of the struggle because of circumstances.
4. Women as shelter provider. Women who provide food, shelter to combatants either as sympathizers or through coercion but either way are extremely vulnerable.
5. Women as victims of sexual physical abuse. These are mostly uninvolved, innocent civilian and also any other group targeted by both and non-state abuse.
6. Women as peace negotiators. The community does not always support women leader who have taken the initiative. They are extremely vulnerable to suspicion and are attacked by all factions of non-state and state actors.
7. Last but not the least many young girls are involved with terrorism not due to any ideological commitment. Some group has joined terrorism to escape poverty at home, and family members even support an idea. Lack of access to political power and equal justice has left them with such desperation that they have no better option. Neither the Government nor the NGO's have

made any genuine effort to improve their present economic status.

Sexual violence against women is constitutive of social and political disorder in India. Widespread violences against women were witnessed at the time of partition of India with thousands of women abducted and raped. After more than 50 years of independence the situation has not improved much. While entire civilian population is increasingly affected and suffer the consequences of armed conflict the impact on women and girls is far worse because of their status in the society and their sex. Widely committed and seldom denounced rape and sexual assault of women in situation of conflict have been viewed more as spoils of war than an illegitimate act of violence. Feminist research for the decades has highlighted the way in which rape has been used as a tool for conquest in conflict throughout history and across the world. Rape is a sexual assault on women where individual man assaulting a single women even with murder is not uncommon. In Assam in the last three decades police and army personnel engaged in law and order duty created havoc on uneducated helpless women and even minor girls of rural areas. The growing number of rape incidents has eroded the idea of 'harmonious' and 'effective' family life and the question of women worth in the family is overcast with concern. In many areas of the Northeast states President's rule has been imposed due to the problem of insurgency. Along with President's rule various repressive measures and armed acts were promulgated. These acts have now been able to bring back peace and stability to the areas, on the other hand provide unbridled power to army *jawans* and police personnel. Following the example of Nagaland, Tripura and Mizoram rural Assam now faces the similar problem of army atrocities.

Rape has been a political instrument not only of subjugation of women bit off all the community of which the victim is a member. It is symbolic of male domination and control. It started with the Naga movement. The message was "people who could not protect their own women is considered to be lacking in 'manhood'". The victimized community tries to being back the 'honour' by all means. In most cases as we have seen the aggressor has been the Indian army representing the power of the state. Similarly in Bodo dominated area, the Assam Police.

These are a few member of recorded cases out of the lot others which will explain the extent to which women are harassed at these difficult times of conflict. In January 1991 at Chakati village, which is located six kilometers from Lakhimpur town, military personnel in the pretext of raid harassed women of all age groups.

Nayanmoni Hazarika, mother of two children was raped when she was breast-feeding her one-month-old baby. The army-men came not to raid but to loot and rape women. The community in the village was cosmopolitan, comprising Hindus, Muslims, Christians etc., people were panicky and in great distress. Women felt insecure as the state had simply carried out investigations without any concrete measures for their safety.

In Madhya-Phulbari village two young girls, Rashmirekha and Jyotirekha Dutta were molested in front of their parents. Military persons surrounded the house of Someshwar Saikia for two successive nights leading to harassment of the inmates. Youth of different age groups were beaten up and harassed. In the family of Nijumoni Saikia an 18-year-old girl was raped when the army came in search of her brother who was to be an ULFA activist. They arrested the other son of the family who was working as a home guard. The army men dug up their compound in the search of weapon. As a result of this incident the mother of Nijumoni went into a state of shock as her whole family was disintegrated. Due to these kind of incidents the villagers fled from their houses to take shelter in Namghars (the local places of worship) and in some school complexes.

In *Bihpuria* subdivision of Lakhimpur district Dongibill was an area inhabited by ex-tea garden labourers in that area on the 4th and 5th of December 1991, two girls, one 15 year old Phulmoni Tapna another 20 year old Karuna Tani were raped during which the male members of the house were forcefully made to stay outside the hut. In Chamma village a student of 12th standard was the first victim of rape. Later a political party took up the case and in the pretext of helping her used her case for election propaganda. Thus they seek to make political gain out of the most reprehensible crime without offering any practical help and reassurance against recurrence of the same.

On 5th April 1995 a group of 18 soldiers based at Bahadur Chitli after drinking alcohol visited a local village. They told the men of the village to leave because senior officers posted nearby wanted them. During the absence of men they raped five women in the space of two hours. Most of the women are illiterate so they do not know how to complain. Local authorities like police usually express their inability to deal with army. Another reason is that victims live in an inaccessible region. Moreover court has taken years before a final ruling is given. Thus majority of cases of torture on women go unreported.

Similarly after a bomb explosion in lower Assam at a place called Nalbari there were army atrocities in the area. Most of the male members of the families were taken into custody and the women were under tremendous economic hardship. The families staying near the area of blast were tortured and the male members were indiscriminately arrested, the condition of the villagers was pathetic. This similar situation was repeated when Mr. Nagen Sharma, the then Minister of PWD and Forest, Govt. of Assam was killed after a bomb explosion at Nalbari. The entire picture demonstrates how the army men harass the innocent villagers in their attempt to look for a militant and is similar to the picture, which occurs during any war. The depth and dimension of violations suffered by women is always more severe. It has also been found that there is lacuna in the existing legal system in ensuring justice to women. Of the various incidences at places like Nalbari have proved that women lack the capacity of self-defense, especially women from rural areas who are poor and are dependant on others. Nalbari is an area where many of the youth are involved in terrorist activities, military and para-military forces are used to maintain law and order. Amnesty international recorded that rape often occurs during raid on village in search of militants. In March 1989, members of Assam Police task force who had raided the village raped 15 tribal girls at Rupnathpur, Kokrajhar district.

In these areas women are deprived of their basic freedom. They are confined to their homes not allowed to visit other family members and friends so forced to live in an atmosphere of fear and uncertainty. Whether it is in Nalbari or upper Assam as in Sibsagar these women live constantly in an unrelenting terror that their loved ones may become victims of militants or police whatever the case may be.

There are stray incidents of terrorist causing violence to women and girls in different parts of Assam and few other states of Northeast. These terrorist groups usually take shelter in different households in the villages. Women do not consider this to be a personal threat. They are expected to extend their hospitality to these men by serving them food whenever they come even if they do not have adequate means to do so. Some give them shelter due to threats and some even do so out of goodwill for the organization or because of motherly feeling for the youths. The activist even sends an informer to give prior notice about their visit to the respective family. In the meantime if army men arrive these women are interrogated and at times abused.

The effect of violence on women has different dimensions. Psychological trauma associated with sexual violation and with the loss and disappearance of family members last long even after peace returns. The conflict in various forms has extended to every home, neighbourhood and community. Normal social and economic life has been compromised. There is constant threat and anxiety of living in an atmosphere of aggression and fear. Over and above the direct impact continued violence has long lasting effect on disruption of society. The family life is affected to such an extent that it may lead to disastrous consequences like starvation, prostitution, drug addiction etc. Moreover, this violence is affecting the livelihood in rural areas leading to lack of personal security, lack of food, education, etc. As a consequence there is widespread migration to the urban areas, an example is the migration of Bodo people from their area to various towns in Assam. Even from places like Nalbari people are migrating to towns as a result of the terrorist activities. Moreover, whenever the concentration of terrorist army becomes, very active violence of different forms take place.

In any area where there is prolonged conflict health implication is tremendous. In Assam as lion's share of the revenue is spent on maintaining law and order developmental activities and healthcare activities have come to a standstill. Health personnel are reluctant to work in the conflict areas for security reasons. As a result women are affected especially as women's need of reproductive healthcare. A tendency to underplay women's health need already exist and these conflict situations exaggerate the situation. Women are often unwilling or physically or financially unable to travel.

The increased violence in Northeast politics has led to the increasing dominance of men in both political and social sphere. Women lose their earlier social power given by their productive rights (A. Mahanta). Thus in a situation of armed conflict there is marginalization of women's right as both the armed forces and militant group reinforce patriarchal values. Women in such situation are expected to uphold cultural and ethnic identities.

The peacekeeping world is still a military world. Since 1980's the shift in the focus of peace operations to include social or human dimensions has resulted in an increase focus on the role of civilian. Civilians are increasingly recognized as essential "tools" in the peace building process. Women's uniquely female values and capacities such as cooperative and less hierarchical leadership and management style need to be incorporated in the mechanism of conflict resolution. Despite enormous impact on conflict on women they have not yet played a decisive role in conflict resolution or post-conflict reconstruction. Women are perceived either as victims or as healers. The peace intervention made by women in Assam was largely issue based. During the army atrocities in Nalbari and North Lakhimpur in 1989 and 1991 respectively, a number of women's groups for peacekeeping sprung up. Opposition from insurgent groups forced that women's unequal power relation must end. Discrimination is socially constructed. As highlighted in the PFA 1995 violence against women is manifestation of historically unequal power relation between man and woman, which had led domination over and discrimination against women by men and to the prevention of women's full advancement.

There are still women groups in interior villages that work for legal awareness, agitation against security raids in villages etc. Opposition parties, rebel groups, student's organization sensationalize state sponsored rape case victims and make political mileage out of it. Once the incident loses its value, neither the state nor the rebel groups are sensitive to the plight of these women. One such example was gunning down of Gulapi Basumotary who was the founder member of North-East Coordinate Community on Human Rights. She was also the first secretary of the Bodo Women's Justice Forum. She was initiating Assamese-Bodo dialogue on peace. Thus Gulapi's assassination caused lot of controversies. There were various allegations and counter allegations on the issue. The government blamed the militants. So in Assam, due to these community conflicts, situation is deplorable for rural women. When women try to negotiate between two communities, both the communities isolate that person and she becomes a political target. These women are in the peace process because of their own initiative. When the state government wants to involve them the women are asked to play the role of a healer but there has been no example of women being involved in the actual negotiation.

The lack of documentation of violence of women's rights reinforces government's silence. In Assam, like many other places, without concrete data government has been able to deny the fact and their responsibility for gender-based abuse. Government pays no political or economic price in refusing to acknowledge the problem.

The government should review legislation and practice to eliminate discrimination on the basis of sex. Government should also implement existing laws and policies that protect women and guarantee them remedies for gender-based violence. In 1999 in the global forum it has been remarked that in a world of continuing instability and violence, the implementation of cooperative approaches to peace and security is urgently needed full involvement of women in all effort for prevention and resolution of conflict are the need of the day. In different parts of Northeast women are still living in the relief camp due to ethnic conflict refugee, displaced and migrant women in most cases have displayed strength, endurance and resourcefulness. Inspite of demands by volunteer organizations women are not involved in the decision that affect them. To solve the problem of conflict care should be taken to socialize people to foster a culture of peace that upholds justice and tolerance for all. To do this as suggested in the Global Forum promotion of peaceful conflict resolution have to be encouraged through education, training, community action and youth exchange programme particularly for young women.

REFERENCES

Report of FWCW Platform for Action Women and Armed Conflict and Beijing+5 Global Forum.

Negotiating Difference: The Indian State and Its Women in Borderland, Paula Banerjee, Unpublished paper.

Democracy and Authoritarianism in South Asia, Ayesha Jalal (New Delhi,) Cambridge University Press, 1996).

Reinforcing Subordination- Rashmi Goswami, Women in Action, 1999.

Emerging Patriarchies: A Critique of nation-building process Northeast India- A Mahanta, In Politics of Nation Building, NE India, South Asian Publishers 1997.

Puspa Ghimire (Nirula) & Neera Shrestha

14

Changing Profile of Women in Nepal

INTRODUCTION

Women make up more than half of the total population in Nepal. Since early times they are contributing for the economic social, cultural and political development of the country. In accordance with time their roles are changing so, it is necessary to explain their roles chronologically. History shows that it is very difficult for a Nepalese woman to come out from the household chores. Though they are contributing for social and political changes. In this concern, what women did in the past is very important than what women are doing at present, as they were the door openers for this generation. So in this paper an effort has been made to show the changing profile of women in Nepal incorporating social-cultural, economic, political and legal aspects because, these issues are closely interrelated, one reinforcing the other.

In order to explain changing profile of Women in Nepal the paper has been divided into 4 phases based on changing political scenario. They are as follows:

1. Before the Advent of Democracy in 1950
2. After Democracy (1950 to 1965)
3. Party Less Panchayat System (1965 to 1990)
4. After the Restoration of Democracy in 1990 Onwards.

Gender Related Demographic Indicators

Facts	*Total*	*Female*	*Male*
Total population (in million)	18.49	9.22	9.27
Population Growth Rate	2.30		
Fertility Rate	4.60		
Maternal Mortality Rate (per 00,000)		539.00	
Infant Mortality (per 000 live birth)	74.70		
Life Expectancy (in Year)		53.40	55.00
Proportion of People below Poverty line	45.00		
Literacy Rate	39.60	25.00	55.00
Dependency in Agriculture (%)		90.50	81.00
Women Headed Household (%)		13.20	
Women Married at the age of 19 (%)		44.00	
Pregnant Women with Anemia (%)		64.00	
Economically Active Women Population		40.40	
Women in Decision Making		4.40	
Women in Parliament (%)		3.41	
Women in Local Government Bodies (%)		54.00	
Women in Administrative and Managerial Position		15.06	

Source: C.B.S., 1991, UNFPA, 1997, Nepal Human Development Report, 1998 and The Ninty Plan, 1998.

Before the Advent of Democracy in 1950

Before democracy there was Rana Ragime in Nepal with strict political & social Structure. There was rigid caste system highly influenced by (Hindu) religion. Conservative social practices like: "Sati Pratha", Slavery, polygamy, early child marriages were prevalent. Late first Rana Prime Minister Jang Bahadur Rana promulgated the first Civil Code to demarcate 'Sati Pratha' by announcing that it is not compulsory to go sati for women who are below 16 years of age, pregnant, mother of infant child, etc. The "Sati Pratha" was completely abolished during the period of late Prime Minister Chandra Samsher J. E. Rana in June 28, 1920 (Dahal, 2057 B.S. pg. 229.)

At the time, the women who were in power were directly related with Royal family, such as mother of the King, Queen etc. They never became the Leader formally but actively participated in political and economic activities of the country. In this regard, the name comes Rajendra Laxmi, Raj Rajeswari

Devi, Samrajya Laxmi was for unification (Asmita, 2056 B.S. Pg. 21).

In 1917, women started to organize especially for women's political right. Late Yog Maya Koirala was the chair of women's organization. During 1910 to 1940, she and her colleagues struggled with devotion against traditional social practices like: caste system, untouchability, etc. which were prevalent in contemporary Nepalese society. They went different places of Nepal and India for religious and social reforms with creating awarness. As a result they got imprisonment, home arrest, etc. by Rana rulers. At that time more than 240 peoples were actively working with her (INSEC, 2055 B.S. Pg. 11-12). In 1941, she and her 68 colleagues took 'Jal Samadhi' (Suicide in Water) as a form of resistance.

During the decade of 1930 the leading women concerning women's awareness started to give emphasis on women's education. In 1933, Chandra Kanta Malla established first women's school. After that Kamachhya Devi opened another school in Banepa for both boys and girls. She then started to teach there as a teacher. Later the school was banned. Again these women opened another schools in 'Tyauda' of Kathmandu valley. It was also banned later.

Formally Rewant Kumari Acharya was contributing for women's political awareness. In her leadership a committee was formed named "Adharsha Mahila Samaj" in 1947 at Kathmandu. The committee demanded for women's education, adult education, appointment of women in government, training for women, health post, women police, etc. In 1948, the prominent women who passed SLC examination for the first time in Nepal are Sahana Pradhan, Sadhana Pradhan, Angoor baba Joshi, Bhuvan Chanda, etc. (INSEC, 2055 B.S. Pg. 11).

During 1940s a woman figure appeared in the field of Nepalese literature named "M. Laxmi". Her first story "Rodan" was published in "Sharada" (literary paper) in 1945. She wrote essay, poem, story, etc. in both Nepali and 'Newari' languages too. She became the first literary woman for writing modern stories and essays through Nepali and Newarai languages (Mandala Book Point, 1997, pg. 316-319).

Before Democracy, Shahana Pradhan, Sadhana Pradhan (Adhikari), Snehalata, Kanak Lata and many other women organized civil right movement and procession for women's civil right. The leaders got imprisonment. In 1947, "Nepal Mahila Sangha" was formed under the chair of late Mangala Devi Singh. After that women's organization started to work continuously for women's issues (INSEC, 2055 B.S., Pg. 12).

In 1947 late Rana Prime Minister Padma Shemsher promulgated constitution called "Nepal Sarkar Ko Baidhanik Kanoon 2004". This was the first constitution of Nepal too. The constitution was more favourable to "Rana ruler. However, there were few good provisions for the people also. Some fundamental rights were mentioned in the law like: provision of free education & equality before the law, freedom of speech, freedom of press, freedom of association, voting right and so on. But he did not follow the constitution in practice (INSEC, 1994 Pg. 74).

Women actively participated for the advent of multiparty democracy in Nepal. In this regard, the name comes Mangala Devi Singh, Sahana Pradhan, Kanak Lata, Dibya Koirala, Indira Acharya, Kamini Giri, Nalini Upadhyay etc. Among them Dibya Koirala, Indira Acharya, Kamini Giri, Nalini Upadhyay participated in Labour movement of 1946 at Biratnagar. Later they were imprisoned and tortured in various ways.

AFTER DEMOCRACY (1950 TO 1956)

With the collective effort of both men and women, democracy was introduced in Nepal in 1950 A.D. Since then women's participation in political, social and economic activities were increased. Though women's participation in economic activities was not effected very much before and after democracy because, women's all economic activities were concentrated in subsistence agriculture and household production. Some educated women started to work outside the household chore.

After democracy, many women's organizations were formed under Mahila Sangathan, Akil Nepal Mahila Sangh, Nari 'Chetana Kendra etc. For the first time in 1953, Sadhana Pradhan was elected as a ward chair of Kathmandu municipality. In 1955 Punya Prabha Devi Dhungana presented women's right protection bill in the advisory committee & Tara Devi presented Nepal Marriage Bill. Both bills had rejected by the Advisory committee. In 1959, Dwarika Devi Thakurani elected as the women parliamentarian and became the first women minister of Nepal (INSEC, 2055 B.S., Pg. 12). Moreover, in between 1951-1961 few Nepali women have got opportunity to participate in decision making.

In legal aspect the constitution of the kingdom of Nepal 1959 was promulgated by late King Mahendra Bir Bikram Shah. The fundamental rights for women guaranteed by this constitution were-equality, personal freedom, prohibition of human trafficking and forced prostitution. It was also mentioned that no gender discrimination would be made in the appointment of women in government services (INSEC, 1995, Pg. 75).

After the advent of democracy, first five year plan (1956/57) was introduced for the planned economic development of country. The main objective of the plan was to build infrastructure for economic development. Few industries were established in some selected urban areas of the country. Though women's economic activities increased to some extent, their condition did not increase. In rural areas women's dependency in agriculture remained the same.

After democracy emphasis was given to improve the educational structure of the country. Many government schools and colleges were started providing free education or in nominal free system. Before democracy right to education was limited to Rana ruler and some powerful elites. Some girl's schools and women's colleges were also established for providing easy access to education for women. In this regard the effort made by Angoor Bala Joshi, Chandani Joshi, etc. are remarkable. Angoor Bala Joshi is the first Woman Principal of the Padmakanya Multiple Campus of Tribhuvan University.

PARTY LESS PANCHAYAT SYSTEM (1965-1990)

In 1965 when late King Mahendra Bir Bikram Shah banned multiparty system and announced party less Panchayat system, many women came out to the street opposing the system. At that time Sailaja Acharya was leading the women's group in Kathmandu. During the 30 years of Party less Panchayat system many women's organizations were banned by the king. Those women who were working informally for the downfall of Panchayat system got imprisonment and exiled from the country thereafter.

Within Panchayat system, some women, who were in power also worked for women's issues to some extent; they were Shushila Thapa, Bhadra Kumari Ghale, Chandra Shah, Sabitri Jangam etc. In spite of the banned of party politics with freedom to speak and write, literary person "Parijat" (Bishnuf Kumari Baiba) contributed a lot for women's issues through literature. Her contribution on novel, poetry, stories, etc. were related to contemporary women's movement (raising awareness & Fighting for women's right). Her novel "Shirish Ko Phool", awarded by "Madan Puraskar 1966", has been included in contemporary leading women figures fighting for women's issues were Dr. Meena Acharya, Dr. Beena Pradhan, Durga Ghimire, Asta Laxmi Shakya, Durga Pokhrel etc.

In International arena the decade of 1970's was very much supportive for women's issues. When United Nations declared the year 1975 as International Women's subordination & oppression. After than, women's issues come into existence in the eyes of policy makers and consequently Nepal started to participate in women's from at home and abroad.

The 'First International Women's Conference 1975' held in Mexico city decided to do a study of the status of women worldwide. According to this for the first time in Nepal an intensive research conducted by Dr. Meena Acharya with the help of Linn Bennett. The study was conducted through Center for Economic Development and Administration (CEDA), Tribhuvan University, Kathmandu, Nepal. The team studied the economic, social, political and legal status of women in Nepal. The outcome of the research was published in 1981. The report opened eyes of the policy makers and also women activists, academicians, researchers, etc. For the First time, working hours of both men and women were counted. The finding of that research showed that working hours of Nepalese women is calculated as 12 to 16 hrs per day depending upon the economic & geographical situation of the country. Where as men's working hour is calculated as 8 to 10 hrs per day (Acharya and Bennett, 1981 and Shadow Report of CEDAW, 1999).

Observing the outcome of this research and voice of women activists, government of Nepal incorporated women's chapter in its 6th five-year plan (1980-85). Government started to give emphasis on women's education, training, health, nutrition etc. Several women development programs were launched through formal and informal sectors. Women started to come out from household economy and got employment in industry and other sectors. A few educated women became economically independent in urban areas, but in Nepalese context economic independence does not mean independent in taking decision.

During that period some educated and active women raised the voice for women's social, political, economic and legal rights. Dr. Santa Thapalia, Kalyani Shah etc. contributed in legal sector. The same way Sahana Pradhan, Mangala Devi Singh, Sailaja Acharya, Meena Pandey, Sama Shahi, Kabita Bhattarai, Ambika Pant etc. struggled for women's political rights and further women's right movement in Nepal.

Since 1970s Dr. Meena Acharya, Dr. Beena Pradhan, Ambika Shrestha, Laxmi Kashari Manandhar, Dr. Leela Devi K.C. etc. are contributing through different ways for the advancement of Nepalese women. Similarly, Angoor baba Joshi, Suprabha Ghimire, Dr. Leela Devi K.C., Laxmi Keshari Manandhar are working continually for women's education. Nepalese Women delegates participated Second and Third World Conference on Women in 1980 and 1985. Though most of the participants were nominated by the government who could not voice the real situation of Nepali women in such world forum.

Among several active women, late Mangala Devi Singh, Sahana Pradhan, Sailaja Acharya, Suprabha Ghimire, Kalyani Shah, Hishila Yemi, Pumpha Bhusal, Meena Pandey, Kabita

Bhattarai, Kalyani Shah, etc. directly contributed for the restoration of Democracy in 1990.

AFTER THE RESTORATION OF DEMOCRACY IN 1990

After the restoration of democracy in 1990, many women's organizations were formed and reorganized under the leadership of Sahana Pradhana, late Mangala Devi Singh, and other women leaders. Many other active women came out from household chore and raised the voice for women's political, legal and socio-economic rights. In this regard the name comes Anuradha Koirala, Chandra Bhadra, Durga Ghimire, Santa Laxmi Shrestha, Geeta Sangrual, Sapana Malla, Dr. Aruna Upreti, etc. They also participated in the Fourth International Women's Conference (Beijing conference). Besides them, many other women from different political, social sector, GO and NGO sectors took part at that conference.

The conference strongly focused 12 critical areas of concern for the empowerment of women. To implement these declarations the government of Nepal immediately (in 1995) formed the Ministry of Women, Children and Social Welfare. Among 18 ministries it cannot be imagined that only one women's ministry can deal women's issues and lunch programs related to women's empowerment. However, it has been a milestone in this regard.

Still Nepali society is patriarchal and dominated by male. Women are not involved in decision-making processes. Nepalese women do not have access to property right and with that no access to credit and entrepreneurship. Still they are not getting equal rights and equal opportunities in spite of the equality before the law. Constitution of 1990 has granted many fundamental rights to women but the implementation aspect of the law is very poor. None of the big political parties are committed to provide equal property right, reproductive right, citizenship rights for women. The prime minister of Interim government Mr. Krishna Prasad Bhattarai ratified the CEDAW without reservation immediately after restoration of Democracy in 1991. But no special effort has been made to implement the agendas of CEDAW in practice. Therefore, all the women's organization including NGOs are struggling of the implementation of CEDAW.

In this regard, the effort made by Women's Studies Program of Central Department of Home Science, Padmakanya Multiple Campus, Tribhuvan University is praiseworthy. The post Graduated Diploma in Women's Studies has been started from 1996 and now the fifth batch is going on. The program is going to upgrade up to Master level very soon. It has been established by the leading scholar of the country with a view to create awareness among Nepalese citizens about the condition and position of women in Nepal and abroad. Dr. Meena Acharya, Dr. Beena Pradhan, Dr. Leela Devi K.C., Laxmi Kashari Manandhar, etc. are actively contributing to this program. Since it's inception, sixteen trained teachers from different department including one male teacher of this campus are facilitating in this course along with several guest lecturers.

In Accordance with changing development concepts, now Nepal is following Structural Adjustment Policy/Globalization in its national development policy. Many macroeconomic changes have been occurred along with globalization like: privatization and liberalization of the economy, opening the border for multinational companies, export-led growth, etc. Due to these, migration particularly from rural to urban and national to international are taking place. As a result, women headed household have increased with increased work burden of women especially in rural areas.

In urban areas too, women are coming out from household chore in order to fulfil the increasing need of family. Job opportunities are scarce in formal sector especially for women because, formal sector requires skilled and trained human resources. Most of the Nepalese women lack education and training so, they are going to informal sectors where their status is considered very low. A few trained as well as elite women are conducting their own business-enterprises. These are Ambika Shrestha, Laxmi Sharma, Saraswoti Shrestha, Jyoti Tuladhar, etc.

Those who are employed in tourism sectors (Travel, Tours, Hotel, Restaurant) are occupying very low position. Most of them are suffering from sexual harassment. Though the practice of trafficking of women and girls children is observing in the country since more than 100 years. Now after the restoration of democracy some positive effort has been made to control it especially through the initiation of some NGOs. They are also taking initiation to bring out the women from different brothels and rehabilitating them. In this regard Nepalese society will never forget the contribution made by Anuradha Koirala (founder of Maiti Nepal), Durga Ghimire (ABC Nepal) Renu Rajbhandari (WOREC), etc.

In this way women of Nepal are struggling for their rights and better position in the society.

REFERENCES

Acharya, Meena and Bennett, Lynn (1981), "The Rural Women of Nepal, An Aggregate Analysis and Summary of Eight Village Studies", The Status of Women in Nepal, Vol. 11, Part-9 Center for economic Development and Administration, Tribhuvan University, Kathmandu, Nepal.

Acharya, Meena (1998), "Women and Economy: Key Issues", Kathmandu, Nepal.

Acharya, Meena (1994), "The Statistical Profile on Nepalese women: An Update in the policy context", IIDS, Kathmandu, Nepal.

Acharya, Meena (2000), "Democracy and Gender Equality: The Economic Aspects" A Paper presented in a Workshop on Democracy and Gender Organized by Padmakanya Campus, Tribhuvan University, Kathmandu, Nepal.

Acharya, Meena (2000), "Labor Market Development and Poverty with Focus on Opportunities for Women in Nepal", Tanka Prasad Acharya Memorial Foundation in Cooperation with Frediric Ebert Stiftung Foundation (FES), Kathmandu, Nepal.

Acharya, Meena (1995), "20 Years of Women in Development-What we have Gained", a paper presented in a Teachers Training on Post Graduate Course on Women's Studies, Padmakanya Multiple Campus, Tribhuvan University, Kathmandu, Nepal.

Asmita (2056 B.S.), "Asmita 50-Swarna Anka" Year 12, Anka 50, Kathmandu, Nepal.

Asmita Publications (2000), Asmita, November, Kathmandu, Nepal.

Dahal, Pesal (2057 B.S.), *"Nepal Ko Itihas"* M.K. Publishers and Distributors, Kathmandu, Nepal.

Forum for law, women and development (1999), "Shadow Report on the Initial Report of the Government of Nepal on the Convention on the Elimination of all Forms of Discrimination against Women". CEDAW, Kadhmandu.

INSEC (2053 B.S.), *"Rajnitik Mahila Parichaya"*, Informal Sector Service Center, Kathmandu, Nepal.

INSEC (2055 B.S.), *"Netritwama Mahila, Mahila Janapratinaidhi Rastriya Behela", Pratibedan,* INSEC, Kathmandu, Nepal.

INSEC (1996), "Women in Politics: National Conference or Women", Informal Sector Service Center Report, Nepal.

Mandala Book Point (1997), "Studies in Nepali History and society" Onta Pratyoush, Chene Mary Des, Onta-Bhatta Lazima. Linchty mark Ed, Vol. 2, Nepal Human Development Report (1998) UNDP, Kathmandu, Nepal.

National Planning Commission (1998), "The Ninth Plan (1997-2002)", His Majesty's" Government of Nepal.

Sangraula Geeta (1998), "Law and Exiting Reality of Nepalese Women".

Sharma Kamal Raj (2056 B.S.), *"Nepali Samaj Ra Sanskrit: Samajsastriya Tatha Manabsastriya Dristikon"* Kathmandu, Nepal.

Stri Shakti, (1995), "Women, Development, Democracy: A study of Socio-Economic change in the status of women in Nepal (1981-93)". Prepared for USAID, DANIDA, CCO, Kathmandu, Nepal.

Aparna Mahanta

15

Woman in Discourses of Nation and Community and the Politics of the Personal: A Study of Northeast India

In the late Nineteen-Seventies and early Nineteen-Eighties when the latest phase of the Women's Movement was sweeping over India and even percolating into sleepy nooks and corners of the country, there was a sense of new beginnings and the dormancy of the Fifties and Sixties. As a matter of fact the pre-Independence women's movement had not died away completely but survived as a bastion of conservatism, or so it appeared to the radical young bloods of the new feminist-oriented women's movement. The representatives of the older women's organization dating back to the pre-Independence and immediate post-Independence period were mainly associated with social welfare activities and seemed like an unpaid extension of the Government.[1] Now, twenty-five years on after that new phase of the New Women's movement, with the then fiery feminist activists provably graying grandmothers the situation looks somewhat different. There have been a lot of changes in the ground realities. Women's groups, activated wings of political parties, and NGOs are highly visible. The rhetoric of women's empowerment has entered the state discourse, with 2001 being officially declared the Year of

Women's Empowerment. But things do not appear to have really changed apart from the cosmetic changes, and even these are not very apparent. The talk is of women's empowerment but the speechmakers are male.

Has there really been a paradigm shift in the perceptions of the state and society in general policy of women's role and place in society? Has the women's movement and women's studies in particular succeeded in bringing about this paradigm shift? Wisdom, like Minerva's owl comes late. However with the aid of a process of hindsight by placing the present against the recent past and the further past it is possible to get a perspective on the issue. It thus appears that there has not been so much a process of any radical change as a continuing dialectic of two opposing conceptions of women's role and place in society. On the one hand there is the continuing attempt to fit women into universalistic frameworks of discourage to serve male determined agendas whether defined as rationalistic, humanist or Marxist. On the other hand there is the movement of feminist self assertion, the attempt to create a radical separatist agenda for women that is separate and woman-oriented. This can be seen even at the origins of feminism if one studies the writings of Mary Wollstonecraft. It is reflected in the zigzag path of the women's movement itself as periods of struggle and optimistic self-assertion are followed by the periods of bleak realization of the need to accommodate and adapt to the status quo, albeit in new configurations or opt out, whether struggling or quieten. Even the path of revolution is no longer as straightforward as it used to be.

Despite all the struggles, woman continues as the subject of discourse, whether it is the discourse of nation or now with the rise of ethnic-based self identity movements and fundamentalist politics in the discourse of community.[2] The feminist politics of the personal, women's search for self-identity and struggle for self assertion is caught between the two dominationg forces. Woman's struggle for self determination at work, at home and for the collective goals of women's rights and status has seemingly not altered the place of woman in the official discourses as subject and not an agent.

The tantalizing goal of empowerment dangled before women remains a chimera. Even those who have the materials for empowerment, the capabilities as they are now called ala Amartya Sen such as education, employment, information fail to use those for self-empowerment because of the old mindset in which women have been trained, to sacrifice themselves to family, nation or community. After all empowerment has to come from within and is not something which can be 'given'. Hence the spectacle of women working hard to prove themselves equal to men, trying to ignore the fact that they are in Simone de Beauviour's sense 'women', made and not born so. As in *Alice's Wonderland* one has to run harder in order to be able to remain in the same place.

These thoughts come to mind in reviewing in historical perspective the course of the women's movement in Northeast India, the former undivided Assam of colonial and immediate post-Independence India and the present Northeastern States. While arguing for the continuity of the movement one can divide it into three distinctive phases.[3]These are in the period of the Nationalist struggle, the post-1975 women's movement and in the ethnic identity movements of the eighties and nineties. Except in the post 1975 phase women organised themselves, on the other occasions, on nationalist issues, with the overt or covert backing of the main sponsors of the mass movement. In the National Movement it was the National Congress Party. In the Autonomy movements it was the various student or youth organizations like AASU (All Assam Students Union) or ABSU (All Bodo Students Union) or ASDC (Autonomous State Demand Committee). In each case the women responded often in a mass way to the liberative potential of the movement, as they perceived it on their own terms. Again it was the convergence of many factors which made this mobilization possible. The movement becomes a space for defining an effective self-dignity, subsumed under the general febric of self-determination. The women could organize on a specifically feminist agenda bringing in time specific issues like women's education, widow remarriage, child marriage, rape, atrocities on women and so on. In each case women organize themselves with full zest and involvement but ended each time with a sense of betrayal and disenchantment.

A closer study of women's involvement in the nationalist movement and the struggles for ethnic identity in the context of the Northeast would bring out this point more clearly. In Assam and the Northeast generally, the ethnic based identity movements, which started in the early eighties overlapped with the women's movement of the time. In this case there was either a pooling of personnel of the two movements or a conflict of interests. At that time I was editing a women's magazine *Aideour Jonaki Bat* (1983-88) and had to face flak from students (male) as being anti-national for publishing news of women in Pakistan and other countries. At the same time some of my colleagues in the group were active in the Assam Movement. As the women's movement as such as opposed to women's mobilization in the identity movement was very small I will concentrate only on the latter in this paper.[4] Thus I will concentrate on the roles of women in the freedom struggle and in the recent identity movement.

WOMEN IN THE FREEDOM STRUGGLE

In Assam the period of woman's actual involvement in the freedom struggle as an organized group starting from 1926 with the formation of the Asom Mahila Samiti is preceded by a period of mobilization since the second decade of the 20th century. As elsewhere in India in Assam too the groundwork was laid by the discourse of Social reform, which brought up issues like women's education and widow marriage in the mid-nineteenth century. The educational and literary efforts of the Baptist missionaries and the educated progressive Assamese youths as well as the proselytizing efforts of Brahmo preachers popularised girls' education in Assam. It was the educated women themselves who organized themselves on women's issues like girls' education and self-help. According to the main spirit behind the pre-Independence women's movement in Assam, Chandraprova Saikiani, the first women's organizations in Assam were started in Dibrugarh (1915), Nowgong (1917) and Tezpur (1919) (Saikiani, pp. 2-3). All the three places especially the first two were noted centres of girls' education. Dibrugarh had the first full fledged girls' school in Assam established in 1885, becoming a high school in 1911. Dibrugarh, a military outpost and railhead for the first railways in the region, had a sizeable Brahmo presence. Under their influence a magazine named *Alochani* was started which patronised education, encouraging many local girls to go to Brahmo schools in Bengal for study. In Nowgong the Baptist missionaries had started a coeducational school for orphans with the aim of conversion as early as 1842. This became a solely girls' boarding school imparting normal schools training to girls in 1857, when the orphan institution was closed down (Bora, p. 223). While Hemprova Das, the headmistress of the Dibrugarh school took the lead in organizing women in Dibrugarh, Saikiani, an alumnus of the Nowgong school, and later schools teacher successively in Nowgong and Tezpur, was instrumental in establishing the other two (Saikiani, p. 2-3) In a parallel manner, in fact a year earlier, in 1914, the progressives among the men-folk aligning with a rising congress wave took the initiative to organize women around the iconic figure of Sati Jaymati. The Sati was a 17th century Ahom princess who is supposed to have sacrificed herself to save the political fortunes of her fugitive husband who became later founder of the most successful of the Ahom dynasties and ruled Assam prior to the British takeover. She was iconised as the very epitome of a patriotic woman who was simultaneously a chaste and virtuous wife. The future leaders of the Congress party of Assam (formed in 1920) in the first annual Jaymati Day organized in Sibsagar in 1914, exhorted the assembled women to emulate the virtues of Jaymati (*Banhi*). Sibsagar was the headquarter of the Baptist missionaries who were the first to provide opportunities for the education of girls in their areas of work after their entry into Upper Assam in 1836. Moreover their journal, Orunodoi published since 1846, supported the education of girls. The local elite, though shying away from conversion, was appreciative of their efforts and soon started opening girls' school on their own account. Thus an open assembly of women would not be such a strange thing there in the early decades of the twentieth century. Though the men took the initiative, the women participated spontaneously. When later the AMS was formed in 1926 the Sibsagar unit was very active and published between 1928-1930 a magazine by women for women named *Ghar-Jeuti* (Light of the House).

Thus it can be seen that the groundwork for women's organization was the spread of women's education and the consequent rise of consciousness that made them amenable to new ideas about women's role in society. This can be particularly seen by reviewing the career of Chandraporva Saikiani, the founder of the *Assam Mahila Samiti*. Incidentally the *Assam Pradeshisk Mahila Samiti* (as the Assam Mahila Samiti was renamed in 1945) is celebrating the birth centenary of Chandraprava Saikiani (1901-1972) this year with a lot of fanfare on an all Assam basis. Paradoxically, while the Nationalist leaders following Gandhi's lead were holding up the Sati-Savitri ideal as the symbols of "Bharatiya Nari", the Assam women's organization was led by a social rebel like Saikiani. Born in an interior village to a poor socially inferior caste family, she trudged to a village boys school with her sister (Assam's first lady medical graduate of Calcutta medical college) before gaining admission to the Nowgong Mission boarding school for girls. After passing the Normal course she started working as a school teacher first in Nowgong and later Tezpur, living alone. In 1919 she joined a few lady delegates at the Annual conference of the *Assam Chatra Sanmelan*, the then All Assam Students' Union. She gave her first speech, the first by any woman in Assam in that conference. In 1921 Saikiani fell under the spell of Gandhi, then on his Assam tour when he also visited Tezpur (Das). Saikiani abandoned her school job to work full time for the struggle. At the time she also got pregnant and gave birth to her son who was never publicly acknowledged by his father. Her lover abandoned her under family pressure as she belonged to a lower caste. Undaunted, Saikiani brought up the son as a single mother and he grew up to be a respected public figure, a trade union leader. While organising the women in the early years Saikiani carried her son about with her a fact she mentions in the official history of the organization (*mahila samitir ittibritti*, p. 8).

The Assam Mahila Samity was formed in 1926. But the nucleus had existed from 1915, and it was these same women who came forward to form this organization. In forming the AMS Saikiani had the organisational experience as a member of the *Chatra Sanmelan* and the *Asom Sahitya Sabha,* (ASS) the national literary organization of the Assamese people founded in 1917. In fact the first conference of the AMS was held on the occasion of the annual session of the *Assam Sahitya Sabha* in Dhubri in 1926. The organizers of the *Sabha* made all the arrangements for the meeting and the President of the ASS himself presided over the session. However all the *Sabha* members were not sympathizers of the feminist cause like the President. In the previous session of the Sabha held in Nowgong in 1925, Saikiani as an official delegate to the *Sabha* had called upon the women members of the audience to come out from behind the bamboo screen, which served as *"purdah"* for the separate *zenana* section. The women heeded the call and consequently the screen was smashed. Enthused by the response the ladies planned to have their own meeting on the last day of the session. When they arrived in thousands as planned they found the organizers hastily demolishing the pandal to prevent the meeting. The ladies held their meeting in an open field and took the resolution that bore fruit the next year (*ittibritti,* pp. 4-5).

The support that Saikiani received from her co-workers in the movement, many of whom were the wives of prominent Nationalist leaders, may have been due to the exigencies of the large struggle, but she was basically a rebel, a feminist. In her reminiscences of Gandhi written in 1969 she rationalises her attraction for Gandhi in his espousal of Harijans, she herself being a member of a despised caste (Saikiani, 1969, p. 324). It is obvious that for her as for many others of her co-workers the struggle offered a space to express their personal grievances and aspirations. The AMS in its formative years between 1926-1930 with regular annual conventions held in Jorhat and Golaghat worked zealously for causes which the women considered important like girls' education, raising age of consent, setting up weaving centres, ending untouchability and so on. The Sarda bill was a hot topic of debate and later direct action as conservative mothers battled with defiant daughters. In 1927-29 the Sibsagar unit of the AMS brought out a mouthpiece, *Ghar-jeuti* which reported on activities of the communities and its several branches besides news from all India organizations. It also contained stories and poems on Jaymati besides articles on the Russian and Chinese (Sun Yet Sen) revolutions. One of the editors of the journal was a woman who walked out on her husband when he remarried. The flurry of activity ended in 1930 when the Non-cooperation movement started. Saikiani and most of the active women workers were imprisoned for long periods. The next Annual session could only be held in 1934 in Guwahati. It is interesting to note that while the previous sessions were presided over by women, even if wives of prominent men, the president of this session was a noted supporter of the Nationalist cause, the *Satradhikar* of Garmur *Satra*. In place of Saikiani the secretaryship of the AMS went to a young educated woman. As an active force the AMS disintegrated as all the active members were totally involved in the general struggle. In 1945 at a meeting held in Guwahati, the AMS was totally reorganized as the Assam Pradeshik Mahila Samiti with a constitution modeled on that of the Assam Pradeshik Congress Committee, and drawn up by a Congress functionary (*ittibritti*, p. 13). By now Saikiani is totally dependent on the Congress leaders, virtually a camp follower. The next full conference of the APMS was held in Nowgong in 1947. It was now an institution in the familiar process of co-option, an appendage of the Social Welfare Board formed in 1952. It is an irony of history that a woman, who had struggled for the political and social identity of women as an articulate student, working woman and single unwed mother should end her days concerned with setting up rescue homes for unwed mothers and distributing relief in floods and famines, but she could not fight against the establishment. Politically Saikiani was totally sidelined. It was not that she was not politically ambitious. She was eventually given a Congress ticket in 1957, after having been passed over several times in favour of younger more educated candidates, but she failed to win

(Mahanta, 1998, pp. 174-175). She was eventually given a *Padmasri* in 1972 on her deathbed. She became a totally forgotten figure. It was only after the resurgence of the women's movement in the Eighties that her radical past was unearthed and she has been reinstated as a pioneer of the women's movement in Assam.

WOMEN IN ETHNIC-BASED IDENTITY MOVEMENTS

Since the inception of the Assam Movement in 1979 women have again come to the forefront of the political scene of the Northeast as a sizeable force. For many in the early eighties its seemed to be a comeback of the Gandhian movement with words like satyagraha, non-violent movement and picketing returning to the political vocabulary and large scale involvement of women. Following on the Assam Movement, in other ethnic-based identity movements like that of the Bodos and the Karbis women are visible as both the subject and object of the discourse of community. This is true also in the states where the political movement is not of a mass character but which have to grapple with problems of ethnic identity which is the basis of their statehood such as Meghalaya and Arunachal Pradesh. As in the National movement there is a dichotomy in the conceptualization of women's political role. While they are projected as being necessary for the struggle and their participation is encouraged, at the same time there is the perception of the need of control within patriarchalist frameworks of family and community honour. The situation of the Northeast is piquant because in the tribal based societies women have a high social visibility, due to their economic activities, which has also influenced their participation in education and professions. While Assam is an exception as not being a tribal state, it has a sizeable tribal presence, which is only glossed by the predominance of the Hinduised upper castes.

During the six year Assam Movement (1979-1985) thousands of women participated which was noted at the time (unfavourably) by most outside observers. Both rural and urban women joined the movement, as it appeared to be a fight to save the nation from foreign infiltrators. At the same time communal feelings were raised by the alleged atrocities by the Indian army personnel on villagers and women, especially rape. There is a distinct difference between the spontaneous involvement of the women and the manipulation of communal emotions by the rape allegations or incidents. The familiar nationalist identification of the woman's honour with the nation's honour is evident here. As during the freedom struggle women are reified as the symbol of the country's exploitation by the (male, i.e. more powerful) outsider, since woman is the indispensable 'other' of the nation's self-identity. The women's forwardness perceived during the movement as promiscuity (by disapproving outsiders) had to be checked by the male leaders of the movement by appropriate measures like edging them out of the political process once the negotiations began. Thus women's mass involvement rather than leading to greater empowerment led to greater conformity to the status quo, the pervasive patriarchal setup of the nation state. In the ten years since the student leaders came to power there has just been one woman state minister and that too a tribal woman. Apart from her, all the women MLAs of the AGP party-ticket happen to be widows of former MLSs. A similar situation prevails in the Bodo and Karbi movements where involvement of women in mass programs goes alongside virtually powerlessness in decision making. The only woman issue that crops up is rape which underlies the helplessness and vulnerability of women.

Interesting examples of the perceived threat to ethnic self indentity (which needless to say is perceived as male), that is posed by women comes from the states of Meghalaya and Arunachal Pradesh. In Meghalaya customary law follows the matrilineal system of inheritance. In Arunachal society women are traditionally cultivators and traders with access to communal land and forest resources. Yet in both states, politics is traditionally strictly taboos for women. After Independence the Sixth Schedule of the Constitution provided protection for customary law. However the exigencies of modern state craft and the consolidation of power through ethnic assertion has created a rift between women's economic and social independence and male political dominance. Thus in both states there is an attempt by male legislatures backed by student groups to curb the rights of women and bring them under legal and patriarchal control in the interests of a perceived ethnic identity. The essence of customary law is that it changes with time and circumstances, in consonance with the traditional environment. Bringing it within a legal framework within male dominated abimance of the present political setup while ignoring the women's viewpoint would destroy many the customary safeguards of women's rights in marriage and property. This is the point being made by the Arunachal Pradesh Women's Welfare Society (APWWS) in its resistance to this tendency. They were opposing, for instance, a bill placed in the AP (Arunachal Pradesh) Assembly in 1994 for legalizing polygamy as customary. The APWWS contended that while polygamy had been practised in some areas it was only confined to a few wealthy and influential people, but making it a law would be a denial of the rights of all women forced into such marriages in the name of law. As in the case of Gandhi's attacks on the Western-educated Indian women as a violation of the concept of *'Bharatiya nari'*, the opposition to such biased interpretations of customary law would be exposed to the charges of anti-tribal behaviour (Ete, p.).

The case is even more blatant in Meghalaya. There the almost wholly male State Assembly, backed by student and youth organizations, again overwhelmingly male, is making an attempt to interpret customary law against women. Again the very fact that state like Meghalaya are based on the concept of linguistic or ethnic identity hastens what appears to be a process of ethnic consolidation. The legislation in question is the "Khasi Custom of Lineage Bill, 1997". The bill was intended to codify the Khasi system of matrilineal inheritance. The item which raised the ire of Khasi youth as being inimical to the protection of Khasi identity, was the clause relating to the rights under the matrilineal system of Khasi women married to "outsiders". While Khasi men married to non-khasis did not risk losing their Khasi identity and the rights thereby accruing, Khasi women in the same situation risked doing so unless they conformed to some conditions like continuing to speak Khasi or follow Khasi customs. Particularly the children of such marriages were at risk, thus going against the whole concept of matriliny where descent is traced through the mother. The students' opposition was that the conditions given were not stringent enough. The student and youth organizations argued that "recognising such women (Khasi women married to outsiders) and their children as Khasi not only exposed the population to economic risks but also tarnishes their ethnic identity" (Nongbri, p. 380). This too when it is a well known fact that the Khasi women are economically self sufficient and often even support the men economically. Only a women's organization, the Meghalaya Women's Alliance took up the issue as involving the rights of women both to free choice in marriage and to ethnic identity if she chose the former. However most other affected women remained silent for fear of being branded as anti national and unpatriotic (Nongbri, p. 381), the common argument in all societies to bring women to heel.

The process of patriarchal consolidation, through nationalistic and communal based ideologies is one where women are made the objects of the discourse and denied their agency, even where it exists. The process started with colonialism and its related ethos has gradually subverted and destroyed the existent gender relations in tribal society. The Indian state with its policies of the regional consolidation of the state system has only intensified this process. As Nongbri puts it, "colonial rule... has made gender identity a politically charged affair. The woman's body has become an ideological terrain around which identity and entitlements are reconstituted and reworked" (Nongbri, p. 388). This is true of the entire Northeast. The fluidity of earlier patterns of gender relations in predominantly tribal or tribal influenced societies is being replaced by rigid constructions of gender identity mediated by self perceptions of national and gender identity. In the accompanying discourses of Nation and Community women are seen as the repository of the nation or the community's honour. Hence their rape or despoliation (in the real or symbolical sense) by outsiders becomes a rallying point for national or ethnic consolidation. Thus women are trapped in the myths of nation or community, perceived as vulnerable and hence to be protected and controlled and saved from themselves. The resulting scenario of violence and counter violence has silenced their voices, as in history the real issues espoused by women like Chandraprova Saikiani have been perverted and elided in a sanitised version of women as devoted social workers. While the outer violence is magnified the violence turning inward on the women is hidden. As is the case with the rape of Bhanwari Devi, the killing of women as witches in Bodoland or the murder of women activists in the same area goes unnoticed in the more powerful discourses. These are the signs of the threat of violence, which ensures women's conformity to the status quo, in any age and in any place.

In the universalizing discourses of Nation and Community the politics of the personal, of woman's identity as an individual and not as a member of any nation or community appears to have got lost. Similarly in the present state discourse of women as agents of development the empowerment of women is constructed as essential to the development process. Hence it is argued that the empowerment of women is necessary so that they can be good mothers by having less children, educating them better and providing for the nutrition and health needs of the family (a la Amartya Sen). The empowerment of women for self-development is ignored or lost sight of. Developing the study of the politics of the personal in women's studies could restore this lost dimension.

NOTES

1. "The Emergence of New Women's Groups in Assam in the Decade since 1975", in Neera Desai, ed. *A Decade of the Women's Movement in India*, Himalaya Publishing House, Bombay, 1988, P. 131.
2. See Partha Chatterjee, "The Nation and its Women" and "Women and the Nation" in *Nation and its fragments: Colonial and Postcolonial Histories*, Delhi, OUP, 1994 and Tanika Sarkar, "The Woman as Communal Subject: Rashtrasevika Samiti and Ram Janambhoomi", *Economic and Political Weekly*, 26:35.

3. It is a gain of the feminist movement and women's studies that we are able to see this continuity. Earlier each phase was seen as separate, part of other movements. The feminist content was thus ignored. But a closer study of the movements show that there was a convergence of various interests in the course of the movement of which the feminist interest was certainly to some extent at least very important.
4. This aspect has been dealt with in the article cited above in note 1.

REFERENCES

Shiela Bora, 1998, "The Nowgong Orphan Institute: A Reflection on Miles Bronson's work for Women (1843-1854)," M.N. Karna, Ed. *Social Movements in North-East India*, Indus Publishing Company, New Delhi, 1998.

Puspalata Das, *Agnisnata Chandraprova*, National Book Trust, 1998 Jarjum Ete, 1996, "Empowering Women", *Seminar*, 441.

Aparna Mahanta, 1988 The Emergence of New Women's Groups in Assam in the Decade since 1975", in Neera Desai, ed. *A Decade of the Women's Movement in India*, Himalaya Publishing House, Bombay, 1988, p. 131.

———, 1998, "Working of Parliamentary Process and empowerment of Women in Northeast India", in G. Phukan and Adil-Ul Yasin Eds. *Working of Parliamentary Democracy and Electoral Politics in Northeast India*, South Asian Publishers, New Delhi, 1998.

Tiplut Nongbri, 2000, "Khasi Women and Matriliny: Transformations in Gender Relations" in *Gender, Technology and Development 4:3*, Sept-Dec. 2000.

Chandraprova Saikiani, 1961, *Mahila samitir ittibritti*, Guwahati, 1961.

——— 1969, "Moi Gandhijik Jenefore dekhichilo" in C.P. Saikia, Ed. *Gandhijir Sowaranat, Assam Prakashan Parishad, 1969.*

Laxmi Keshari Manandhar

16

Women Development and Gender Equality Towards Twenty-first Century-Issues, Challenges and Opportunities (Case Studies of Nepal)

BACKGROUND

The concept of women development across the globe particularly in the western world arose more than a half century ago. Several movements in favour of women were mobilized by women activists, professionals, labourers but still an unequal power relation exists between men and women even at the present context. In spite of several efforts taken nationally and internationally with numerous conferences, Workshops/seminars, interactions for changing policies, incorporating, women's issues in planning and programming, there still exists a wide gap between the two sexes throughout the world. But we can observe the most affected and neglected countries are South Asian countries facing the fundamental problems of gender inequality particularly in basic rights such as education, healthcare, economic rights, political rights and legal rights.

We cannot say there is nothing been progressed in the field of women development since 1975 (beginning of international Women's year) there had been some efforts to incorporate women development policies formulating in plans and programmes of South Asian Countries which was a result of International Women Conferences took place in Copenhagen (Denmark), Mexico, Nairobi during the decade of womens' year.

Although the basic and fundamental problems of gender inequality is the same for all human race but only it's nature, and expressions differ from country to country. The women of South Asian region, have many common problems, as we have a similar culture, similar pattern of socialization, family and gender construction, patriarchal society. It was thus felt that we should try to be more united to seek solutions to our own problems and overcome the constraints. The fourth world women conference (Beijing conference) in China brought the South Asian women more united and together to advocate, pressurize and lobbying by approaching the voices to the government or state level.

According to the Beijing commitment, the 12 concerned areas were identified to enforcing towards implementation in their respective countries.

In Nepal after Beijing Conference we found lots of initiatives taken from NGO's and other private organizations, even from women activists and political leaders but the achievements are not upto the mark. This is because of some weaknesses of the organizations which have not been able to motivate and put much pressure on the political parties to speak and act strongly for enforcement to bring in action. This again refers the patriarchal society which allowed only the 5 per cent women members in the parliament.

WOMEN DEVELOPMENT AND GENDER EQUITY/ EQUALITY IN NEPAL-ISSUES AND CHALLENGES

Nepal is a land locked country of South Asia, situated between India and China, the biggest populated countries in the world. Total population of Nepal is 20 million (1991 census) of which 50 per cent are women. Historically deep-rooted patriarchal structure practiced traditionally in Nepal due to which male dominated society subordinated women as second class citizens. Men have controlled Women's labour, power, reproduction, sexuality, mobility, economic resources and rights. This is still existing in various degrees through many improvement efforts have been made to implement.

After the establishment of Human Right Commission in Nepal in 2000, the consideration of women's right as human right has come to the public sphere as one woman was appointed as the member of the commission.

Nepalese women are lagging behind men in all spheres of life due to dominant patriarchal structure as shown in HDR (Human Development Report 1997).

Towards the issues of 12 concerned areas, if we analyze after Beijing + Five Review there are some achievements of progress that have been found such as:

VIOLENCE AGAINST WOMEN AND TRAFFICKING

- Government has formulated national policy in close coordination with NGO's. It has also initiated the awareness programmes for prevention in 25 districts.
- Repatriation of 124 young girls from Bombay in July 1996.
- 228 women were liberated from police raid action.
- NGOs are implementing programmes, for domestic violence against women (SATHI).

WOMEN AND ENVIRONMENT

- Government established ministry of environment and population in September 1995.
- Ninth 5-year plan expresses the commitment to involve women and the underprivileged people while preparing and implementing environmental programme and promote women NGOs (WEPCO)

The involvement of women through NGOs, local communities and consumers has been increased. However the lack of decision making power of women at policy level does not ensure gender integration in the programmes which hinders to bring gender equity among the two sexes.

WOMEN AND EDUCATION

- Male and female literacy rate is— 66% (male) and 30% (female).
- Even there is no disparity between boy's and girl's education, there is big disparity in villages where girls are send to cheaper and ordinary schools and boys are send to nearby boarding schools. Dropout rate of girls from the schools after primary education is very high due to their assignment of household responsibility to help their mother to care siblings.
- Government has initiated (Ministry of education) non-formal literacy classes for women and girl child all over the country.
- Scholarships for girls.
- Vocational trainings are also integrated to literacy classes.
- Primary education is free but not in practice in most of the places.

WOMEN AND ECONOMY

A large proportion of women's labour devoted to eking out a living for their families still goes unreported and unrecognized (Acharya, Meena).

- There is some progress in Nepal's per capita income i.e., US$ 210 (HDR 2000 Report) but women are becoming poor and poorer in rural areas though government initiated the recognition of marginalization of women in the national economy, a gender mainstreaming strategy has been adopted to reduce gender gaps and disparities at all levels.
- Efforts are underway to include women's contribution in national economy in the census of 2001, which has not been reported yet.
- NGOs have also contributed significantly to uplift women's economic status through saving/credit loan schemes, skill trainings for self-employment (Business and Professional Women).

Government lacks political will or commitment to enforce existing laws as well as introduce new legislation in favour of Women's Right such as property right—the bill is hanged in the parliament since a long time.

WOMEN IN POWER AND DECISION MAKING

- There are only 12 women members (5.85%) in the parliament (House of Representatives) out of total 205 members.
- Deputy Speaker in the parliament is woman.
- Only 9 women (15%) in National Assembly out of total 60 members.
- Only one woman in the cabinet out of 25 members.
- One woman state minister for women, children and social welfare, established after Beijing conference in 1995.
- One woman in secretary post in the Ministry.
- Out of 75 chief district officers only one woman as CDO.

No woman has been yet appointed chief of any constitutional bodies and in the national planning commission.

- In the university level nearly 35% of women are in teaching but nobody in the higher authority level such as Vice-Chancellor, Rector, Registrar, Dean.

WOMEN AND HEALTH

- Maternal mortality rate of women as high as 539 per 1,00,000.
- The life expectancy for women is 53.5 years for men 55 years less than that of men (only the country).
- Government has initiated for strengthening the reproductive health and safe motherhood.
- NGOs and INGOs are involved in upgrading women's general health and reproductive right of women but there has been no evaluation of the efforts made by these organizations.

WOMEN AND POVERTY

- The globalization of the world's economy and deepening interdependency among nations present challenges and opportunities for sustained economic growth and development. This is the prioritized area towards alleviation of poverty among women.
- Women are the poorest among poor people (least developed countries).
- Women's work burden from early in the morning to late night but not getting any income.
- Women are considered only servicers, houseworkers (without money in hand).
- Gender inequity in Intra-household distribution of food and nutrition, many women and girl children die due to malnutrition.
- Women have no inheritance right, hence their access to control over land and other capital assets is severely limited (4.4% only).
- The incidence of poverty is found to be higher in female headed households (13%) than in male headed.
- Majority of women work in agriculture as unpaid workers.

NON-AGRICULTURE SECTOR

- Self employment– 2.68 (Daily wage difference–Rs. Women in organized sector has increased upto 23% in 1991, but declining in 1996-97 to 21%. 77 for male and Rs. 58 for women).
- Women Entrepreneurial activities gradually emerging for small scale enterprise establishment.
- Government initiated Gender Equality and Women's Empowerment policy in the 9th five-year plan through provision of land right, technical skill training's saving/credit provision, income generating activities and marketing opportunities can be taken as positive impact.
- Allocation of separate fund for women's economic empowerment through income generation i.e., Jagriti

programme has been launched by the ministry of women, children and social welfare in most of the districts.

Other areas of concern like women and Media, women and Human Rights the girl child, women and Armed conflict, Institutional Mechanism for Advancement of women have also achieved. Some have positive results but some have negative results.

HOPE TO HAVE OPPORTUNITIES

- In the rapid changing circumstances in the world and modernization, opportunities of womens' empowerment and womens' equality helps to meet gender equality. At the macro level women's equality implies significant representation in the leadership and management in both government and non-government level (industry)
- Mobilization of NGOs (men and women) through advocacy, lobbying reinforcing the government for implementation of existing laws and bring change in gender bias policies.
- Women's changing economic roles.
- Increasing women's interest in political participation from grassroots level.
- Legal literacy for women.
- Bring the changes in attitudes of men towards gender equality through continuous dialogue/interactions with men folk who are gender sensitized.
- A successful democracy required the equality in all the spheres of life.

REFERENCES

Kahne Hilda and Giele Janet Z. Women's work and Women's lives, Westview Press – Boulder, San Francisco, Oxford, Copyright 1992.

Achary Meena (Dr.) – Gender Equality and Empowerment of Women, A Status Report published by UNFPA, 1997.

A key note paper on South Asia Gender Network, December, 1997.

Beijing + 5 Review papers presented in workshop in Nepal, May 2000.

Marieta Bañez-Sumagaysay

17

Correlates of Married Women's Labour Force Participation in Private Sales and Service Sectors

Women's role in society has greatly shifted from the wife-for-the-home-only syndrome to the working woman who harmoniously combines home production with gainful employment outside the home. Along with the onset of industrialization, women have become juridically and ideologically equal to men (Schultz, 1991). Married women at work have become more common and their employment has become more accepted as a legitimate alternative for them to help their respective husbands increase the family welfare. Among married women, participation rates in the labour market have significantly increased in recent years, particularly as far as part-time work is concerned) Blau and Ferber, 1992). American census estimates indicate that while 19% of all women were in the labour force a century ago, it has jumped to 60% at present (Goldin, 1990).

In less developed economies, the increase in female employment remains largely confined to the informal sector and activities left over to them by the men (Israel-Sobritchea,

* Marieta Bañez-Sumagaysay University of the Philippines in the Visayas UPV Tacloban Collage, Philippines.

1991 in Mananzan, 1991; Angeles, 1990 in Evasco, et al., 1990). With the serious setbacks suffered by the Philippine economy in the eighties, female employment growth rate reflected wild fluctuations between 1983 to 1986 compared to male employment, implying that women were the first victims of layoffs (Amatong, as cited in Suliek, 1990). Women form the bulk of the reserve army of labor, to be pulled in when needed, and discarded when not (Pineda-Ofreneo, 1990 in Kintanar, 1990). Women comprise 37% of the country's total employment and 40% of overseas contract workers usually hired as domestic helpers.

According to the NSCB (1998) and NSO (1999) data, among the paid own-account workers in Eastern Visayas, only 27.91% are females. However, among the unpaid family labor, a large proportion of 59.62% are females. These women comprise 62.83% of the 191,000 in the wholesale/retail industry. They also comprise 56.31% of the 222,000 in the community, social and personal services. The labor supply of women is low at only 36.8 work hours per week.

The low participation rates of women, their being limited to "feminine" jobs, their short working hours, and the high incidence of unpaid female labor contribute to low cash incomes brought home by women. The crucial question then is how to improve women's access to economic resources such that her labor supply decisions become more favorable toward more paid work in the informal sector. Hence, improving the financial status and standards of living of the families.

An insight into these realities and the identification of demographic, economic, and socio-psychological parameters that will boost employment and work hours of women motivated the conduct of this study. What factors might change and alter a married woman's decision regarding the extent of paid work hours that she offers in the informal market?

Findings will be of interest to women's groups, employers of women and policymakers who want to chart a plan of action dove-tailed to efforts in integrating women in development, by increasing their labor force participation, their output, and their productivity. The data gathered will also serve as baseline data for academicians and researchers. Results will add to the body of knowledge related to women's work and gender development concerns. Students in economics and the social sciences can likewise gain insights. Moreover, research results can serve as instructional inputs and teaching materials in gender-related courses, and in engendering the curriculum.

SPECIFICATION OF THE MODEL

The conceptual model is cast in the income-leisure choice model where the married woman who opts to offer her labor services in the market consciously decides on the number of work hours spent for pay or profit.

The Labor Force Participation Decision

The decision to work is ultimately a decision of how to spend time. This participation decision is the choice between being in the labor force or being out of the labor force. The former refers to the use of one's available time in work for pay. The latter is to spend one's available time in non-market activities. One can work for pay and use his earnings to purchase childcare, food and clothing. Alternatively, one can work around the home performing such household production activities as raising children, preparing meals and sewing (Ehrenberg and Smith, 1994). Because working for pay and household production are two ways of getting one thing/job done then labor force participation decisions can be aptly characterized as the choice between leisure and income (that is, working for pay).

A neoclassical time allocation model advanced by Becker (1965) and Mincer (1962) has been used to explain how an individual decides on the allocation of his or her time between the home and the labor market (Blau and Ferber, 1992). Known as the New Household Economic Model, it assumes that adult members of the family make informed and rational decisions that result in the attainment of maximum utility or satisfaction. Individuals decide whether or not to participate in the labor market by comparing the value of their market time, w, to the value they place on their time spent at home, w^*. Labor force participation, that is, the choice of whether or not to work or seek market work, is based on a comparison of market opportunities and the benefits of staying at home (Filer, et al., 1996).

If w is greater than w^* an individual participates in the labor force; if w is less than w^*, he remains out of the labor force. The term w is measured by market wages, while w^* is the reservation wage. This reservation wage is the amount of extra earnings that the worker would require to be willing to give up one hour of leisure when he is not working at all (Filer, et al., 1996). Individuals with high potential wage rates are more likely to be in the labor force. On the other hand, people who place high value on leisure time (have a high reservation wage) and are less likely to be in the labor force (Anderson et al., 1994).

Participation decisions depend on changes in economic variables that influence the values of both market and nonmarket times. Factors that influence market time (w) include; woman's education, changing levels of economic activity, increases in overall labor productivity, and higher wages brought about by urbanization. Increases/improvement in these areas have caused rising trends in the labor force participation of married women (Blau and Ferber, 1992). However, this trend cannot entirely be ascribed to higher wages and to overlook those changes that influence the relative value of non-market time (w^*). These variables include: demographic trends, tastes, rising husband's income, availability of mother-substitutes, and presence of nonlabor income (Blau and Ferber, 1992).

The Labor Supply Decision

Once in the labor force, how much time do workers spend on their jobs? The labor supply decision refers to the number of hours per time period that workers are willing to work. The income-leisure choice model that is used to analyze how a rational decision maker chooses whether or not to participate in the labor force can similarly be applied to analyze how such a decision maker chooses the number of work hours to supply (Filer, *et al.*, 1996).

Assume utility maximization behavior of a worker, where his satisfaction depends on income and leisure. That is, income is payment for work performed by him and leisure refers to non-market time. Both income and leisure are desirable. The worker derives utility from the commodities he purchases with his income, and from the improvement in welfare brought about by nonmarket/leisure activities.

The Empirical Model

A married woman's labor supply behavior is, then, basically a rational decision concerning a trade-off between benefits derived from working for pay or profit, on one hand, and the benefits derived from undertaking nonmarket activities at home, on the other hand. In order to determine the significant correlates of married women's differential labor supply behavior, the model to be empirically tested is written as:

EMPW = *f* (AGEW, EDUC, CHIL, LAST, HHSI, SUBS HUSY, OTHY, WIFY, ATTI, WOCO, WOMB, FERT)

Where *EMPW* = woman's work effort (average work hours per day)

AGEW = age of the married woman

EDUC = married woman's educational attainment

CHIL = presence of children less than six years old

LAST = recency of last childbirth

HHSI = household size

SUBS = availability of mother substitutes

HUSY = husband's average monthly income

OTHY = contribution of other family members to family income

WIFY = wife's average monthly income

ATTI = husband's attitude towards female work

WOCO = wife's work commitment

WOMB	=	premarital work experience
FERT	=	future fertility plans

MEASUREMENT OF VARIABLES

Data source is primary information derived from a survey conducted for the purpose. The dependant variable, ***EMPW,*** is measured in terms of work hours offered in the labor market for wage or profit on an average monthly basis. A woman is defined to be a market participant if she worked for money sometime in the survey period.

The employment of the woman includes both primary and secondary jobs. Employment can either be for other employers or self-employment activities in the informal labor market. Average work hours per day during the month immediately preceding the conduct of the survey is the relevant data. Specifically, the measure of work effort is the number of days worked per week multiplied by the "average" or "usual" hours worked per day. This measure avoids the kind of sample bias that arises when one uses only the reported hours on the day the survey is conducted. This specification is derived from the model used by Hechman and Macurdy (1980) in analyzing the life cycle labor supply decisions of married women in an environment of perfect certainty.

The independent variables include demographic, economic, and socio-psychological factors relevant to the working married woman and her family. ***AGEW*** is the chronological age of the married woman. Her age at nearest birthday was recorded.

Education may affect a wife's productivity in the household or in paid work. ***EDUC*** is measured by the number of years of formal schooling completed by the married woman. The presence of children and their age composition affect the value of women's time in the home. ***CHIL,*** the number of children less than six years old who are living with the mother influences the value of her nonmarket time. So, too, is ***LAST*** or the number of years to last childbirth (Heckman and Macurdy, 1980).

Household size, ***HHSI,*** is the headcount of people dwelling in the same unit and sharing in the budgeting and decision making activities. This includes non-nuclear family members who stay wit the family nucleus. The availability of mother substitutes, ***SUBS***, releases the wife/mother to the labor market. They incldue grandparents, spinster aunts, nursemaids, and older siblings who are old enough to take care of the babies and younger children. This is a dummy variable equal to 1 if there are available mother-substitutes; zero, otherwise.

HUSY is measured as the husband's average monthly income from all sources. Other family members may also contribute to the family income. Their average monthly contribution, ***OTHY***, likewise consists of incomes derived from all sources. ***WIFY*** is the estimated average monthly income of the wife from all sources.

Socio-psychological factors include attitudinal, premarital work experience, and future fertility plans. ***ATTI*** is the husband's attitude towards female paid work. A Rating Scale measures ***ATTI*** where lower scores mean that the husband favors female employment, as perceived by the wife. ***WOCO*** is the wife's work commitment. This is measured as the total score of the woman in a Work Commitment Index where a higher score means higher commitment of the woman to work for non-familial reasons.

WOMB, a dummy variable, is the wife's premarital work experience which is equal to one if she worked before marriage, and zero otherwise. ***FERT***, is the wife's future fertility plans. A dummy variable equals one if she plans to bear a child in the future; zero, otherwise.

SUBJECTS

The subjects of the study consisted of women who have been continuously married to the same spouse during the past year. They have been working for pay or profit during the month immediately proceeding the week when the survey was conducted in December 1999 to January 2000. The nature of their employment may be on a full-time or part-time basis in the informal labor market. Unpaid work was excluded.

The research locale were purposively chosen for this study. This comprised the six provincial capital towns/cities and two other cities in Eastern Visayas. Centers of business and

Table1
Measurement of Variables

	Code and Name of Variable	*Measurement*
EMPW	Woman's work effort	Days worked per week multiplied by the "usual" hours worked per day during the month immediately preceding the survey.
AGEW	Age of married woman	The chronological age at nearest birthday.
EDUC	Married woman's educational Attainment	Number of years of formal schooling completed.
CHIL	Presence of children less than 6 years old	Number of children less than 6 years old who are living with the mother.
LAST	Recency of last childbirth	Number of years since last childbirth.
HHSI	Household size	Headcount of persons dwelling in the same Unit and sharing in the budgeting and Decision-making activities.
SUBS	Availability of mother substitutes	Dummy variable: 1 if there are available Mother-substitutes, 0 otherwise.
HUSY	Husband's average monthly Income	The husband's average monthly income from all sources during the last 12 months.
OTHY	Other family members' Contribution to family income	Sum of other family member's average monthly income from all sources during the last 12 months.
WIFY	Wife's average monthly income	Sum of the wife's income from all sources During the last 12 months.
ATTI	Husband's attitude towards Female work	A Rating Scale adopted from Layo (1977) will be used.
WOCO	Wife's work commitment	The score taken from a Work Commitment Index adopted from Herrin (1979).
WOMB	Wife's premarital work Experience	Dummy variable; 1 if wife worked before marriage, 0 otherwise.
FERT	Future fertility plans	Dummy variable; 1 if wife plans to bear a Child in the future; 0 otherwise.

administration, degree of modernization, and locus of convergence of people's activities were the parameters used in choosing the specific villages for study. Six hundred married women (600), randomly distributed across the eight research areas, and who were working in the informal labor market became the respondents. About 76.33% or 458 of these women were in the private sales sector (Table 1). The remaining 23.67% or 142 women were in the services sector (Table 2).

Table 2
Distribution of Respondents as to Type of Activities Engaged in, Private Sales Sector (N. 458)

Specific Activity	*Sub-Total*	*Total Frequency*	%
Processing and Vending			
Food Items:			
• Rice rolls	8		
• Viand	40		
• Smoked fish	6		
• Dried fish	18		
• Native delicacies	4		
• Banana cue/chips	8		
• Squid rolls/chips	10		
• Barbeque	16		
• Rice cake	22		
• Cassava cake	4		
• *"Tablea"* (native chocolate bars)	2	138	30.13
Non-food Items:			
• Firewood	2		
• Nipa shingle	30		
• Mats	6		
• *Abaca* (Manila hemp) Items	6	44	9.61
Vending/ Peddling (on commission basis)	*48*	*48*	*10.48*
Buy and Sell (for Profit)			
Food Items:			
• Dressed chicken	4		
• Meat	28		
• Fruit	10		
• Dried fish	2		
• Vegetables	18		
• Fish	8		

Contd....

Vending/ Peddling (on commission basis)	*Sub-Total*	*Total Frequency*	%
• Rice	4		
• Eggs	2	76	16.59
Non-food Items:			
• Dry goods	24		
• Cosmetic products	14		
(Avon/Herway)	2		
• Religious items	8		
• Hollow blocks	2		
• Newspaper	2		
• Cigarette/tobacco	8		
• Flowers	6	66	14.41
Sari-sari Store (Variety store):	86	86	18.78
Both food & non-food items			
Total for the Private Sales Sector		458	100.00

The informal labor market, also known as the secondary economic sector, is characterized by the absence of a screening process for incoming employees, by employees not being covered by civil service laws and other relevant rules and regulations of the Department of Labor and Employment. There may be no minimum educational requirements, nor protection of laborers from the government. Terms and conditions of employment may be more wanting and inferior than it is in the formal labor market.

Economic activities in these areas range from processing and vending/peddling food items and non-food items, to domestic service, dressmaking, laundry and/or parlor (beauty) services, and direct selling of various consumer items (such as cosmetics), among others.

INSTRUMENTATION

A rapid appraisal survey schedule was prepared based on instruments used by researches reviewed, but appropriately modified for the purposes of this study. This consists of three parts. Part I is composed of survey tables and matrices which enabled the researcher to gather quick information on the independent and dependent variables specified in the model. Part II attempts to measure the attitudes, interests and perceptions of married women. Two Scales were constructed: one to measure the husband's attitude towards female work (adopted from Layo, 1977), and another to measure the wife's work commitment (adopted from Herrin, 1979). Part III is a questionnaire designed to gather qualitative data and in-depth information that were significant inputs in analyzing and explaining the behavior of married women towards their decision to participate in the labor market and the extent of their participation.

Table 2
Distribution of Respondents as to Type of Activities Engaged in, Service Sector (N=142)

Specific Activity	*Sub-Total*	*Total Frequency*	%
Services			
Self-employed:			
• Beautician (home service)	12		
• Hair stylist (home service)	6		
• Dressmaker (shop at Home)	19	37	26.06
Employed by Others:			
• Laundry	43		
• Cook	4		
• Cashier/bookkeeper	4		
• Domestic help	16		
• Beautician (parlor)	8		
• Sales lady	22		
• Dress the chicken	2		
• Repacking	2		
• Quack doctor	4	105	73.94
Total for the Services Sector		142	100.00

Data gathered from Part II was analyzed based on rating scales. The Rating Scale to measure a husband's attitude towards wife's work (Layo, 1977) was scored as a continuum with 1 for strongly disagree and 5 for strongly agree. A lower score is interpreted as a husband's attitude which is favorable to wife's participation in the labor market. A score of 25 is considered least favorable.

The work commitment index (Herrin, 1979) was measured as the total responses of the woman to the following scaled items. Responses to items 1, 3, 5, 7, and 9 were scored in a continuum where 1 is strongly agree and 5 as strongly disagree. On the other hand, responses to items 2, 4, 6, 8, and 10 were in a similar continuum with 1 as strongly disagree and 5 as strongly agree. The highest score is 50 and the lowest is 10. The higher the score, the higher is the woman's commitment to work for non-familial reasons.

DATA PROCESSING

Data gathered were encoded. Correlation and stepwise multiple regression were used to determine significant correlates of married women's labor force participation. Four (4) alternative regressions are run for each sector. That is, models that include demographic variables only, economic variables only, socio-psychological variables only, and finally, all the identified variables. This is an attempt to determine significant predictors per identified category of the variables used.

RESULTS AND DISCUSSION

A set of variables deemed to explain the extent of paid work hours offered by married women in the labor market was identified based on priord relationships from the literature reviewed.

RESULTS

The Profile of Married Women

The number of hours spent by a married woman in paid work or work for profit partly depends on the nature of the market or the occupational group that she belongs to. In formal markets, labor laws have set that an employee's regular work hours is 8 hours per day for 5 days per week, or from 176 to 184 hours per month. Using this as the base point, then it is safe to consider any number of work hours which is lesser or more than this figure as shorter or longer work hours, respectively.

Research results show that married women in private sales and service sectors work for as short as three hours per week to as long as 70 hours per week. Hence, an average of about

46.90 per week or roughly 6.70 hours per day. Tables 1 and 2 show the specific activities engaged in by the women-respondents.

The vector of explanatory variables on EMPW are categorized into three. First are the demographic variables: age of the woman, her highest educational attainment, the size of her household, the number of years since last childbirth, the number of children in the family who are less than six years old, and the presence of mother substitutes at home. Second are the economic variables: her husband's income, the other family members' combined income contribution, and the wife's income. Third are the socio-psychological variables: her husband's attitude towards female work, her work commitment, her fertility plans, and whether or not she has worked for pay or profit before marriage.

Demographic Characteristics: Married women engaged in sales and services exhibit a profile which is typical of participants in informal sector (Table 3). They are as young as 17 years old and as old as 83 years old with a mean age of about 42 years. There is no minimum age requirement for entry nor maximum age requirement for retirement from paid work.

Educational attainment does not serve as a screening device in informal markets. While there are college graduates (those with 16 years of formal schooling), there are as well women with no completed year of schooling. There is a mean educational attainment of women of 8.61 years, a level which reflects attainment of a second year of secondary education.

Household sizes are as small as 2 and as large as 13. The former refer to cases of old families where the couple are left alone, or in female-headed families with a child or grandchild to take care of. The latter refers to extended families, or in some cases, to nuclear families with many children. The average household size is 5.

The life cycle of the family can be indicated by the number of children less than six years old, and the number of years since last childbirth. Data shows that the more recent is the last childbirth, the greater is the number of children below six years old. On the average, the women have barely one small kid (that is, 0.75) who was born within the last six years. This is corroborated by another finding showing that the average number of years since last childbirth is 8.67 years.

Table 3
Demographic Profile of Married Women in Private Sales and Service Sector (N=600)

Variable	*Minimum*	*Maximum*	*Mean*	*SD*
EMPW (dependent variable)	3.00	70.00	46.90	20.34
Age of woman	17.00	83.00	41.57	11.91
Highest educational attainment	0.00	16.00	8.61	3.43
Household size	2.00	13.00	5.30	2.04
Years since last childbirth	0.00	60.00	8.67	7.80
No. children less than 6 years old	0.00	4.00	0.75	1.16

Economic Indicators: The families of the women in this study are poor, and generally fall below the poverty threshold as reflected by selected economic parameters (Table 4). Husbands earn an average monthly income of PhP 4,390.42 (about US$87). The individual distribution, however, shows wide disparities, with the highest earner having Ph. P 30,000.00 per month (about US$589) and the lowest one having a zero value. The former are cases of seamen-husbands, the latter are eight older men, sickly men, or simply unemployed. The latter gives rise to female-headed families, where the wife usually becomes the primary breadwinner. In a lot of cases, all able-bodied family members get employed in order to augment family incomes.

Data reveal that contributions of other family members to family income is relatively low. The mean values are as low as PhP 785.42 (about US$16). It seems that where there is a higher child labor incidence, higher incomes contributed by other members of the family is registered. Mostly from employment in the informal sector, and due to multiple employment by as many able-bodied members of the family, these other family members contribute as high as PhP 19,000.00 per month (about US$ 373). At the other end of the continuum are zero values for young families.

Table 4
Economic Profile of Married Women in Private Sales and Service Sectors (N=600)

Variable	*Minimum*	*Maximum*	*Mean*	*SD*
Husband's income	.00	30000.00	4390.42	4289.35
Other family members' contribution to income	.00	19000.00	785.42	2451.60
Wife's income	160.00	13600.00	4039.77	3599.18

Wives have low incomes as well. They are either self-employed or employed by others. They tend sari-sari stores, maintain a dress shop, vend and peddle cooked-unprocessed food items/fish, or offer labor services as domestic help, beautician, nanny, laundry woman, sales ladies, or cook. Depending on the number of hours worked, the number of work engaged in, and the nature of the job, wives can earn as high as PhP 13,600.00 per month (about US$ 267) but as low as PhP 160.00 per month (about US$ 3). There are few cases of wives whose primary employment is in the formal sector.

Socio-psychological Considerations: Perceptions and social nuances attached to particular economic sectors affect a married woman's decision as to whether or not she will get a paid work and to what extent. In a Rating Scale where a score of 25 reflects the least favorable attitude of the husband towards his wife's labor supply decisions (as perceived by the wife), a mean value of 14.56 can be construed negatively. Husbands generally would disapprove female work had they enough income for the family. Given no better option, husbands then find themselves appreciating wives who help earn for the family's upkeep.

Women's commitment to work for non-familial reasons reveal a mean of 34.63 (Table 5). In a scale of 1 to 50, this score does not seem to reflect a very strong desire of the married woman to work for reasons not directly related to family welfare considerations. Hence, what moves married women to work is basically the need to uplift the family's standard of living over their desire to reach self-fulfillment and self-realization brought about by the use of her potentials/capabilities.

A married woman's labor supply decision may also be affected by her pre-marital work experience. About 60.67% of the 600 women-respondents claimed to have worked for pay or profit before marriage.

Fertility plans among married women is low at a value of 25.67%, representing 154 out of the 600 respondents. Weaker future fertility plans may significantly give more work time for the wife.

Table 5
Socio-Psychological Profile of Married Women in Private Sales and Service Sectors (N=600)

Variable	*Minimum*	*Maximum*	*Mean*	*SD*
Husband's attitude toward female work	5.00	25.00	14.56	4.07
Woman's work commitment	19.00	43.00	34.63	3.82
Pre-marital work Yes=364 (60.67%)				
Fertility plansYes=154 (25.67%)				
Presence of Mother-substitutes= 356 (59.33%)				

A similar effect may hold for another finding which reveals that more families have mother-substitutes. Out of the 600 respondents, 356 or 59.33% claim to have mother-substitutes. A large family can usually provide for this. Older children and the presence of non-nuclear family members releases mothers to the labor market.

Significant Predictors of Married Women's Labor Supply Behavior

The computed statistics reveal the expected relationships of the identified variables as shown in the literature review, WIFY, EDUC, SUBS show positive relationships with EMPW, being significant in some regression specifications. On the other hand, HHSI, HUSY, OTHY and ATTI are negatively associated with EMPW. Other variables turn out to be insignificant. This result can be explained by the high correlation between the identified explanatory variables.

Four regression models were run. These include: demographic variables only, economic variables only, socio-psychological variables only, and all variables considered in one equation. The importance of running the first three specifications is to determine significant predictors per category. The fourth specification aims to identify the significance of the combined influence of all the independent variable on EMPW.

A stepwise multiple regression found in the SPSS software was used to determine the minimum number of predictors needed to explain the maximum variance in the criterion, and to estimate the likely score of a criterion from the predictors identified in the study (Table 6).

Regression 1: Demographic-Variables-Only Model

Results show that EDUC and HHSI significantly predict the extent of paid work hours offered by the married woman in the market.

$$\text{EMPW} = 50.317 + 0.498\text{EDUC} - 1.477\text{HHSI}$$
$$(2.074) \quad (-3.667)$$

The work hours of a married woman increases by 0.498 per unit change in her educational attainment, and decreases by 1.477 per unit change in household size, holding other factors constant. Household size seems to be a better predictor as indicated by the beta coefficient of 3.667.

The adjusted R^2 though significant is very low. Only at most 2.6% of the total variance in the labor supply behavior of married women is explained by the demographic predictors. A major proportion of the total variance can be explained by other factors that are excluded in this demographic-variables-only model.

Regression 2: Economic-Variables-Only Model

Alternative income level parameters were used in the model. Husband's income, the wife's income, and the income contribution of other family members are significant predictors of EMPW, with WIFY as the better predictor as indicated by the beta coefficient.

EMPW = 42.504 − 8.642E-04HUSY + 2.133E-03WIFY − 6.97E-04OTHY
(−0.182) (0.376) (−0.084)

That is, work hours decease by 8.642E-04 units per unit change in the husband's monthly income, and by 6.971E-04 units per unit change in the monthly income contribution of other family members, all other factors held constant. On the other hand, work hours increases by 2.133E-03 per unit increase the wife's monthly income. This variable, WIFY seems to be the best economic variable-predictor, as seen by its beta coefficient.

The adjusted $R^2$is low, at a value of 14.6%. This indicates that the identified independent variables are not enough to explain the total variance in the criterion. An economic-variables-only model, therefore, leaves so much of the total variance of EMPW to be explained by factors excluded in the model.

Regression 3: Socio-psychological-Variables-Only Model

A third regression model that includes socio-psychological variables only reveals much lower adjusted R^2 values at 6.6%. Though significant, the model does not give a good explanation of the total variance in the work hours offered by a married woman in the labor market. Obviously, it excludes many possible good predictors as identified in the literature cited in the review.

EMPW = 52.857 − 0.641ATTI + 5.115SUBS
(−0.128) (0.230)

ATTI shows a negative association with EMPW. This reveals that a lower ATTI value (that is, a more favorable attitude of the husband towards female work) is associated with increased work hours of the married woman. That is, EMPW decreases by 0.641 units per unit change in ATTI. On the other hand, the presence of mother-substitutes has a positive effect on EMPW. A married woman's work hours increases by 5.115 units per unit change in SUBS, all other factors held constant. SUBS turns out to be the better predictor in this regression run.

Regression 4: All-Variables Model

In a fourth regression specification, all the identified independent variables are included in a stepwise multiple regression analysis. The variable which is most highly related to the criterion variable is entered first into the regression equation followed by variables which are the next most strongly related to the criterion once their relationship with the other variables is taken into account. If later variables are strongly associated with the variables already entered, then it is less likely that they will independently account for much more of the variance than those previously entered and so they are unlikely to be included as predictors (Cramer, 1997:301).

Regression results show that WIFY is the best predictor with a beta coefficient of 0.341. This is followed by SUBS, HHSI, HUSY, and ATTI in descending order.

$$\text{EMPW} = 53.997 - \underset{(-0.163)}{1.625\text{HHSI}} - \underset{(-0.162)}{7.721\text{E-04HUSY}} + \underset{(0.341)}{1.932\text{E-03WIFY}}$$

$$- \underset{(-0.081)}{0.404\text{ATTI}} + \underset{(0.203)}{4.515\text{SUBS}}$$

The predictor and criterion variables show expected relationships. A married woman's work hours tend to increase by 1.932E-03 units per unit increase in her monthly income, and by 4.515 units per unit increase in SUBS, all other factors held constant. It increases by 0.404 per unit decrease in ATTI value, that is, when husband's attitude toward wife's labor supply decision becomes move favorable. On the other hand, EMPW decreases by 1.625 per additional increase in household size. It also decreases by 7.721E-04 per additional unit of husband's income.

Table 6
Significant Predictors of Married Women's Labor Supply Behavior in Private Sales and Service Sector (N=600)

Regression Specification	*Significant Predictors*	*B*	*SE B*	*Beta*	*T*	*Sig t*
Demographic Variables Only	EDUC	0.498	0.240	0.084	2.074	.000
	HHSI	-1.477	0.403	-0.148	-3.667	.038
	(Constant)	50.317	3.129		16.082	.000
	Adjusted R^2= 0.026F= 9.128 p value= .000					
Economic Variables Only	HUSY	-8.642E-04	.000	-0.182	-4.726	.000
	WIFY	2.133E-03	.000	0.376	9.726	.000
	OTHY	-6.971E-04	.000	-0.084	-2.197	.028
	(Constant)	42.504	1.327		32.026	.000
	Adjusted R^2= 0.146F= 9.128 p value= .000					
Socio-Psychological Variables Only	ATTI	-0.641	0.198	-0.128	-3.238	.001
	SUBS	5.115	0.879	0.230	5.816	.000
	(Constant)	52.857	3.042		17.378	.000
	Adjusted R^2= 0.066F= 22.025 p value= .000					
All Variables	HHSI	-1.625	0.375	-0.163	-4.340	.000
	HUSY	-7.721E-04	.000	-0.162	-4.352	.000
	WIFY	1.932E-03	.000	0.341	9.093	.000
	ATTI	-0.404	0.186	-0.081	-2.179	.030
	SUBS	4.515	0.823	0.203	5.487	.000
	(Constant)	53.997	3.292		16.404	.000
	Adjusted R^2= 0.207F= 32.246 p value= .000					

The regression run still reveal relatively low adjusted R^2 values, at 30.7%. However, this is the highest value among the four regression runs made. As it is, the multiple linear regression model as a whole does not explain nor "fits" too well the variance in the dependent variable. It shows that only a small proportion of the linear variance in the criterion is explained by all the independent variables acting together.

The adjusted R^2 is only a descriptive statistic, where a high value is associated with a good fit of the regression line, and a low value with a poor fit. A low value of the adjusted R^2 can occur for several reasons.

First, in cross-section studies a lower squared multiple correlation may occur even if the model is a satisfactory one because of the large variation across individual units of observation which is inherent in the data (Pindyck and Rubinfeld, 1991). This suggests that the R^2 alone may not be a suitable measure of the extent to which a model is satisfactory. Pindyck and Rubinfeld (1991) further suggests that a better overall measure might be a statistic which describes the predictive power of the model given another data set.

Second, in general in social research, particularly high values of R^2 should not be expected. This is because there are so many things which might contribute to influence a variable that one cannot reasonably expect to be able to analyze or even measure (Rose and Sullivan, 1996). As a rule of thumb, the R^2 depends obviously on individual circumstances.

Third, a low R^2 does not necessarily mean that there is no association between the variables, nor is there the absence of significant predictors of the criterion (Norusis, 1985). Instead, it may indicate that there is no linear relationship.

To depend solely on the use of the R^2 as a measure of the explanatory power of a regression equation can be misleading because of the sensitivity of this parameter to the choice of dependent variables (Pindyck and Rubinfeld, 1991). The standard error of the regression is often more useful as a measure of the predictive power of a regression equation than is the R^2.

Results of this study further reveals that based on the F statistic, the computed R^2 is significant. It is possible for R^2 to be significant at a given level even if the value is low, and/or even though very few of the regression coefficients are found to be significant according to individual t-tests (Pindyck and Rubinefeld, 1991). This situation arises if the independent variables are highly correlated with each other. The result may be high standard errors of the coefficients and low t-values, yet the model as a whole may fit the data very well.

DISCUSSION

Several results from the regression runs/models using the SPSS stepwise multiple regression analysis may be interpreted as follows:

AGEW was not found to be a significant predictor. This may be due to the possibility of a potential non-linear relationship between AGEW and EMPW. Young mothers and older women have relatively lesser work hours in the market. It is the middle-age woman who finds more hours in the labor market. Young mothers withdraw from the labor force when children start coming and the couple starts to build a family. The older women withdraw from the labor market because of age. The older women are first to be fired but last to be hired in an arena where masculinity dominates the hiring-firing decisions.

The recency of last childbirth, LAST, is neither significantly related to work hours. This may be caused by the variable's high correlation with other demographic variables such as CHILD and HHSI, and other economic variables such as HUSY, which has shown significant contribution in explaining total variance of the criterion. It is noted that collinearity results to high standard errors of coefficients.

On the other hand, HHSI and HUSY significantly do. In the literature cited, HHSI may either have a direct or an inverse relationship with the labor supply behavior of married women. On one hand, a woman may increase work hours to improve the financial position of a large family whose needs are increasing. Or, it could be viewed as a larger family reflecting a not-so-young family whose children can be left on their own, hence, releasing the mother to more paid work hours. Or still, a larger family implies the presence of mother-substitutes that similarly enables the woman to seek longer paid work hours. On the other hand, a woman may decrease work hours if a large household size mean that more able-bodied family members are significantly contributing to family income. In this study, it is the positive relationship which is revealed.

With regards to economic variables, HUSY is a significant predictors that show negative relationship with EMPW. When husbands can financially support his family, the wife decreases her work efforts. This behavior may be voluntary on the part of the woman specially if she has a low educational attainment since offering her labor services in the market does not open to her a variety of employment opportunities. The informal sector may not require minimum educational qualifications but it cannot provide stable, regular and better-paying work.

EDUC is a potential good predictor, having emerged as significant in one of the regression models. A higher educational attainment improves the productivity of women in the workplace. It also improves the women's understanding of the production process and new techniques/technology of the trade. A higher educational attainment widens the opportunities for better-paying work (such as the employment in the formal sector), and increases the probability of multiple employment.

OTHY, another significant predictor of EMPW affects in a negative manner. That is, even if other family members contribute to the total family income a woman will desire to work for shorter hours. This may reveal that such contributions meet a minimum level which is set by the family as a requirement to stay on a target/desired welfare position of the family. In the study, therefore, it seems that the contribution of other family members to total family income is significant. This is expected in the informal labor market where alternative job opportunities are available, and where the human capital is not a necessary condition for employment. However, jobs may not provide stable, regular and better terms/working conditions. On the other hand, a possible non-linear relationship between OTHY and EMPW is worth considering.

WIFY is another significant explanatory variable. A wife's worth in the market, as reflected by the market wage that she can command, and the possible multiple self-employment activities that she can engage in, affects the woman's decision on the extent of work hours offered.

Among the socio-psychological factors, only ATTI came out as significant predictor. Decreasing her work hours in the market may be simply dictated by cultural norms or by the husband's unfavorable attitude towards female work, ATTI. As revealed in the study, women perceive their husbands to have a generally unfavorable attitude toward female work if only the financial position of the family warrants for her voluntary unemployment. Husbands in the research locale would rather have their wives stay at home and take care of domestic concerns. Moreover, at low family incomes, nursemaids cannot be hired. So, the mother stays at home. Oftentimes it is this reality which pushes husbands to ultimately consider favorably the decision of wives to spend more hours at work for pay or profit.

On the other hand, FERT and WOMB do not significantly explain the total variance in the criterion, EMPW. Future fertility plans is highly correlated with household size, the number of children below six years old, and the recency of last childbirth. The first two of which have been found to be significant predictors. This multicollinearity may also explain why premarital work experience failed to emerge as a significant predictor.

The empirical analysis moreover, showed that the combined influence of the various factors resulted to higher R^2 values and more significant predictors of the labor supply behavior of women. Obviously, the addition of independent variables that are based on a priori theoretical framework, and the absence/ minimum multicollinearity of the predictors will increase R^2. Based on the beta coefficients, it seems that the educational attainment of married women is the best predictor of her labor supply behavior.

CONCLUSION AND RECOMMENDATION

Women in the informal private sales and service sectors generally have low educational attainment with a mean of about only six years of formal schooling. They come from medium-sized households of about six family members, at least one of whom is below six years old. They are married to husbands who, with a similar educational profit, do not bring home as much cash income as necessary for the family to stay way above the poverty threshold. Other able-bodied family members contribute to family incomes, but said incomes come irregularly and at low levels.

As related to Becker's (1965) neoclassical time allocation model, the labor supply behavior of married women is a decision concerning a trade-off between the benefits derived from working for pay or profit, and the benefits from undertaking nonmarket activities.

The following conditions influence a married woman's tendency to offer lesser work hours for pay or profit: larger household size, higher income derived by the husband, higher income contribution of other family members, and a husband's unfavorable attitude toward female work for pay or profit. On the other hand, the following conditions may influence a married woman to offer more work hours for pay or profit: higher offered wage in the market, higher human capital, and the presence of mother-substitutes.

The empirical results further show that the significant predictors are mostly economic in nature, with WIFY as the best predictor. Demographic variables are not far behind though.

The aforementioned predictors are consistent with the findings of the literature reviewed in this paper. The empirical results also validates the utility maximization behavior of a worker whose satisfaction depends on a desirable income-leisure mix. The dominance of the income effect of higher wage rates and higher incomes for the family on the demand for leisure over the substitution effect decreases further demand for income and, therefore, a decrease in work hours.

Along these findings, the following recommendations are made. To address the issue of low R^2 values, further studies can be undertaken in the following areas:

(a) possibilities of a nonlinear relationship between EMPW and the independent variables.

(b) a new set of data on married women working for pay or profit in other economic sectors, namely: the formal economy where work terms and conditions vary markedly with the research locale, and in other informal labor markets including farming, fishing, the industries and the fast-emerging nonprofit sectors.

(c) the inclusion of a more direct predictor which has a strong priori theoretical framework such as the alternative wage offers to the married woman

All of these can be done for academic purposes such as to develop instructional materials. These are expected to improve/ contribute to the existing local literature on women and work.

In aid of legislation and policy-development formulation, the following entry variables that will improve the married women's status in the labor market and in the domestic arena, seem to stand out from the empirical results:

(a) a smaller family size so as to enable the married woman to offer more paid work hours

(b) more regular and stable sources of income that provide better pay specifically for the husbands

(c) better and greater access to the means of production/ economic resources through a mechanism that will enable the family to derive regular incomes throughout the year

(d) re-orientation through barangay/village public forums on a gender-sensitive and gender-fair economy.

Anil Bhuimali

18

Women in Education: An Emphasis on Disadvantaged Women

I

INTRODUCTION

Education is one of the finest means of reducing inequality in every society. Social status of a person can be improved through education. Education helps a person to acquire knowledge, skills, values and attitudes. These help one to lead a desired quality of life. Education for both men and women is important in every walk of life. The present article gives an overview of women education in India. Several indicators like measures of literacy, enrollment, and years in school education reveal important patterns and trends in women's education in a developing country like India. Since literacy is one of the principal goals of education around the world over our discussion here will be mainly concentrated towards explaining female literacy in the pre and post independent India. In the course of our analysis we have tried to explain the rural-urban disparity among females. We have also tried to explain female literacy scenario of disadvantaged group of people in the urban and rural India.

II

THE BACKGROUND

Women constitute almost half of the total world population. Like men women are equally essential in every sphere of life. They play a vital part in economic and non-economic activities throughout ages. In the primitive society before the advent of agriculture women engaged in household activities while men had to gather necessaries by gathering, hunting or fishing. Women's span of activities expanded with the advent of agriculture. In the hunting and pastoral societies the concept of property was not there and naturally there was no difference between men and women in relation to the ownership of resources. After the establishment of ownership the rights to property went in favour of men. Industrial and agricultural revolutions helped multiplying women's participation at work throughout the world.

Historically, in the ancient society the position of women at home and society was high. In ancient China, for example, women were greatly respected. But since the 11th century BC their position in the society came down sharply and the emergence of clan relations empowered men more than women. In the vedic period, Indian women were highly respected and no ceremony was completed without the presence of women. According to mode of work the society was subdivided into four distinct sections, each being involved to play a specific role. Education was specially confined to men and naturally not much attention was paid to the education of women. In the north-west of India there was a University at Takshashila. In that University only men were allowed to study. From this evident it can be inferred that women had little or no access over education.

After the Afghan conquest of India an unfortunate development took place in Indian society. This was purdah custom (privacy of women). Its effect on the society was devastating. The custom grew during the Mughal period. It spread among the elite Hindus and Muslims of great central (Delhi, UP, MP, Rajasthan) and eastern block (Bihar and Bengal) of India. The purdah custom had kept women backward and underdeveloped for centuries. It also hindered the development of children and men. It had negative impact on the social life of India as a whole. The position of women went on deteriorating until in the 19th century some philanthropic and social reformers like Raja Rammohun Roy and Iswar Chandra Vidyasagar made efforts to ameliorate their condition. They raised their voice against the anti-women practices existed in the male-dominated society. The efforts continued in the 20th century when Mahatma Gandhi and others gave women equal status with men. Men like Jyoti Rao Phule of Maharashtra and B.R. Ambedkar came forward for preading up of education among women especially the disadvantaged group of the society. But the orthodox society went against women's education. The people of male-dominated society thought that an educated woman would refuse to subsuit to man. As a result, the sincere efforts of the social reformers remained ineffective for a long period of time. This is evident from the literacy position among the women. In 1881-82, for example, women literacy was only 0.2 per cent. In 1901-02, it slightly rose to 0.69 per cent. In 1911-12 it just crossed one per cent. In 1946-47 the position improved to 6.0 per cent. In 1952-53, women literacy was 8 per cent. The tables from 1 to 4 clearly show the literacy position of Indian women from 1881 to 2001-02.

Table 1
Women Education Scenario in the Pre-Independent Era

Year	*% of women literacy*
1881-82	0.2
1901-02	0.69
1911-12	1.05
1921-22	1.81
1931-32	2.93
1946-47	6.0

Source: Various Issues of Census of India.

III

POST INDEPENDENT SCENARIO

Since independence women's literacy rate started improving with the constitution giving equal rights to women in every sphere, including education, and with continued government efforts. Table 2 below represents a post-independent position of women literacy in India.

Table 2
Women Literacy Position in the Post-Independent Era

Year	*Literacy Rate*
1951-52	7.93
1961-62	12.95
1971-72	18.72
1981-82	24.82
19991-92	39.29
2001-2002	54.16

Source: Various Issues of Census of India.

The Table 3 shows gross enrollment (male-female) as percentage to total population.

Table 3
Gross Enrollment as Percentage to the Total Population

Year	*Age 6-11years*			*11-14*			*14-17*		
	M	*F*	*T*	*M*	*F*	*T*	*M*	*F*	*T*
1950-51	60.6	24.8	43.1	20.6	4.6	12.9	8.7	1.5	5.3
1955-56	68.2	31.0	50.0	24.6	6.6	15.9	—	—	7.4
1960-61	82.6	41.4	62.4	32.2	11.3	22.5	18.0	4.4	11.4
1965-66	96.3	56.5	76.7	44.2	17.0	30.8	24.3	7.7	16.2
1970-71	92.6	59.1	76.4	46.5	20.8	34.2	27.1	10.2	19.0
1973-74	100.1	65.6	83.5	48.4	22.2	35.6	29.9	12.0	21.2
1974-75	98.2	66.1	82.7	48.0	23.1	36.0	30.3	12.2	21.5
1975-76	95.7	62.0	79.3	47.0	23.8	35.6	25.1	10.6	18.2
1977-78	97.4	62.6	80.5	48.6	24.4	36.5	25.2	11.0	18.3
1979-80	99.3	65.0	82.7	52.0	26.4	39.6	29.9	13.9	21.9
1981-81	95.8	64.1	80.5	54.3	28.6	41.9	24.8	11.5	8.4
1981-82	98.9	66.2	83.1	56.0	29.7	43.3	21.1	9.3	16.0
1982-83	104.0	69.4	87.2	56.3	30.6	43.9	—	—	—
1983-84	110.3	75.5	93.4	62.7	34.4	48.9	—	—	—
1984-85	110.7	76.7	94.1	64.0	36.3	50.6	—	—	—
1985-86	108.8	77.1	93.4	65.0	38.1	52.0	—	—	—

Source: Education in India, Ministry of Human Resource Development M: male; F: Female; T: Total.

The growth of women enrollment in institutions of higher education in India, 1950-51 to 1986-87 is shown in Table 4.

Table 4
Growth of Women Enrollment in Institutions of Higher Education

Year	*1950-51*	*1955-56*	*1960-61*	*1965-66*	*1975-76*	*1981-82*	*1984-85*	*1986-87*
Total women enrollment (in thousand)	40	84	150	271	595	817	992	1125
Number of women per hundred men	14	17	23	24	33	38	41	44

Source: UGC Report for the year 1986-87.

IV

RURAL-URBAN LITERACY

The census report of various issues as depicted in tables 1 and 2 illustrates the state of female literacy and education at the last decade of the last century. The data on women literacy presented in tables 1 and 2 show a dimensional picture of women literacy. The great divide in literacy and education in Indian history came in 1951. Literacy statistics show that before independence the pace of women literacy and education progressed at a snail's pace. But after 1951 it started improving spectacularly.

Table 5
Rural Female Literacy

Year	*Literacy Rate*
1961	9.10
1971	13.08
1981	17.96
1991	24.6
2001	Not available

Source: Various issues of Census of India

The progress of women education is not even throughout the country. The progress of women literacy in rural India is very bad still today. The causes of such slow down growth rate may be many. But the most important and immediate cause is the massive poverty in the rural India. Table 5 shows rural female literacy rate.

The position of urban female literacy rate is slightly improved. This is depicted in table 6 blow:

Table 6
Urban Female Literacy

Year	*Literacy Rate*
1961	37.4
1971	42.08
1981	47.82
1991	53.7
2001	Not available

Source: Various issues of Census of India.

Since the beginning of the last century, Indian women have been lagging behind men in literacy level in all the states. Table 7 shows that the disparity in general literacy has decreased in all states among general scheduled castes and scheduled tribes female population. The decrease is substantial in Himachal Pradesh and Punjab even among the SC and ST female population. Higher disparity persists in the low literacy states of Bihar, M.P., Rajasthan and U.P.

VI

CONCLUSIONS

Education improves the status of women by enhancing their productivity both in the farm and non-farm sectors. Education of women has an inverse relation with population. The decision on education depends on both benefits and costs. Almost one-third of the total population of our country living below the poverty line are not in a position to bear the costs of education. These costs include the direct financial costs. Direct costs are

Table 7
Rural-Urban Disparity in General Literacy among Females

India/ State	*General Population*				*SC Population*				*ST Population*			
	1991	*1971*	*1981*	*1991*	*1961*	*1971*	*1981*	*1991*	*1961*	*1971*	*1981*	*1991*
India	24.3	31.1	37.6	45.9	25.0	30.0	34.7	45.2	21.5	24.4	24.9	34.3
Andhra Pradesh	23.6	30.1	33.9	41.6	23.6	21.8	26.9	37.0	28.3	19.6	19.7	27.8
Assam	28.0	32.4	—	49.8	59.3	51.6	—	68.5	29.4	25.2	—	51.4
Bihar	16.0	20.0	25.5	31.0	19.5	12.7	16.5	23.8	15.4	18.0	23.3	30.3
Gujarat	31.7	38.4	47.1	56.0	61.2	49.6	56.5	69.3	50.0	41.3	54.5	59.1
Haryana	—	22.3	32.5	49.3	—	31.3	41.0	70.3	—	—	—	—
Himachal Pradesh	—	34.7	48.9	62.0	—	33.3	50.2	64.9	—	17.3	26.8	40.6
Karnataka	26.1	34.9	41.4	51.7	17.0	18.6	24.2	39.2	28.1	32.6	33.9	45.5
Kerala	79.1	87.6	89.0	94.5	60.0	74.5	82.1	90.9	40.2	44.8	43.1	77.8
Madhya Pradesh	6.4	16.5	21.3	32.4	17.0	17.3	20.3	37.2	18.8	20.8	21.0	31.1
Maharastra	27.9	37.7	45.5	56.4	25.2	38.3	47.1	61.5	24.6	27.3	26.6	36.7
Orissa	19.9	33.5	43.2	49.6	40.5	50.0	59.2	60.4	25.0	25.5	31.7	33.5
Punjab	24.8	43.8	55.66	65.9	36.7	57.8	71.4	76.6	—	—	—	—
Rajasthan	9.9	13.6	15.8	22.5	11.1	10.9	12.1	20.6	6.5	9.3	10.7	16.7
Tamil Nadu	35.2	41.8	46.1	59.4	30.0	39.5	44.1	58.1	7.1	32.5	50.5	46.8
Uttar Pradesh	8.3	21.0	26.8	36.8	9.1	14.4	19.1	30.7	—	20.3	19.2	33.3
West Bengal	20.6	31.4	40.2	51.8	29.7	39.2	45.7	59.2	16.7	15.4	25.1	43.1

Source: NCAER Report No. 4,2000.

the costs of food and clothing, expenditure on books and learning materials, transportation, tuition fee etc. Of the direct costs an amount is borne by the government; but the substantial amount is met by the households. This is beyond the reach of the unfortunate people living below the poverty line. The other form of cost is the opportunity or indirect cost. They cannot bear the opportunity costs and thus they send their children to the farm and non-farm sectors to earn money in order to maximise their household income. To this section of the society there is no discrimination between boys and girls by parents but they all are discriminated by the society as a whole. In spite of engaging in multifarious activities by all the family members the poor families cannot even maintain their bare minimum necessaries. This is became of low-paid wages. For the around development of this country the government should take up such projects by which all children can come under the umbrella of education. In this context, a hundred per cent costs should certainly be borne by the government. For this government should impose some amount of additional tax to the taxpayers. At the same time government should reduce expenditure on defence purposes by establishing cordial relationship with neighbouring countries.

REFERENCES

Benhabib, J. and Mark M. (1994), "The Role of Human Capital in Economic Development: Evidence from aggregate Cross-Country Data"" *Journal of Monetary Economics.*

Bhuimali, A., Sumangala Damodaran and Others (2002), "Gender and Empowerment", a paper presented at the Refresher Course as part of the programme at Jawaharlal Nehru University on 24th January, 2002.

Bhuimali, A (2004), "Empowering Rural Women: How and When?" in A., Bhuimali (ed) in Education, Employment and Empowering Women. Serials Publications.

Buvinic, M and Margaret A. Lycete (1989), " Women, Poverty and Development in the Third World", in John P. Lewis (ed.), *Strengthening the Poor: What Have We Learned?* Overseas Development Council.

Chakraborty, G and P.K. Ghosh (2000), Human Development Profile of Scheduled Castes and Tribes in Rural India. NCAER Reprint.

Dixon, B.R. (1978), Rural Women at Work, John Hopkins University press.

Hammer, J. (1986), "Population growth and savings in LDCs: A Survey Article", World Development 14.

Hill, M.A. and Elizabeth M. King (1993), "Women's Education in Developing Countries: An Overview", in Elizabeth King and M. Anne Hills, (eds.), Woemn's Education in Developing Countries: Barriers, Benefits and Policies, Baltimore: John Hopkins.

International Labour Office (1985), Women in the Labour Force, World Labour Report, Vol. 2, Oxford University Press.

Jawaharlal Nehru: Discovery of India.

Psacharopoulos, G. (1991), The Economic Impact of Education Lessons for policymakers, San Francisco: ICS Press.

Sainsbury, D. (1996), Gender, Equality and Welfare States, Cambridge University Press.

Shariff, A. and N. Ahu (1999), Mother's Education Effect on Child Health: An Econometric analysis of Child Anthropoverty in Uganda, NCAER Reprint.

R. K. Bhadra

19

The Changing Status of Women in India: The Areas of Role Conflict

Roles are socially defined attributes and expectations associated with social positions (status) of individuals in a society. Role conflict is usually very common in the societies in transitional phase which pass from tradition to modernity. This is true in case of Indian society which has been undergoing rapid process of social change towards modernity. In the traditional society Indian women used to play roles in domestic sphere only, and thus, role conflict was not the usual feature. Today, women are playing two or more roles at one time that make compatible demands. This is happening with those women who are working outside home along with their traditional domestic roles. They have to satisfy simultaneously the role expectations as employees, wives and mothers which may conflict with each other. This happens due to clash between the traditional and modern values. The traditional position of Indian women is very difficult to ascertain. To analyse the traditional position historical data are needed which are almost absent due to the historians' lack of interest on social history of Indian society. This paper limits its focus on the changing aspects of status of women in Indian society where roles of women have been visibly changed, and now roles are incorporated along with the new status of women. These, led to contradictions conflict, dilemma, confusion and loss of roles. The emerging situations associated with the changing status pushed the Indian women into much social criticisms. These have made the Indian women restless, confused and helpless. This paper enquires about the changing status of women due to employment and areas of role conflict.

TRADITIONAL STATUS OF WOMEN

The traditional position of women in Indian society is very difficult to ascertain due to lack of historical data. However, in ancient India the position of a woman in society was low as revealed from various literatures. Her roles in the society were not considered as important and, therefore, she was not required to actively participate in any socio-political and religious occasions and perform any roles.

The concept of a wife in the Hindu religious literatures suggested that role of a woman was only centered around her family and only for procreation of descendants. The most favoured descended was male in the eyes of the Hindus. The roles of a woman were determined by the belief, and she played a passive role in the family. The patriarchal ideology put a man in the family in the highest position having importance to perform every kind of role considered superior to those of a woman. A woman considered her husband as her first god known as 'Pati-devata' and showed all sorts of respects to him. But when a woman became a mother her position in the patriarchal society family considerably improved. Her sons obeyed her, respected her, and were responsible for her maintenance. A woman, if she became a widow, lost considerable social status. She was not allowed to marry for the second time. The widow Remarriage Act of 1856 provided her a legal status to marry again, but still it was considered to be immoral. She was not allowed to participate in sacred occasions. For a widow sacrificing her life on a pyre of her husband was considered to be an ideal (Devendra, 1985).

The Hindu marriage laws put a woman in a low social status. The principles of hypergamy showed plight of a woman as she could not break out of her low position in the society.

Polygamy was an important practice which gave lower status to Indian woman. It was practiced in Bengal, Uttar Pradesh and Punjab. In Baroda an Act in 1942 was passed against polygamy, in Bombay in 1946, in Madras in 1947, and in Saurastra in 1954 (Debendra, 1985).

The custom of Sati indicated low status of Indian woman in traditional society. The widows were inhumanly treated. During the first quarter of the 19th century widow remarriage became the centre of activities of the social reformers. In the actual practice the custom force a widow, young or old, to immolate herself on the husband's pyre.

The inheritance and property rights of the Hindus revealed that a man had unlimited property rights which included land, houses, cattle, and all movable property, sons, wives, etc. (Mies, 1980). Traditionally a woman was excluded from the right to inheritance. The inheritance of landed property went along the male lineage. Theoretically, although a woman was a co-owner of the property with her husband, practically she did not enjoy any rights over it and could not dispose of any part of it. A widow could enjoy the property of her husband but did not have any legal rights to inheritance.

The Purdah was practiced by some upper caste Hindu women that provided them considerably lower social status in the society. Where Purdah was practiced a woman virtually became a slave. She could not mention name of anybody of her husband's family (Devendra, 1985, Mies, 1980). Purdah was actually seclusion of a woman, as a result, she was considered as "Chattel", i.e. movable property and reduced her to her sex function only (Mies, 1980).

The system of Devdasi and courtesans prevailed in the traditional Hindu society was an evidence of low social status of woman. Here a woman was considered as an object of sex only; only a woman could be a Devdasi or a courtesan (Mies, 1980).

FACTORS OF CHANGES IN THE STATUS OF WOMEN

The significant changes in the status of Indian women began to take place since their participation in the National Movement against the British Government. This had enhanced their political status in the society which they did never enjoy earlier. Political emancipation could be traced in the 20th century when they took an important role along with their males in the freedom struggle. During the 19th-20th centuries emphasis was laid on the introduction of laws for social reforms and on women's education. English education helped men in changing their attitudes towards women. The practice of killing of female children, *satidaha*, prohibition of widow marriage and child marriage had been discouraged. These age-old practices along with social values had started to decline considerably. In 1795-1802 female infanticide had been prohibited in Bengal. Social reformers fought against the discrimination against widows. The Indian Divorce Act of 1869, the Hindu succession Act of 1865, the Special Marriage Act of 1872, Abolition of Child Marriage and Child Marriage Restraint Act of 1929 were introduced. The Hindu Marriage Act of 1955 and Hindu Succession Act of 1956 introduced the women's rights to divorce and women's rights to inheritance (Devendra, 1985, Devi, 1982).

Various Hindu revivalistic organizations provided an impetus to the awakening of womanhood. During 20th century various women's organizations took a leading role to abolish purdah and child marriage. They also encouraged widow re-marriage (Devi, 1982).

The independence movement during the early part of the twentieth century had brought tremendous impact on the status of women. The movement helped the women to come out of the family into the field of politics. The participation of women in politics improved their status considerably.

Formally, they were given equal rights and status with men as the Indian Constitution ruled out any discrimination against women. Changes were more noticed due to the impact of spread of education. The legal reforms could not bring many changes in their status. These changes were noticed mainly among the middle class women of the urban areas. The urban middle class educated women had taken up employment. Women's economic horizon expanded and opened to compete with their males. They were employed as teachers, doctors, lawyers, engineers, journalists, officers, entrepreneurs, etc. Under the economic pressure and for better living standard opposition to the gainful occupations had declined considerably. They were burdened with both family activities and work outside home. They had to face dual social situations. During the period since 1911 onwards proportion of working women started to decline due to expansion of industries and private sectors, but proportion of women increased significantly in various service sectors. During the last two decades women's education increased significantly which had further accelerated the increasing proportion of women in the service sectors. In the recent years growth of electronic industries has attracted a large number of women in the employment. Therefore, though there has been decline of participation of women in the heavy industries, there has been rise in their participation in the electronic industries and service sectors. The employed women, particularly who are married, face tremendous difficulties to adjust themselves both in family life in home and working life outside in the work place. When women are increasingly participating in employment, family conflicts are arising. These conflicts are due to scarcity of time to compete both types of works on the one hand and clashes of values, perception, beliefs and roles of traditional society with those of the modern society, on the other.

ROLE-CONFLICT OF INDIAN WOMEN

The educated working women face conflict primarily within their family. Traditionally the upper castes did not permit their women in any economic activities outside home. But women in the economic activities within the household, except women of a very low-status who even in traditional society worked outside. However, the social values encircled women with less mobility outside their domestic environment. Therefore, women were not expected to earn outside home. The significant structural changes came about with the introduction of industrial economy. These structural changes brought separation of production from the consumption and reproduction of labour force. Along with this structural changes women are disassociated from their productive function within family, whoever use to participate in the traditional society. Mies (1980) has observed that women after industrial revolution has not produced anything in the domestic place for market, rather they have only produced for own consumption. They are also not able to participate in the industrial labour force for biological reasons. With this exclusion from the productive spheres a new social category- the housewife has emerged who depends on their husband's income.

Gore (1968) has observed a woman's status in family is directly related to her exclusion from economic activities. The woman of lower castes participates in gainful activities and has considerable amount of freedom. But the upper caste woman does not enjoy such freedom because she is excluded from economic activities.

The improvement of status of a woman at home is due to her education and participation in employment. Wife's income has become necessary to maintain the family's standard of living. Woman at this situation assumes male's role. Unmarried girls often play a role of a brother by financing their younger siblings Thus a new trend is noticed in the conception of division of labour in the family and society (Madan, 1976, Ross, 1973). Earning means control of money to a certain extent by the working women. It provides them some amount of economic independence. But they never get full control over their incomes (Goldstein, 1975).

CONFLICT OVER ROLE AND AUTHORITY IN FAMILY

The question of conflict is relevant to the women of middle class who have taken up employment. This is due to the roles they have to play in their home and workplace. Women of the lower classes, who are working in agriculture and also in blue colour sectors, may not face such problems of role conflict. This role conflict appears to be class specific mainly confined to the middle class working women. The problem of role conflict is not generally visible among the lower class women.

We shall try to see the situation of role conflict among the educated middle class working women. Role conflict of the middle class working women is determined by the family situation- type of family and size of it, and number as well as age of children living in a family.

The socio-economic status of middle class families is determined by the income of the male members. Now, with the increasing participation in the economic activities by women, socio-economic status of the family is greatly influenced. A new pattern of family living and redistribution of familial functions gradually emerge. This situation brings changes in the pattern of relationship between members in the family. Mies (1980) has pointed out that role conflicts are generally found in a family where wife's income is low. In another situation role conflicts are very common where a wife earns more than her husband. Here, the wife aspires for more independence both in the economic and social spheres resulting into a threat to the traditional authority structure. It is also a common feature that taking up of jobs by women is not dependent on the economic status of the family. Women also work where their husband's income is very high. However, women's income is generally considered to be supplementary to the income of their husbands. This is very much true in case of the lower middle class where women have to earn to supplement the men's income. Although women's earning is badly needed for the lower income families, this generates role conflicts.

The consequences of employment of women is farreaching. This leads them to neglect their obligations to families and children. It is very common that working women prefer to live in the nuclear family. Living in the nuclear families provides them with a greater freedom and independence. The nuclear family is free from all types of restrictions on women which are traditionally considered to be very important and expected types of behaviour of women. Working women do not prefer to live in joint family because of the authoritarian position of the in-laws, particularly the mother-in-laws. They understand the practical advantages of the joint family living for rearing up of their children, but do not come under the traditional subordination of their in-laws in the joint family. The cases of maladjustment of women are higher in the joint family.

The middle class mothers who are employed prefer to have a small number of children. But marriage and small children are not the barriers to take up jobs by the middle class women although there may intensify the situation of role conflict as they still largely adhere to the traditional cultural values of a mother.

Domestic help from relatives may help women to take up jobs outside where small children may not create problem for adjustment both in domestic and working places. Lack of domestic help generally creates problem in the family. This leads to domestic conflict. In this situation middle class working women often take help of parental family for looking after their children. But this brings break in the character of patriarchal society. They continue to stick to their traditional sex-based division of labour. They try to take extra burden and may take help of servants. They do not get any help from their husbands in the domestic work. So long they continue this traditional value pattern there is not conflict seen to be emerged. But working women who try to break this traditional pattern of division of labour conflicts are bound to emerge. In Indian situation it is more acceptable that domestic activities are done by employing servants for performing domestic works where women work in the offices. Thus, domestic conflicts may be avoided through adjustment of division of labour. The western values related to the sharing of domestic works by husband and wife are not acceptable even when women spend a large portion of her time for earning in outside work.

Women's employment, higher education and economic independence are the main sources of tensions in the family and work place. Role conflict of Indian Women, therefore, emerge also in the work-place and working situation. Types of profession, occupational pattern, job motivation, attitudes of family members and attitudes of their own are the various factors which generate conflict in the working place.

Several studies have shown that women are equal with males in efficiency and performance in any jobs (Ross, 1973). Some studies have been indicated women as more efficient in some jobs. The majority of women engage in teaching profession as it becomes easier for them to adjust in the family life involving less conflict. The second largest occupation of women is office work, health services and technical profession. They prefer full-time jobs although more time and work-load with strains are involved in it. Teaching profession is considered to be respectable for a woman, but there are certain prejudices against the profession of secretaries, typists, etc. The woman office workers have more marital problems than teachers and doctors. The middle class women do not consider marriage as a break in their professional career. Along with the traditional obligations they try to continue their career. Familian obligations are the primary barriers for the working women.

The reasons for taking up jobs by women may be many. The main reason is to support her family with additional finances. Both middle and upper middle class women take up jobs among whom a considerable proportion of unmarried women take employment for accumulation of dowry money for their own marriage. Many of them are willing to add finance to the income of their husbands for maintaining a higher life style. Some women are very much conscious of their own status and for raising it they take up prestigious professions. But a large number of women of the middle and upper middle class are not in a position to emancipate themselves from the traditional roles and social values which may be the reasons for conflict in the family.

There are women, particularly, from among the upper middle class who deviate, to a certain extent, from the ideals of Indian womanhood. They aspire for own status and independence from husband's income. Role conflicts are very common to be found among them in the large cities and modern metropolis. Yet husbands of many of such women do not want their wives to work. They feel it to be low dignity and cause of threat to the traditional authority structure in the family. Some women are therefore to be found to take up voluntary works and hobbies to avoid conflict in the family. A minority women of the upper middle class are interested to take up professions to spend leisure time for avoiding their family environment. The women who take up jobs may feel for equality with males in terms of their work in the workplace but continue to be dominated by the male members in the family (Mies, 1980).

Even under this situation where women have to face criticism for taking up of employment they accept it as a challenge to break the traditional authority pattern for establishing their own position firmly on a better position. There has been a significant change in the attitudes of women today. The majority of middle class women are of the opinion that women's work and family responsibilities are harmoniously complement to each other. They do not feel any problem of adjustment. While the highly qualified women feel that their professional work is that majority of women give equal importance to domestic works and professional works. To avoid role conflicts they are found to take extra load of work and try to balance the situation. Attitudes of working women towards employment is always on the positive side. They prefer to be employed rather than to be confined in the domestic environment.

However, taking up of a job does not depend on a woman because the decision largely depends on her husband, if she is married. Still in the urban middle-class families husband is found to be the central authority whose decision is final. Husband's opinion towards wife's employment is of decisive importance. A high proportion of husbands show positive attitudes towards their wife's employment. Sometimes, husbands are to be found to influence wives to take up employment. There are the families where role conflicts are less or sometimes absent. In the reality it is also found that although a husband possesses a positive attitudes towards his wife he does not cooperate actively or share responsibility equally with his wife. He may be found to hold the authority in the family in terms of traditional values. The wife has to perform dual role in home and outside. This is the situation where role conflicts are to be found inspite of husband's positive attitudes towards wife's employment. Where women's employment is directly opposed by their husbands, marital problems may arise. Quarrel, role conflict, maladjustment etc. are the causes of day to day conflict in the family. In the recent years status of women has changed considerably, but the patriarchal authoritarian structure of the family has not changed. There is constant conflict to be found between role performance by women and role expectation of the patriarchal ideology.

REFERENCES

Devendra K., *Status and Position of Women in India*, Shakti Books, New Delhi, 1985.

Devi, U.L., *Status and Employment of Women in India*, B.R. Publiashing Corporation, Delhi, 1982.

Goldstern R.L., "Tradition and Change in the Roles of Educated Indian Women", in D. Narain, (ed.), *Explorations in the Family and other Essays*, Thacker and Co.bay, 1975.

Gore, M.S., *Urbanisation and Family Change*, Popular Prakashan, Bombay, 1968.

Madan T.N., "The Hindu Women at House," in B.R.Nanda (ed.), *Indian Women: Purdah to Modernity*, Vikas Publishing House, New Delhi, 1976.

Mies, M., *Indian Women and Patriarchy*, Concept Publishing Corporation, New Delhi, 1980.

Ross A.D., *The Hindu Family in Its Urban Setting*, Oxford University Press, Delhi, 1973.

Soumyajit Samanta

20

Feminist Response to Cultural Imperialism: A Study of Some Selected Indo-Anglican Women Novelists

Post-colonial discourse contains a nascent tension between the colonizer and the colonized within the problematics of its imperial-colonial dialectic. Against such a relationship can the issue of de-colonizing the culture of the empire be effectively mooted? This dialectical encounter between Europe and the other has been given post-structuralist orientation in the works of Edward. Said and Gayatri Spivak. Both, Edward. Said in his *Culture and Imperialism* and Homi Bhaba in his *Nation and Narration* have stressed in their own ways the hybridity of culture and history and their interactive issues. Said has stated cultural experiences partake of many often contradictory experiences and domains, cross national boundaries, defy the police action of single dogma and lowd patriotism. Far from being unitary or monolithic or autonomous things, cultures actually assume more 'foreign' elements, alterities differences than they consciously exclude (Said, 1994, 15).

In this manner all matter of discourses may be open to radical rethinking/appropriations under different cultural milieu. In this way Imperialist ideology and much of European thought, history, ancestry or the past become modified and reappropriated in Indian narrative patterns where as Les Murray has indicated 'time broadens into space' (Murray, 1969). Thus linear history and epistemology in colonial rhetoric has been re-assembled in Rushdie's *Midnight's Children*. European notions of historiography and the ordering of time has been violently butchered. Bhaba has noted the collusion between narrative patterns, history and mimetic reading of texts. In a sense culture must be liberated from the destructive dialectics of history by overcoming the politics of binarism, between that of dominance and subservience. This can only be done when Indian writing in English reflects the multi-cultural, syncretic nature of Indian society and culture as against the exclusive, ethnocentric and authoritative character of colonial discourse.

Imperialism has led to the cultural validation of British literature and vice versa. Gayatri Spivak has drawn our attention to this fact in her essay *Three Women's Text and a Critique of Imperialism*.

It should not be possible to read nineteenth century British literature without remembering that imperialism, understood as England's social mission, was a crucial part of the cultural representation of England to the English. The role of literature in the production of cultural representation should not be ignored.

The proliferation of English in India as the sole metropolitan language in the nineteenth and twentieth centuries' was due to its incessant employment in the dominant systems of administration, education and communication. The use of language and the popularization of literature not only led to the centralization of the bourgeois state in the colonial period but also made possible the continued literaty pre-eminence of English in the post-colonial period as well. Aijaz Ahmed notes that even after decolonization we have never outgrown the political ideology we have inherited from the European bourgeoisie, especially the dialectics of the centre and region by inventing more heterogeneous forms of unity or by obviating such centralized narrative patterns which have been usurped by the stifling logistics of phallocentric discourse. Post-colonial discourse carries in the tensions of the culturally subversive; the undermine of master narrative by the periphery, the marginalised voices. The attempt of cultural domination by the colonizer over the colonized becomes an apt metaphor for the annexation of feminist narratives by male-oriented discourse in Indian writing in English. The feminist perspective in Indian English novels is socially, politically and ideologically dominated by the male quest (the same) and its domination of an Other. In other words post-colonial discourses sometimes becomes a patriarchal construct, functioning to confine and lable women to a particular sphere and thereby inhibiting the full evolution of women as human beings.

The image of the women as the protecting mother and as a repository domestic bliss who nurtures and feeds her husband comes alive in Kamala Markandaya's novels. Jayamma in *A Handful of Rice* (1966) feeds Ravi in spite of him breaking into her house this idea of women as a protecting, benevolent authority persists through her novels *Some Inner Fury* (1956) becomes a prey to an Englishman's love and Maya in Anita Desai's *Cry, the Peacock* (1995) suffers from fear which is resolved only in deary. In all these instances the woman merely suffers from the consequence of male domination. Thus Ira lives with her albino child, Mira has to desert Richard in favour of her own people and Maya can only hope for death.

Often in Markandaya the woman is portrayed as the silent *pativrata* (as a devoted and a chaste woman) who is likely to accept *atmasamarpana* (annihilation of self) in spite of male despotism. Shirwadkar has commented that much of Indian writing in English has adhered to the image of the woman as *Sita, Savitri* and *Shakuntala*. In feminist narrative the positive characteristics of the woman has been highlighted. Chastity, self-sacrifice and personal sanctity have been stressed in *Rukmani (Nectar in a Sieve,* 1980) and Premala (*Some Inner Fury,* 1956). On the other hand the male novelist's representation of women is centered on stereotyping the female as the subservient wife, the evil temptress, the doting mother, the authoritative grandmother. In women writers the qualitative difference in their presentation of women lies in their depiction of the multifaceted women through an illustration of her strength and resilience which shines through her vulnerability. This change in the perception of feminine discourse from the stasis of cultural stereotyping and arbitrary labelisation to the legitimization of the independent, modern woman who becomes conscious of her multiple dimensions is a step taken towards dismantling male presumptions within logocentricism and which forms the crux of a patriarchal society.

The axiomativs of male narrative patterns in post-colonial discourse like that of R.K. Narayan (1955, 67, 71, 72, 79 a, b and c) or T.S. Pillai (1976) are woven round well defined categories, leaking to the oversimplification of woman. The Indian woman is portrayed as either strong/promiscuous; as either silent/suffering/rebel-malevolent type. Such narratives gloss over the human weakness and strength of the Indian woman. The question often raised by women writers like Markandaya, Desai and Sahgal are how valid is the image of the *pativrata* in today's would, who never forgets that a woman's place is with her husband? If we take the case of Rukmani in *Nectar in a Sieve* as a test case we are sure to note that although she qualitatively superior to her husband as regards her education and social status but in spite of everything she has been marginalised by her husband. Again, male possession of woman has been illustrated in Ravi's control over Nalini, the 'bashful neutra' virgin in *A Handful of Rice*. In the final stages Nalini is driven out from the house because of Ravi's constant abuse of her (Uma, 1989).

The traditional *Sita-Savitri* images of the woman have been reduplicated in Vasantha in Markandaya's *The Nowhere Man* (1975), in Premala in *Some Inner Fury* (1956). Anita Desai's heroines evince a similar note of resignation and acceptance. Tara in *Clear Light of Day* (1980) accepts her loss of identity as well as her subordinate status almost like the English woman in *Bye-Bye, Black Bird* who turns submissive once she'd married to an Indian. For the Indian woman as envisioned by Desai, Markandaya, Sahgal or Bharati Mukherjee there can be no total rebellion or radical rethinking of her orthodox role. Assaults may be made by the wife against her depersonalisation but she always accedes to phallocentric authority. Sita in Desai's *Where Shall We Go This Summer* and Saru in Shashi Deshpande's *The Dark Holds No Terrors* (1980) are rebels against the male system but live to see such revolt being aborted.

In most of her novels Desai is preoccupied in highlighting the disintegration of the female psyche and sensibility under the stress of marriage. The deconstruction of the women is effected when she realises that she is not courageous enough to challenge the outmoded remains of an age-old tradition. In her critique of the institution of marriage Desai's narratives image the evolution of the modern woman. The untying of male discourse patterns have been symbolically enacted by Maha's murder of Gautama in *Cry, The peacock*. Through her loss of sanity she realises that marriage is unlikely to lead to reconciliation and compatibility between sexes and have conjugal harmony remains a fiction-allusion-maya.

The evolution of the woman from her position of acceptance to the role of a rebel has several implications within the context of female discourse patterns. For the female rebel, several options remain open. On one level as Bharati Mukherjee in *Days and Nights in Calcutta* (1977:268) has indicated that 'a young Bengali woman could rebel by simply reading a book or refusing to fast'. On another level it could lead to suicide in a moment of sheer desperation as may be seen in the fate of Manisha in Desai's *Voice in the City* (1965). She can also break free by divorcing her husband as in Smriti's divorce settlement in Nayantara Sahgal's *The Time of Morning* (1965). Divorce may lead the woman 'toward freedom, toward goodness, toward a comprehensive world' as in Saroj in Saghal's *Storm in Chandigarh* (1968), (Jain 1978: 145). All this is the result of male brinkmanship which margnialises the voice of the female, who, like a mountain climber is always grasping the next moment and the next. It's like clinging to a precipice, to all the dangerous places, by every hand and foretold, and never giving up (Sahgal 1986:86).

In most of these instances we find that the rebel woman paradoxically makes use of a second man in her life to break the pall of failure and despair and to usher in a new life. A different class of women have been portrayed by Raj Narsimhan (1979) and Markandaya who, as rebels have the confidence and authority to battle life alone, without the anchorage of a second man in their lives. Can a woman be free in existential terms? This question may be asked of Shyee and her mother when they have gone through their usual gamus of sexual relationships with men and have been rid of them forever. Knowledge brings awarness but does it lead to freedom? Saroja controls her sexual urges and stays at home whereas Lalitha revels and leaves her home in Markandya's *Two Virgins* (1977: 6) Freedom in women is to understand not merely in terms of cultural and social forces which contain her persona but also in terms of her own psychological biological needs which may be controlled for a period of time but rarely repressed.

The ambiguous character of feminine discourse in Jhumpa Lahiri allows the woman to move in and out of male discourse patterns at her own will. In *A Temporary Matter* Shōba drifts aways from her husband not merely because she is shattered after giving birth to a dead male child but primarily because her husband is unable to share her torment, physically and psychologically. Sexual incompatibility breaks up a meaningless marriage. The wife consciously speels out her own isolation and moves away from the authority of phallocentric discourse. Sexual incompatibility is once again stressed in Mrs. Jas's alienation from her husband in *Interpreter of Maladies*. She attempts to escape from an intolerable boredom of a failed marriage by having an extra-marital affair with her husband's Punjabi friend. When she discloses her secret to Mr. Kapasi, the 'interpreter of maladies' she expects him to suggest some remedy. But she miserably fails. When he asks her about her guilt and pain she never answers because with a female's instinct' some knowledge seemed to pass before her eyes, and she stopped (66). The male is thoroughly deconstructed. Mr. Kapasi wasn't even considered fit for a proper feminine insult/ assault....' 'It crushed him; he knew at that moment that he was not even important enough to be properly insulted' (66). Narratives rush at cross purposes revealing the distance between sexes.

'Sexy' charts the emotional graph of two extra-marital affairs. Laxmi's cousin's husband deserts his wife and child when he falls in love with a woman sitting next to him in a plane flight on route to Montreal. On another level Miranda has an affair with Jev, who is comfortable and happy with his wife. In both cases the intrusion of the female questions the solidity of marriage and the relations between sexes. The arbitrariness of the male is exposed in his exploitation of women, both as wife as well as the others. However, with Lahiri the era of male domination comes to an end with the feminist reproduction and foreclosing of colonialist/male structures. Sanctioned ignorance and a refusal of subject statute and therefore human-ness. No more can the male conscience validate and consolidate itself (the Same) by imagining the female as the other. It has thus, so to speak, abdicated from its superior position with the downfall of the Europe and its colonialist hegemony. Today the political implications of feminist writing can never be ignored because female discourse legitimizes such a volte face-an arrogance of conscience which opines that only the marginalised can speak for the margin. Hence the need for a decolonization of male narratives which goes in tandem with the dismantling of colonialist hegemony in the Indian political and social panorama.

The woman's liberation may be enacted amongst the medley of discourses in the post colonial scene in a terrifying world running riot with male imperatives through the delimitizing power of love. Arundhuti Roy's *The God of Small Things* illustrates that in the heart of darkness prevalent in post-colonial India the only reality is that of love. Love defies convention, tradition and the linear movements of history only to re-write its own become heroes and heroines of a new historicity founded by an entirely new God, the God of Small Things. Love pours torrentially, wiping away of class consciousness, untouchability, fearfully surging into the mind's dark corners exposing all that has been repressed, hidden, underrated beneath the authority of society, the male, the logocentric ethos. In Roy's novel the revolution by the 'God' of small things becomes a terrifying deconstructive of social, psychological limits, pushing the female beyond the barriers of sense and sensibility, taking her to the realms of the unknown, the undefined in terms of emperience and laying the foundations in her of a new sexuality. The novel celebrates no merely the sexual impulses but speaks of gender inequality and racial discrimination which is the curse of post-colonial remains in Indian society where all sorts of small, insignificant voices have been marginalised and pushed into the periphery. The male presumptions which had been marginalised and pushed into the periphery. The male presumptions which had erstwhile dictated the voices of politics and history have been violated by the exigencies of female discourse which conspires and colludes with the male in order to de-negate and overthrow the authority of (phallocentric) the patriarch.

In the novel the male voices are allowed to deconstruct each other. Velutha symbolises the starkness of nature, the nakedness of the wild, the materiality of a sense of loss. He stands for defeat in the civilised jungle inhabited by master manipulators like comrade Pillai or inspector Thomas Matthew. Post-colonial discourse is full signifiers which both signify as well as intimidate a deeply-felt transition where labelisation of women does not work and gender discrimination becomes self-defeating and negative. Here narratives become fluid and men and women exchange roles as fast as changes in history. Or that history is re-written at this cultural esplanade of post-colonial cross-roads when the female usurps the potentialities of male discourse patterns and the man follows suit like the inevitability and certainty of historical currents.

Arundhati Roy shows that rationality and logical discourse pattern of imperial narratives, which always have a stable fulcrum with the tyrant/benevolent white-skin at the centre have been effectively deconstructed by multicultural openings of post-colonial narratives where ethnicity, casteism, religion as well as gender identities as children's narrative impinge upon the economy of such stable mimetic and realistic appraisal of a world order. It is supremely ironic that with all his sophistication the Englishman fails to posses Ammu whereas Velutha, dark as night and an untouchable commands her love and passion.

The defeat of the colonizer at the hands of the colonized is a culturally subversive act, which can only be enacted through the re-writing of history and colonial legacy and the catalyst which precipitates such a move is the voice of the Indian woman. Feminist narratives Indian English writing, therefore, function socially as well as politically as they challenge the neo-colonialist cultural assumptions of dominating of the West even within the context of the issue of globalisation today.

WORKS CITED

Almeida, R. and Ashcroft, B *et al* 1997: The Post-Colonial Studies Reader, London, Routledge. Originality of Imitation: Indianness in the Novels of Kamala Markandaya, Jaipur: Rawat P.

Desai, A. 1990: Voices in the City. ND: Orient.

——1994: In Custody. ND: Penguin.

——1995: Cry, The Peacock. ND: Orient.

——1998: Where Shall We Go This Summer. ND: Orient.

——1999: Bye-Bye Blackbird. ND: Orient.

——2000: Feasting, Feasting. London: Vintage.

——2001: Diamond Dust. London: Vintage.

Deshpande, S. 1980: The Dark Hold No. Terrors. ND: Vikas.

Jain, J. 1978: Nayantra Sahgal. ND: Arnold Heinemann.

Lahiri, J. 2000: Interpreter of Maladies: Stories. ND: Harper Collin Pvt. Ltd.

Markondaya, K. 1956: Some Inner Fury. NY: NY American Library.

——1966: A Handful of Rice. ND: Orient P.

——1975: The Nowhere Man. Bombay: Sangam.

——1977: Two Virgins. ND: Bell.

——1980: Neetar in a Sieve. Bombay: Jaico.

Mukherjee, B. & C. Blaise. 1976: Days and Nights in Culcutta. NY: Double Day.

Narsimhan, R. 1976: Sensibility Under Stress: Aspects of Indo-English fiction. New Delhi: Ashajanak.

Narayan, R.K. 1975: Waiting for the Mahatma. E. Lansing: Michingan State U.P.

——1979 (a): The Financial Expert. Mysore: Indian Thought.

——1979 (b): The Guide, Mysore: The Wesley P.

——1979 (c): The Maneater of Malgudi. Delhi: Hind Pocket Bks.

Pillai, T.S. 1976: Rungs cf the Ladder. New Delhi. Arnold-Heisemann.

Roy, A. 1997: The God of Small Things. ND: IndiaInd.

Sahgal, N. 1965: The Time of Morning. NY. W.W. Norton.

——1968: Storm in Chandigarh. Delhi: Vikas.

Said. E. 1994: Culture and Imperialism. London: Vintage.

Shirvalkar, M. 1979: Image of Woman in the Indo-Anglian Novel. New Delhi: Sterling.

Uma, A. 1989: Woman & her Family: Sterling.

Index

Y